BLINDNESS AND THE VISIONARY

Sir John Coles, who is non-executive chairman of Sight Savers International, has had a distinguished diplomatic career. He was Permanent Under-Secretary at the Foreign Office and Head of the Diplomatic Service for three years from 1994, after being Private Secretary to the Prime Minister from 1981 to 1984, Ambassador to Jordan from 1984 to 1988 and High Commissioner to Australia from 1988 to 1991. He was also Deputy Under-Secretary at the Foreign Office for Asia and the Americas between 1991 and 1994. Earlier, he had been Head of Chancery in Cairo, 1975-7, Counsellor at the UK Permanent Mission to the EEC, 1977-80, and Head of the South Asian Department at the Foreign Office, 1980-1.

A Daisy Book for All
with CD-ROM

With its specially designed multi-format CD-ROM, in a folder at the back, containing versions of the text and pictures for dyslexic and blind people and other people with a print disability, *Blindness and the Visionary* provides equal access to all readers: in Large Print; Daisy Audio and Full Text; Screen Reader (magnification, speech or Braille); and Braille. See page iv for instructions.

Blindness and the Visionary

THE LIFE AND WORK
OF JOHN WILSON

by

John Coles

dlm

First published in 2006
by Giles de la Mare Publishers Limited
53 Dartmouth Park Hill, London NW5 1JD

Typeset by Tom Knott
Printed by Cromwell Press Limited
Trowbridge, Wiltshire
All rights reserved

A CIP record of this book is available
from the British Library

ISBN 1-900357-25-9 paperback original

How to Use the CD
(in the folder at the back of the book)

With the CD-ROM, you can read and navigate this book using any combination of your eyes, ears and fingers.

You can listen to it on a *Daisy player*, either as a stand-alone or with Daisy software on your computer.* You can follow the text on the monitor of your computer as well as listening to it. People with dyslexic conditions may find this helpful.

To make a *Large Print* or *Braille* copy, place the CD-ROM in the CD-ROM drive of your computer, and follow the menu to use your own home printer.** You can also read the text on screen.

To read the book using your *Screen Reader*, place the CD-ROM in the CD-ROM drive of your computer, and follow the menus to access an HTML-formatted version that is designed for magnification, speech and Braille screen readers.

* A fully functioning demonstration copy of EASYREADER is included on the CD-ROM. A range of Daisy players can be bought from RNIB Customer Services (see below).
** *Blindness and the Visionary* is also available in *paper Braille* from RNIB Customer Services: +44 (0) 845 702 3153 and *cservices@rnib.org.uk*.

(Daisy is a trademark of the Daisy consortium. For information about Daisy, visit *www.daisy.org*.)

Contents

Illustrations

Acknowledgements

I am grateful for the permission I have received to quote from various works. First, from *See It My Way* by Peter White (Little, Brown and Company, 1999) and from *Yesterday's Safari* by Geoffrey Salisbury (The Book Guild, 1990). The quotation from *And There Was Light by Jacques Lusseyran* (1985) is reproduced by permission of Floris Books and that from *An Experiment in Education, the History of Worcester College for the Blind* (ed. D. Bell, 1967) with permission of the Royal National Institute of the Blind. The quotations from *World Blindness and its Prevention* (OUP, 1980), edited by the International Agency for the Prevention of Blindness under the direction of Sir John Wilson, and from *World Blindness and its Prevention, Volume 2*, similarly edited, are reproduced with permission of the Oxford University Press. The passage quoted from *Disability Prevention: The Global Challenge* is included with the kind permission of the Trustees of the Leeds Castle Foundation. The article referred to in the final chapter, entitled 'The Magnitude and Cost of Global Blindness: An Increasing Problem That Can Be Alleviated', by Kevin Frick and Allen Foster, is published in pages 471 to 476 of the *American Journal of Ophthalmology*, Volume 135, no.4, copyright 2003 by Elsevier Science Inc, and is used with permission from Elsevier. It has not been possible to trace the current holders of copyright to John Wilson's book *Travelling Blind* (Hutchinson and Co, 1963), which is much quoted in the text, but we shall be happy to acknowledge them in future editions should they come to light.

I thank Lady Wilson and Sight Savers International for the loan of many of the photographs in the book, and Christina Chelmick for permission to use her photograph of John Wilson on the back cover. The photographs of John Wilson using a Braille typewriter and studying a Braille map of Africa are reproduced with permission from the Advertising Archives, that of Jibon Tari (the Boat of Life) with permission of David Constantine, Chief Executive of Motivation, and that of the young eye patient at Harare Hospital with permission from *The Herald*, *The Sunday Mail* and Kwayedza. Efforts to trace the present holders of copyright in the photograph of the simulium fly have been unsuccessful, but, again, should they be discovered, we shall be happy to acknowledge them in future editions.

Preface

Blind for most of his life, John Wilson did more than anyone else has done to cure and prevent blindness. In his later years, he sought to apply that experience to the prevention of disability in general. He changed more people's lives for the better than many others who have claimed to benefit humanity.

I never met him. I only became aware of his work in 2001 when I was appointed non-executive chairman of Sight Savers International, an international non-governmental organization which he did so much to create and build. His name is well known, indeed famous, to people who work on problems of visual impairment. By any standards, his achievements rate comparison with those of other great humanitarians. I have therefore asked myself why I was ignorant of him until I became involved in this field. It is uncomfortable for me to admit it but I fear that my mind, perhaps like the minds of most people, was closed to the problems of disability for the selfish reason that I had not experienced them either directly or through close acquaintances. A failure of imagination and understanding cuts us off from a large area of human life. The discovery of what disability actually means, and how disabled people deal with it, can become a humbling, thought-provoking and even stimulating and inspiring experience.

This book should perhaps have been written by a visually impaired person, for he or she would certainly have had more insight into Wilson's experience of being blind than I can bring to the task. But blindness was only one aspect of his life. He was a man of action, a global traveller with an extraordinary sensitivity to the unseen world around him, an internationalist, a leader, a source of profound inspiration to many people, an accomplished speaker, a husband, father and grandfather, a puckish humorist and a lover of

life. And of course he had his faults. To some of these things I hope
I can bring insights.

I have learned a certain amount about visual and other impairments in the last few years, though probably not enough to have entirely avoided language of a kind that may irritate some disabled
people who read this account. If so, my apologies to them in advance. As the world has become more conscious of the nature
and scale of disability and as attention has become more focused
on the rights of disabled people, so the language used in discussion
of these issues has become more important. References to 'the blind'
or 'the disabled' offend because they imply a group of people who
are separate from the rest of the human race, and ignore their personality and humanity. This is not a matter of political correctness.
The words used affect the attitude of the user to a person described
in this way. If we think of people largely in terms of their impairments, we do close our minds to their personality, which is invariably more significant and important. As John Wilson often said,
'First, I am a person. Second, I am disabled.'

But this consciousness of the language used in the discussion of
disability is a relatively recent phenomenon, just as the consciousness of disability as an issue of human rights is recent, too.
In writing this book, I have taken the view that it would be un-
historical to change the language used by Wilson and others in
earlier times. Their words must stand. But it is unlikely that any
reader will consider that Wilson himself was guilty of not seeing
disability in its proper perspective. He was one of the earliest cam-
paigners for the rights of disabled people. He often said that his
own blindness was just a nuisance, nothing more. As will be seen,
he lived and worked as though he meant what he said.

In one way it is an advantage that I never met him. His was a
powerful personality. The power was felt by all who met him. As
with other such people, his charisma created a myth. An objective
biography must try to penetrate that myth: an easier task if one has
not been directly influenced by it.

The materials I have used are unusual. For much of his life
Wilson kept a diary in Braille. In his latter years he recorded extracts from this diary on tape, adding reflections and comment as he
did so. He excluded from the tapes the parts of the diary that he felt
to be too intimate or sensitive to publish. I have not attempted to
pry into the unrecorded parts of the diary, not just because I do not

read Braille but because, in the case of someone who died so recently (1999), an invasion of that kind risks distress to those who were closest to him. I do not for a moment believe that the unrecorded parts contain the kind of revelations that are so beloved of the tabloid press. I doubt that, if I read them, I would need to change my account of the man and his work in any substantial way.

For there are other rich sources. In addition to the tapes, which Jean Wilson, John's widow, kindly made available to me (so that I have been able to listen to his voice for many hours), there is much written material. John Wilson says comparatively little on the tapes about his work because he was a prolific writer of memoranda, reports, articles, speeches and letters and, naturally enough, saw no reason to repeat their content in his diaries. The mass of his written work lies unregistered in the archives of Sight Savers International where I have studied it. For the period of his life before the organization which became Sight Savers was established, there are valuable papers both in the National Archives at Kew and in the archives of the Royal National Institute of the Blind, the latter also, for the relevant period, being unregistered. Since so much of this material is not registered, and precise references to documents are not therefore possible, this book is not peppered with footnotes. The location of documents that are quoted will usually be evident from the context. Where Wilson's own words are quoted, they come from the tapes unless otherwise stated.

I have talked to well over sixty people, from many parts of the world, who *did* know John Wilson: to his widow, Jean, and other members of his family, to colleagues with whom he worked in Britain and overseas, to friends and critics. The picture that emerges from all these sources of the man and his work is remarkably consistent.

The book is only broadly chronological. The first two chapters, discussing Wilson's education and upbringing and then his early employment and the events that led to the creation of an organization for dealing with blindness overseas, do progress chronologically. But in Chapters Three and Four, I have adopted a thematic approach, the first dealing with his focus in the 1950s and 1960s on Africa, and the second with his later campaign against blindness in Asia. This handling makes, I think, for clarity but it needs to be borne in mind that his interests spread across the world and that on any given day he could be dealing with Accra, Calcutta, Hong

Kong, Moscow or New York, or virtually anywhere else for that matter. Chapters Five and Six follow new general themes that relate to the second part of his life and work. Chapter Seven suspends the story of his work and considers instead the man in the round; while Chapter Eight assesses his legacy, his achievements and their consequences for today.

My book is not a public relations exercise for Sight Savers or for the International Agency for the Prevention of Blindness or for Impact, all organizations with which Wilson's name will long be connected. They are perfectly capable of presenting their own case to the world. But it is an account, I hope objective, of how they came into being and developed. The story of international non-governmental organizations is for the most part an admirable one, if largely untold. I believe that, in Britain at least, we would benefit from more published work on how these bodies grew from disparate origins into the highly influential and effective instruments that so many of them now are. Perhaps this account will contribute to that work.

I have no medical training or background. Any medical terms which are used are explained in a way that I, and therefore others, can readily understand. If, despite checks carried out by some who have kindly read this text, there are still errors, that is my fault.

The organization which began life as the British Empire Society for the Blind, and which today is called Sight Savers International, was also known by two other names in the course of its development. I shall explain these changes in their proper place. But, to avoid burdening the account with the repetition of cumbersome titles, I shall refer to the organization wherever possible simply as 'the Society'.

I am very grateful to Jean Wilson for encouraging me to write this book and for her help with materials, as I am to others in the Wilson family. I have been determined to write as objectively as I can about John Wilson, as I have said, and they have unfailingly respected that determination. I hope they will find the outcome, in the round, an accurate portrayal. I also thank Richard Porter, Bjorn Thylefors, Carl Kupfer, Donald McLaren, Miriam Benn and Gorindappa Venkataswamy for reading and commenting on various parts of the book, as I thank, though not by name because the list is too long, all those who spoke to me about their memories and assessments of Wilson's life and work.

In my searches in the archives, I have benefited from the professional assistance of staff at the National Records Office at Kew, the Royal National Institute of the Blind and Sight Savers International and I express my gratitude to them.

Any profits from this book which would normally go to the author will be divided equally between Sight Savers International and Impact.

It is largely in the conviction that the personality and achievements of John Wilson should not go unrecorded, particularly in an age when much shallower personalities and accomplishments so easily achieve 'celebrity' status, if only for a fleeting period, that I have written what follows.

Chapter 1

A Different Upbringing

One rainy morning in late October 1931, a twelve-year-old boy, John Wilson, walked as usual from his home in Murchinson Street, Scarborough, to his school – the Scarborough High School for Boys. The day's timetable included a chemistry class. The pupils were to carry out an experiment. Wilson later described what happened: 'There was a rubber tube leading into a retort filled with water. The idea was that the oxygen, when it was produced, would come bubbling up into the water. It was my turn to heat the test-tube with a Bunsen burner. I was sitting on a high stool very close to it, playing the blue flame from the Bunsen burner on to the test-tube when it suddenly exploded. The chemicals had been wrongly labelled and produced an explosive mixture. It must have been quite an explosion because they say it shattered whole rows of bottles and wrecked part of the room.' A classmate confirms this: 'There was a huge bang. We got peppered with glass. Everybody was bleeding. I got some glass in my face, but they managed to remove it.' One boy present was blinded in one eye. John Wilson was blinded in both.

The school building has been used for various purposes in the last seventy years and now houses the School of Creative Arts of the Yorkshire Coast College of Further and Higher Education. It has been much refurbished and modernized but in the corner of one classroom there remain some of the sinks and cupboards of the old chemistry laboratory, clearly the area where the accident happened. Wilson remembered being carried downstairs after the accident and taken to hospital, though he soon lost consciousness. 'When I woke up, there was no pain. All I could see was a ragged star-shaped ink pattern like an ink-blot.' His parents – George, a Methodist minister, and Norrie – arrived. His mother kissed the only part of his face not covered by bandages. John stayed in the hospital until Christmas 1931, when Norrie insisted that he should come home.

Wilson always said in later life that he did not at the time think of the event as tragic. It was, he said, catastrophic for his parents and much effort was spent in soothing their anxieties. But his own attitude was more one of accepting his blindness as a fact and entering with energy and zeal into a life of which blindness was only a part. A sighted person may find that hard to believe, but others who lost their sight at a young age have said similar things.

Jacques Lusseyran was a French underground resistance leader during the Second World War. He survived incarceration in the Buchenwald concentration camp for fifteen months and eventually became a university professor in the United States. He was blinded when seven years old, in a school accident like John Wilson, and in the same year. He wrote in his autobiography that he thanked heaven for making him blind then, at a time when the habits of body and mind had not yet been formed, when the body was still 'infinitely supple, capable of making just the movement the situation calls for and no other; ready to settle with life as it is, ready to say yes to it.' 'Grown-up people,' he adds, 'forget that children never complain against circumstances...For an eight-year-old, what "is" is always best...A child's courage is the most natural thing in the world...A child does not think about the future, and so is protected from a thousand follies and nearly every fear' (*And There Was Light*, Floris Books, 1985).

The case of the blind philosopher and activist, Martin Milligan, is admittedly different in that he lost his sight at eighteen months. But his retrospective comments chime with those of Wilson. He did not regard it as a terrible blow, nor a devastating deprivation: blindness just did not seem to be a problem for him as a young child. He took it for granted and learned to live with it (*On Blindness* by Bryan Magee and Martin Milligan, OUP, 1995).

There is another reason why Wilson did not feel the full impact of the event in his youth. Although he was totally blinded by the accident, and never saw again, a distinguished ophthalmologist led him to believe that there was a good chance that he might recover. Later in his life Wilson practically never complained about his blindness, but this false prospectus did leave bitter feelings. 'It was a very cruel thing to do because it must have been perfectly obvious at that time that there was no chance of recovery. I was for a time something of a visitor to the world of the blind.' The uncertainty made his subsequent rehabilitation and the learning of Braille considerably more difficult because he long laboured under the impression that his blindness was a temporary phase. Not until his late teens did he begin to accept that it was irreversible. Unsurprisingly, he came to insist always that ophthalmologists should tell their patients the truth.

Before the accident John's father, George, had already announced his intention of preaching the following Sunday on the biblical text 'All things work together for good for them that love God, to them that are called, according to His purpose' (Romans 8.28). Following this severe blow to the family, those around him suggested that he might prefer not to preach at all, or at any rate not use that text. George insisted that he would deliver his sermon as planned, a statement of faith and optimism in the face of adversity which his son would remember and return to.

George Henry Wilson was born in 1872 into a farming and lead-mining family. He married Norrie (Leonora Carrick) in 1901. As a child, John Wilson was brought up in a series of manses – in Nottingham, Chorlton near Manchester, Bakewell in Derbyshire, Scarborough in Yorkshire and Belper in Derbyshire. The Methodist influence was a significant strand in his upbringing. Although later on he would have a distinct leaning towards Anglicanism, there was a tension between this and his Methodist roots. He would, for example, always feel slightly guilty about having an alcoholic drink for there was never any liquor in his parents' house.

Norrie was a busy, amusing person, devoted to her children. She, more than anyone, regarded John's blindness as a disaster. She came from a musical family and was an accomplished pianist. George was distinctly eccentric, dithery and absent-minded to a fault. One winter evening when he was preaching in chapel the police arrived. Doubtless apologizing for the interruption, they asked him to switch on the lights of his car which he had parked inappropriately. He walked out of chapel, got into the car and absentmindedly drove home, leaving his congregation in extended ignorance of his whereabouts.

A man of strong faith, he was an unusual Methodist minister. He was a keen botanist. But his great passion was archaeology. He was President of the Peakland Archaeological Society; he formed the Peakland Explorers Club whose members conducted expeditions to the caves of the Peak District; and he published two small books

3

and several articles on caving and archaeology in Peakland. He was once told that he should not be in the Church at all since he spoke of events of ten thousand years ago which, some sectors of the Church still considered, was inconsistent with the biblical dating of the creation of the world.

One evening in 1924 when John was five years old he was woken in bed to be told that his father and brother, Ernest, had come home with a great treasure. 'There, on a carpet, glittering in the firelight, was a silver Saxon cross of St Bertram, Saxon jewellery and piles of Saxon coins. It was all packed up later in a large cardboard box and sent to the British Museum. A treasure-trove enquiry resulted in all of it being claimed for the Crown.' The discovery had been made at St Bertram's cave inside a rock cliff called Beeston Tor in the Manifold Valley, in Staffordshire. It was of some significance for the Anglo-Saxon period of British history and received much media attention at the time, locally, then nationally, primarily through the *Daily Mail*, and then internationally. Although most of the items passed to the British Museum, George was allowed to keep a few pieces and received some £70 in recognition of the historical value of his find.

As a small boy John Wilson took part in some of his father's archaeological work and continued to accompany him after his accident when his task was to sift with his fingers through piles of debris in search of fossils, pottery and ancient coins. Ernest, who was seventeen years older, and of whom John was particularly fond, was a keen member of these caving parties. John was the youngest member of the family, and there were three sisters who were a good deal older, but with whom he remained close. Much later he re-called how, following his accident, his sister, Joan, used to take him for walks at night through the streets of Scarborough until he developed enough confidence to go out in daylight.

George's predilection for collecting went beyond his archaeological finds. He was an avid collector of books and would buy whole lots of miscellaneous items in order to acquire the books contained in them. He once returned home with a life-size plastic statue of a nude woman. His wife refused to have it in the house, so he put it in the coalshed where it became blacker and blacker in the dust until it eventually disintegrated. A second acquisition was a large hemisphere map in a frame which was propped up by John's bed, where father and son would trace long, imaginative journeys across Africa and India. Much of the young boy's life would be spent in travelling to these two parts of the world.

Speaking years afterwards of his childhood, Wilson remembered nothing of the house the family occupied in Nottingham, and had only vague memories of the one near Manchester – not surprisingly since he was only some five years old when they moved to the manse in Bakewell, Derbyshire. But he had vivid memories of this house and of pre-accident Scarborough. 'When I think of Bakewell, and the early days in Scarborough, I see them in full colour. Places we lived in subsequently I think of in terms of sound, and, just occasionally, when I do manage to think of them visually, in monochrome.'

He recalled the 'fine, square house in Haddon Road, Bakewell, looking out onto a recreation ground with the blue River Wye wandering through it'. There was a sizeable garden, which George cultivated expertly, framed by a large hedge. The heady perfume of yellow and gold flowers remained a distinct memory in Wilson's mind. At a deep bend of the river he caught minnows and sticklebacks in a jar and kept them in a bowl in the garden. In Haddon Road itself there were chestnut trees: he remembered their candles, all alight in the early summer, and the polished, deep mahogany nuts in their curious, spiky cases which appeared in the autumn. Each year a circus came to the recreation-ground opposite his house, with merry-go-rounds, flying chairs and a shooting gallery. In the town there was a market at whose entrance 'orators and tricksters' practised their crafts. In the cattle market butchers used white chalk to mark the parts of cows that they wanted to purchase when the beasts were slaughtered.

Many years later, when in Buxton, John Wilson found a box of toys which he thought he must have had when in Bakewell. 'As I touched each of these toys, they came back to me in full and vivid colour, although I was told that many of them had in fact faded in their colour. Perhaps Keats was right in his "Ode to a Grecian Urn": such images are immortal and don't fade like the objects themselves.'

Not all his visual recollections were sunny and comfortable. Two other images came back to him. There was a nunnery nearby. He would look with terror at 'the silent hooded ladies walking along the path. For some reason, probably because of my non-conformist upbringing, there seems something very evil about those nuns.' One day he and a friend saw two dogs copulating. He knew what Siamese twins were, thought these must be Siamese dogs and knelt down and prayed to God that He would allow them to become separate again.

Many seeing children of Wilson's generation would have had similar experiences of growing up. But in their case the early images would have been largely overlain by the multitude of scenes through which they moved as they grew older. For a boy who had no new visual experience after his blinding, the remembered earlier images had a special sharpness and value.

When the family moved to Scarborough in 1930, he at first found the terraced house at 83 Murchinson Street, with its stone floors, dingy and cold after Bakewell, but they made it shiny and cosy. It was a time of acute economic depression. Wilson recalls children walking about in rags with bare feet. It was a very difficult time for the fishing community. In the style of the time, one aristocratic lady descended to harangue the fishermen's wives on the merits of making a nutritious soup from fish heads, which they proceeded to do. Wilson recalls with approval that a fisherman who was present challenged the notion: 'What I am asking is, when we are eating all these fish heads, who is eating the fish?'

The last scenes the sighted Wilson saw were of Scarborough. In 1980 he tried to recapture those memories and wrote: 'The Scarborough sea in winter is sombre and grey. And after one of those great Northern storms the sky is exhausted and the sea running silver. And on the horizon the spectral outline of ships. In the summer the same sea, under the sunshine, flashes golden and purple with highlights on the waves. And that small, beautiful, smelly harbour, where the tubby fishing boats are moored, and the crab pots, and the herring gulls screaming and laughing like drunken barmaids.'

An account of a conventional upbringing might at this point attempt to assess the influence of childhood years and parental personalities on the subject's subsequent development. It is safe enough to say that John Wilson grew up in a loving and close family and retained a strong sense of family throughout his life. The eccentricity of his father and the Methodist environment may connect with the radical streak which is detectable in the later Wilson. The unusual will-power and single-mindedness which would be such marked features in the adult may owe something to the grimness of an economically depressed Britain in his formative years. But the major influences on his personality were still to appear, as he adjusted to his loss of sight.

At home after the accident, he learned how to listen in a different way and how to move without seeing, in part by the use of sound. 'When you walk along the street, you begin to get used to the shadow sound of a tree or a lamp-post, the differing echoes of a wall and a hedge. You build a panorama, a view of those things.'

He began to take his first Braille lessons at home from a blind woman teacher who lived nearby. 'She wore lavender perfume and we sat together on a bouncy, overstuffed, swollen settee in a room full of ticking clocks.' Another visitor to his house was a blind social-worker from Bridlington called Bull Allison, who took him to visit other blind people in Scarborough and well-known institutions for the blind in York, Leeds, Manchester and Liverpool. Wilson would say much later that his early acquaintance with work for the blind in Yorkshire opened up for him an interest which would lead him to join the staff of the National Institute for the Blind (now the Royal National Institute of the Blind). But, as we shall see, there were other, I think more decisive, influences that led him in that direction.

It was certainly Allison who prompted a key decision by George and Norrie Wilson to send their son to a boarding school for blind boys where he himself had been. In 1933, shortly after he went there, John Wilson began writing his Braille diary, which he continued with few gaps until 1943, and then, with rather more gaps, until 1956, producing only an intermittent record in two more volumes after that date. In 1989, when he dictated extracts from his diary onto tape, he said that he had not kept it out of a wish for perpetuity nor because he envisaged that he would later wish to read it. He did it because of 'the itch to write' which was always with him; and sometimes because the exercise provided a type of catharsis. The diary, he stated, is truthful, sometimes embarrassingly so, and he insisted that it was not written for anyone else to read. As I have explained in the Preface, it contains little about his work because he wrote accounts of that elsewhere. He also felt it necessary to leave out material of a particularly intimate nature, especially relating to 'the tangled and deeply felt relationship with a woman at Oxford'. But with all their limitations the tapes do provide rich material, in particular about his formative years. It must be rather unusual for the writer of a biography to be able to listen for many hours to his deceased subject talking about his life. His voice became very familiar in my home during the months of writing.

In June 1932, John Wilson and his parents took a train to Worcester in order to visit the Worcester College for the Blind. This remarkable institution had been founded in 1866 by Reverend R. H. Blair, a local clergyman who believed there was a need for a 'college where the blind children of opulent parents might obtain an education suitable for their status in life, and such as might enable them to become not only useful but even valuable members of society'. John Wilson claims that when he visited it in 1932 there was a notice outside reading 'Worcester College for the Blind Sons of Gentlemen'. If so, it was well out of date because in 1903 the college had exchanged that elitist description for 'a School for the Higher Education of Blind Boys'.

Be that as it may, Wilson was lucky, because he entered Worcester College at a time when it had acquired, and by all accounts deserved, an excellent reputation owing to the efforts of G. C. Brown, the headmaster from 1912 to 1938. Wilson describes him as a scholar with outstanding degrees in philosophy and history, a good amateur boxer and a swimmer of county standard. Brown took the view that blindness was 'not a barrier nor even a handicap, but just a nuisance to overcome' (*An Experiment in Education: The History of Worcester College for the Blind*, ed. D. Bell, RNIB, 1967). John Wilson's attitude, as he came to reflect on blindness years later, was very similar.

He was at Worcester for five years, from 1932 to 1937. It was then a small school – some forty-five boys from the age of eleven upwards, many with multiple disabilities, some mentally handicapped. In his time only about twenty were able to take a full part in college activities. But he was one of that number. Worcester was a decisive influence on his life. A contemporary remembers him arriving for the first term – shy and lost (as generations of new boarders have felt). He had also missed a year's study because of his accident and he was still far from fluent in Braille. By the time his diary starts in 1933 he is already changing. He was, say contemporaries, a born raconteur and he used to regale the other boys in his dormitory with stories practically every night, alternating between high romance and heroism one night, and comedy the next. He had taken up rowing which was a strong sport at the college; he was a good swimmer; he hated running but had to do it; he took piano lessons; and he later played the accordion and saxophone in the school band. He wrote and acted in the school pantomime. He learned to dance at the fortnightly school dance and the termly ball, in which a local girls' school joined.

He says less in his diary about schoolwork but all the indications are that this progressed well. It was not plain sailing. With memories and expectations of a sighted child he was consistently frustrated, then and afterwards, by the limited amount of literature available in Braille and the 'stultifying slowness' of the equipment then used by visually impaired people for calculating, measuring and drawing. By 1935, at the age of sixteen, he was beginning to write poetry, much of it of the solemn, introspective kind to which many teenage minds are prone, and he was asking himself large questions about religion. He was becoming an ardent listener to the radio, a habit which lasted for the rest of his life, and he began to record in his diary key international events – the rise of Nazism, German re-armament, Mussolini's invasion of Abyssinia, German entry into the de-militarized Rhineland, the Spanish Civil War, the abdication of Edward VIII, and much else. He often described these events in considerable detail, but he rarely made a political observation.

When the Silver Jubilee of King George V was celebrated in 1935 he copied the text of the King's speech from the newspaper into his diary. He later quoted a few sentences which had especially struck him: 'I ask you to remember that in the days to come you will be the citizen of a great Empire. As you grow up, always keep this thought before you. And when the time comes, be ready and proud to give your country the service of your work, your mind and your heart.' We shall see that Wilson was often moved by the 'magic of Empire' as well as the concept of the Commonwealth and, though he might have expressed it differently, a belief in service.

Reflecting many years after on his time at Worcester, Wilson commented that he had since visited schools for the blind in a hundred countries but Worcester still seemed to him remarkable, far ahead of its time, not only in education for the blind but in education generally. The academic standards were high, although others found the teaching staff of variable quality. In sport, it never occurred to him that the college could not compete with, and indeed beat, schools like the local grammar school with its hundreds of pupils.

The school motto was 'Possunt Quia Posse Videntur': 'They Can Because They Think They Can.' (Wilson said that the boys translated this as 'Can They Really Be As Queer As They Look?') But for once the motto really did point to the school's principal achievement. It gave disabled boys confidence at a time when they most needed it and the means and tools to develop their lives. Those who were blind learned to compensate for their blindness by developing an acute sense of hearing, touch and smell. They were given little mobility training but were sent off to find their own way, without canes, and walked for miles. The impressive range of sporting activities developed in them a physical courage and, in a few, Wilson included, something close to physical recklessness. School friends remember him as extremely positive in his attitude to life, courageous and adventurous, communicative, at ease with strangers, a boy who had adjusted to blindness as well as anyone who was blinded in his youth. The schoolmaster who taught him to row regards him as the 'best all-round chap as a schoolboy that I ever came across'.

The college may have publicly discarded its earlier class-ridden self-description before Wilson went there. But it still aimed to turn out well-spoken, socially adept young men. Peter White, the blind BBC presenter, who went to the school in 1958, says in his autobiography *See It My Way* (Little Brown, 1999) that even then 'Worcester boys acquired posh accents...(they) thought they were better than everyone else. Unfortunately, they also had a habit of proving that they were...it filled us with so much braying self-confidence that most of us emerged finding it difficult to believe that anything we did could be regarded as less than totally admirable.'

The college's admission system was pretty rigid. It declined to take Ved Mehta, the distinguished Indian writer, because of his lack of formal education, and its examination system was to screen out David Blunkett, the blind Labour Cabinet Minister. But Wilson always spoke with gratitude and pleasure about his time there. He had no doubt that it had given him a strong capacity to believe in himself. The headmaster conveyed to the boys his firm conviction that there need be nothing beyond the reach of a blind person if he or she had talent and confidence. Wilson recorded one of Brown's sayings, 'The reality of the fear is not necessarily related to the reality of the danger.'

While Wilson's positive attitude towards his time at Worcester is attractive, I cannot help wondering whether there were not periods of blacker moods. Only about a year after being blinded he had been sent away from home and family to the inevitably strange atmosphere of a boarding school in a different part of England and was surrounded by disabled boys. It is hard to imagine that there were not, at least initially, times of loneliness and sadness. But when the BBC presenter, Sue Lawley, asked him on 'Desert Island Discs', a few years before he died, whether these huge changes in his life had not been a great shock to him, he denied this: 'I don't remember it that way. You accept it as a child. There was so much to do to adjust to disability.' Whether that stoical attitude was really so firm at the time, or whether Wilson is here in part transposing to his childhood the attitude he adopted to blindness subsequently, is hard to judge.

In January 1937, the beginning of his last year at Worcester, he had a career interview with the headmaster, who told him that his examination marks would fully justify an application to an Oxford college. Brown acknowledged Wilson's current wish to be a writer but told him he would need a settled job as well. Physiotherapy? That, said Wilson later, did not appeal in any way. The Church? No, because it would be wrong to view this as a profession rather than a calling. Business? 'It seemed to me that this would not be suitable,' said Wilson vaguely. Teaching? That appeared to offer quite a lot, but no, because, he said, teaching in a sighted school would be difficult, and the amount of scholarship needed to teach the blind would in most schools be less than demanding (I doubt if he would have subscribed to this remark in later life). Given the view then taken of careers open to visually impaired people, that seemed to leave only the law. Wilson had not thought about this before but was very much attracted to it.

Discussion resumed in July when it was decided that Wilson would seek to go to Oxford, probably St Catherine's College, if it could be afforded. He and his father calculated that with a grant from the National Institute for the Blind, the local authority and a trust, plus a compensation payment to which he was entitled, they might raise £220. The Wilsons were not well off and his father, who was about to retire, had some difficulty finding money to supplement the grant. In the event he was offered places at St Catherine's and Pembroke and accepted Brown's advice to opt for the former on the grounds that it was (then) a non-residential college which would be easier for him than collegiate life.

In 1934, the Wilson parents had moved from Scarborough to Belper in Derbyshire where George Wilson conducted his last ministry, before moving again in 1937 to their retirement home in Buxton. Here John Wilson spent the summer holidays with his family before going up to Oxford in October 1937.

Oxford can be a lonely and somewhat bewildering place for any first term undergraduate, though in most cases the loneliness and bewilderment do not last long. For a blind person there were added problems. Although Worcester had given Wilson considerable self-confidence and physical skill, it was nevertheless a protected environment in the sense that it was entirely geared to the requirements of disabled children. Oxford, of course, was not. When he arrived there in October 1937, his first need was to learn to cope with a large, busy town. He had not used a white stick or cane before, nor would he until much later on. He used no guidance devices to get around but relied on very sharp hearing and what he called his 'obstacle sense' which enabled him to detect at a considerable distance lamp-posts, parked bicycles and entrances to houses and shops.

Looking back on those days, he thought he had appeared very sighted, striding along in his undergraduate gown, and he often provoked angry comments from people as he got in their way. It in fact took him about a year before he was really familiar with walking around the town. After that he had little difficulty finding any building he needed.

He describes a walk he took from the college boathouse on the river through the meadows of Christ Church: 'A bird is singing close to me. An astonishing, startling trill. It must be pleasant to make a noise like that, whether you want to or no ... What a nice laugh that girl's got – a soft contralto. Why do Oxford girls all seem to wear the same perfume? Damn that hole ... Christ Church is very quiet – tea, I suppose. I bang my head on that thing again. I wish people would not be so sympathetic. The children aren't. They just laugh.'

He remembers walking across a tablecloth and picnic in the meadow, but says that the picnickers took it well and they had a beer together. A woman friend who knew him then commented on his mobility: 'In those days the High Street presented many a hazard as a number of the colleges had cellars under the pavements which were often left open for the barrels of beer. Walking with John was somewhat perilous as he refused to take an arm even when crossing the road, and often one's heart was in one's mouth as he strode firmly forward.' Another woman friend says that, physically, he was almost reckless. When they went swimming in the Cherwell he would simply change and dive in without a thought for what might be passing on that often busy stretch of water.

By his second term he was feeling considerably more confident about the geography of the town, and in his diary for early 1938 he set himself an agenda: 'There are many obstacles but I will cope with them. Having now found my way around the streets of this city, I have the chance to enter into the wonderful academic and social life of Oxford. This year I will do three things – begin to become a competent, academic lawyer, develop my gift of writing so that I can make good prose and sensitive verse and also get to know some of those charming, sophisticated girls. That may be the most difficult barrier of all. To overcome the not unreasonable re-pugnance which I suppose a normal girl might have towards a blind man, and at the same time avoid a relationship based on curiosity or sympathy.' He also recorded a foreboding that, as Europe moved closer to war, the gaiety and beauty he now sensed around him might be superseded by a much less agreeable environment.

Work, writing and women. Many undergraduates have set them-selves a similar agenda, if perhaps, in most cases, less consciously than he did. His law tutor was Theodore Tyler, a blind Balliol don, who was himself a product of Worcester College. At that time, there were not many law books available in Braille, so Wilson employed the services of a succession of readers of varying quality at a shilling an hour to read to him while he made notes in Braille. The Braille-writing machines of the time were too noisy to use during lectures and tape-recorders were not available. Fortunately, he had a good memory, and he would make notes on a Braille handframe and then write them up in the evening. Sometimes sighted friends would read law books to him, and in the vacation members of his family would perform the same task. By June 1938, as his Law Moderations exam approached, he was working hard in preparation but was worried about Roman law which was his weak point. Although that proved the most difficult paper in the examination, the others were less taxing and he was provided with the services of a typist 'who got the stuff down with extraordinary speed.' He records in July that he had passed with distinction and that his tutor told him that his papers were some of the best of his year.

The notion that he might make his way in life by writing was still quite strong in his mind. He began to attend the Apollo Club, a poetry society, of which he was to become president for a short period. Here members read their own poems and stories and distinguished writers would appear from time to time. Wilson was present when George Orwell addressed the club on the Spanish Civil War. And one evening Tolkien spoke, 'with his high piping voice and what at the time seemed an unwholesome obsession with elves, dwarves and little hairy men from Middle Earth.' How much poetry Wilson himself was writing at this time is not clear but, as we shall see, when his first emotional relationship with a woman developed, poetry would become a central activity. Meanwhile, he had also joined a history club in college and read a paper to its members on 'legislation and scientific humanism'. The chairman congratulated him on its originality which, says Wilson, 'showed that he had not read Julian Huxley's book, from which I cribbed most of it.' More relevant to his future career, he also joined a group of undergraduates at St Mary's Church who called themselves 'somewhat pompously' 'The Committee for Human Causes' and included people who, he says, later founded Oxfam and the Leonard Cheshire Homes.

But however intent he was on his work and his writing, a desire to get fun and broader satisfaction from life was never long repressed. On arrival at St Catherine's he had written to enquire about rowing. While those in charge seemed at first very doubtful whether a blind man could be trusted in the boat, he was soon rowing practically every day in the Second Eight. This enthusiasm continued throughout his time at Oxford and he eventually rowed at bow in the First Eight for his college.

The sounds of Oxford continued to give him great pleasure. 'In the meadows you hear all the bells. Merton's, strangely incomplete, like an unanswered question; the confident boom of Christ Church; in the distance the clang of Keble, like an alarm clock.' And not just bells. The 'beautiful, patrician voices' of the girls, which he heard as he walked the streets, were a particular attraction.

Like many of his successors he was both irritated and amused by some of the University's rules. Warned on arrival not to drink in public houses and 'common taverns', he promptly gathered a companion and went off to celebrate at the Lamb and Flag. He noted that girls were not allowed to visit college rooms after dinner had begun and were on no account to visit the clubs of male undergraduates. But there were other possibilities. He attended the final service of a Christian Mission run by the Oxford Group which finished with a kind of confessional, during which a girl stood up and confessed that in her first term she had 'lusted'. A New College undergraduate sitting next to Wilson said 'I'm going to invite that girl to tea.'

Once he went to an Oxford pub with four other undergraduates who claimed to be 'professional debauchers'. When they left for 'various destinations', he refused to go with them. 'They said I was a prudish virgin. I'm certainly not a prude and I shall be delighted to have a reasonable chance to lose my virginity, but not on those terms – a squalid encounter in a back street, to buy from a casual stranger something as private and committing as sexual intimacy.'

When recording parts of his diary covering this period, Wilson admitted to his surprise that, although he had three sisters and three attractive cousins, he then knew little about female psychology, to say nothing of anatomy. But was it so surprising? Given his accident, his closeting in a boys' boarding school for the next five years and the *mores* of the time, it would have been more remarkable if he had been knowledgeable in these areas by the time he was nineteen. Many years afterwards, young Englishmen of that age who had moved to university from boarding school would be just as inexperienced. In his case, things were about to change.

He had in fact met his first woman friend the previous summer at a holiday camp on the east coast where his family were staying. During a ladies' night, when women asked men to dance, he was approached by a young woman who turned out to be a good dancer. They spent most of the evening and a good deal of the rest of the holiday together. They met again when he was back in Oxford in the autumn term, went to the cinema and held hands in the dark. 'This was all such new ground for me and certainly for Joan. I ought to have learned more about it years ago.' By November they met for the last time. Another more significant relationship was about to develop. But Wilson reflected that he had been fortunate to find such an affectionate, uncomplicated and sunny person for that innocent first relationship. He hoped that she would find someone else and that their 'brief but chaste' romance had helped her, as it had certainly helped him, to cope with something much more serious.

Towards the end of the autumn term in 1938, a young woman called Miriam Embray was canvassing in Oxford for a Labour election candidate. She entered a student residence, knocked on a door, was called to come in, did so and found a room in complete darkness. When John Wilson put the lights on she realized why. He immediately went into a tirade about the old men who were hopeless as readers of law textbooks and how he could not make sense of his Braille notes. She took the relevant book, sorted out the meaning and stayed for hours talking. During the Christmas vacation, he wrote to her from Buxton and they met again as soon as the next term began.

Miriam was nearly nineteen, a year younger than John. She had come to St Hugh's College, Oxford, on a state scholarship and was reading French and German. That January they began to talk about poetry. John told her that he had always been convinced he could write good poetry and, perhaps, significant literature, but he had read so little, having concentrated at Worcester on the few books he could read in Braille. She told him that she thought he had a rare talent and set out to read poetry to him: Housman, Pound, Coleridge and Shakespeare's sonnets figured early on. Donne, Marvell, Wordsworth, Clare and Baudelaire are mentioned later.

'She has a wonderful way of reading,' wrote Wilson, 'without any affectation of mood, laughter bubbling behind her voice at the pompous passages, and sudden highlights at points which catch her spiritual interest.'

By the end of the month they believed they were in love. John Wilson wrote:

> 'What liar likened the coming of love
> To a tempest of fire and flames?
> Rather it came on white, wide wings of silence
> Dropping into the still air
> To us who fear to speak its name.
> Hold your breath, my love
> This bubble bursts at a breath.'

On Miriam's nineteenth birthday at the end of January, Wilson gave her a beautiful copy on india paper of the *Complete Oxford Shakespeare*, with a poem he had written on the flyleaf. She described it to me as expressing the feeling that they were living a shared dream which would, if the Gods were propitious, develop from its gossamer beginnings into a truer waking experience:

> 'Our song is the frozen laugh of bells
> To rhythms the river taught
> Our dreams are the powder of word dust
> Atangle with gossamer thought
> But these must wake as the rainbow wakes
> From the silver sleep of the rain
> But the lotus draught of the dream god
> Will make them sleep again.'

Miriam had already told Wilson about Charles, another man in her life. He now came to Oxford to meet him, but Wilson found him chilly and unsympathetic and called him 'the old cabbage'. A week after that Miriam wrote to say that Charles was intending to propose to her, that she was bemused but nevertheless knew that the 'horrific rush' of feeling must override all else. It must mean, she thought, that John could not have meant as much to her as she truly believed and hoped. She had made, she said, an appalling mess of reading the significance of her emotions. Wilson recalled decades later his own feelings of loss and blank depression.

A mutual girlfriend tried to help him at the time by saying that she believed Miriam had been very happy with him. She added, in case no one had told him, that Miriam was rather beautiful – blonde and petite – and clever (a photograph of the nineteen-year-old Miriam confirms her beauty). But his depression continued. He sent Miriam a long, bitter letter and an equally bitter poem he had written called 'The Song of the Wooden Man', ending:

> 'But there is a garden
> The immaculate flower is open to the sunshine
> God grant that she may be happy
> She who for a moment truly loved the wooden dancer
> Seeing only its gaiety, not its creator
> And she will laugh and sing

Such a pathetic young man
But he'll grow up
And I did him good.'

Miriam then re-appeared with the news that she and Charles had broken their engagement, envisaging that she and John might resume their relationship. However, he had been badly bruised and made it clear that for him love had to have 'the implication of permanence'. They continued to see a good deal of each other but Wilson says that his diary for this period is too intimate to record on tape: 'For me, it was a time of tenderness, wonder and beauty – seeking for, but never quite finding, the trust of our earlier days.' At the end of that summer term, Miriam, unsettled by the expectation of war and for other reasons, decided to abandon Oxford. In 1941 she married Charles, though the marriage lasted for only seven years, killed by the war, especially the Blitz, which disturbed his mind considerably.

So John Wilson's first love affair lasted less than a year. But its effects were much more long-lasting. During their relationship Miriam had talked at length about what he would do after Oxford. She had, by his account, argued that a lot of people would be blinded and disabled by the coming war, quite apart from the people who were blind already, and that they should together study what could be done. So Wilson obtained a set of books on blindness and disability and Miriam read them to him instead of poetry. Wilson always regarded these exchanges as a turning point in his life.

Miriam is now in her eighties. She remembers John Wilson vividly and with affection: 'He was slender, not tall, attractive to look at, with a pink skin and fluffy hair and a quirky, humorous mouth that would twitch a bit as of a preparation before he said something, especially something comic. His manner was eager; his speech quick, even a little rushed sometimes, as his thoughts would pour out in abrupt little bursts. John was an enthusiast. He was fun. His blindness was only a disability to others. To him it was a spur to achieve everything ingenuity, courage and intelligence could invent or envisage as possible.' When she had first met him he had told her, like others, that he believed he might recover his sight before he was twenty-one, but she considers that before they parted he had realized that this was a fantasy.

I asked Miriam, who was in time to become a university lecturer in English literature, what she had thought of Wilson's poetry. She replied that his poems were often poignant though they were immature, both emotionally and in a literary sense. I am less qualified to judge. But I share that view.

Wilson's remaining time at Oxford was probably the least happy period of his life. He had been disillusioned by his first love affair. In September 1939, his sister Winnie, to whom he was deeply attached, died at the age of thirty-five. And war was approaching. His diary, as at Worcester, recorded factually the main events in the build-up to war but, as before, offered almost no political judgement. In October 1939, he returned to an Oxford which had changed beyond recognition. Undergraduates were drilling in the Parks with rifles and bayonets. The boathouse was locked. There were no crews on the river. 'The city has lost its laughter. Everything seems to be provisional, waiting for some monstrous conclusion.' Each morning when he passed the Divinity Schools, he found people queuing to enlist. He asked a disillusioned sergeant about his own prospects. The latter replied that he was coming to believe that the higher commands of the armed forces were recruited exclusively from the deaf and mentally handicapped, but he did not really think that there was a job for the blind. Wilson buried himself in work, for there was nothing else to do.

At the end of 1939 his tutor encouraged him in his developing view that he should make a career in work for blind people and arranged for him to visit the National Institute for the Blind in London. Its Secretary General, W. McG. Eagar, suggested he should spend a fourth year at Oxford and take a Diploma course in Social Administration and also do some general social work, following which he would take him onto the National Institute's staff.

First, he had to take his final degree examination. Oxford had become a rather lonely place for him. Most of the young people had left the student accommodation where he was living and it was being filled up with army officers 'and their bridge-playing wives'. He worked hard at his law books. His diary – and the tapes – become much thinner. He has nothing to say about his finals. Several of the obituaries of Wilson, published on his death in 1999, stated that he obtained First Class degrees in Law and Sociology. But this is wrong on nearly every count. The University and College records show that he was one of eighteen students who obtained a Second

Class degree in Law in 1940 (there were two Firsts). There was no such thing as a degree course in Sociology at Oxford.

In October 1940, he returned to the University for his post-graduate course in Public and Social Administration. He found its practical aspects depressing. He had to visit mental institutions, orphanages and homes for the old and handicapped which he thought Dickensian and deplorable. 'You got no sense that the show was run in the interests of the residents. Worcester had taught me about participation and I saw none of that.' But academically he found his examination in May 1941 fairly easy and he was awarded a diploma with distinction in Public and Social Administration.

War was the constant background. On Good Friday 1941, he tried to compose his mind for Easter. But there constantly intruded 'the thought of the shattered homes of England and the dead men in the Balkan Passes. I tried to think of the love of God merging with the sins of men through the unresisting suffering of a perfect being. But more contemporary are the thoughts of Gethsemane and the lonely cry of Jesus on the Cross.'

Despite the sadness of his last year or so, and the changed character of Oxford in wartime, he would generally look back on his time at Oxford positively. And so he should have done. He had mostly enjoyed himself, especially on the river. His academic achievements had been respectable. He was more mature emotion-ally. He was a physically confident, determined and focused young man who now knew the direction he wanted his career to take, at least initially. It is perhaps a little strange, given his prowess later on as an exceptionally persuasive public speaker, that he never men-tions the Oxford Union – the university debating society. If he ever attended it, it certainly did not figure largely in his Oxford life. But the Union was not everyone's cup of tea. It was never mine.

As he left the University, he believed that the enchantment and experience of Oxford would stay with him forever. Which they did. He came to be much decorated and honoured. But few things gave him greater pleasure than his Honorary Fellowship of St Catherine's to which he was elected in 1984. Reviewing his life in an obituary, Sir Patrick Nairne, formerly Master of St Catherine's, was to de-scribe him as perhaps the most remarkable of the College's alumni.

Chapter 2

To Work

As John Wilson began his working life at the age of twenty-two, he could have had no idea where his interest in the problems of blindness would carry him. The usual uncertainties confronting any young person at that age were greatly magnified by the fact that his country was at war. Not just Britain but the world in general was racked with doubt, and fear, as to what the future held. But within a few years of his arrival in wartime London to begin work, he moved from the domestic to the international stage, which became his natural arena. In those years, too, he met and married Jean, who was to become his indispensable partner at home, and later at work, for the rest of his life.

He left Oxford in May 1941 and began his first job in June as Assistant Secretary at the National Institute for the Blind, then in Great Portland Street, London. He would often say subsequently, with a touch of bravado, that wartime London was an exciting and stimulating place to be, provided you were not actually being hit by the bombs. He quickly became used to the routine of air-raid sirens, taking cover in air-raid shelters and emerging with the sounding of the 'all clear'. He sometimes slept on a camp bed at the office, on duty in case bombs set fire to the building. 'Between the bursts of fire we heard the spectral whisper of the barrage balloons over Regents Park. Suddenly, an appalling roar of an approaching engine, reaching a crescendo of sound. It seemed as though it must crash into our building. But it flew on and the sound died away. Soon the all-clear sounded. We made a cup of cocoa and went back to our creaking beds.'

But if he became used to this routine there were other adjustments to make. After a night of air raids he always wondered whether the landmarks that he used in order to move around the city would have changed. 'For me as a blind man in London,' he wrote a little later, 'the whole sound and feel and smell of the place have changed. The railings have gone. I have to be careful not to stray from the path into somebody's garden. Where there used to be the yawning, hollow echo of a doorway, there is now the flat, soggy echo of a pile of sandbags. People speak with brisker voices and walk with firmer steps. There's no longer the smell of perfume in the theatre queues. New sounds – the crunch of troops marching down the street, the rush of aeroplanes through the air, the odd whisper of the barrage balloons like the sound of poplar trees in the country.'

It was a stimulating time in another sense. The war had produced in Britain a ferment of ideas about social and economic change. The concept of the welfare state was being debated and there was much discussion of new techniques for involving disabled workers in wartime production and for the rehabilitation of people disabled in war.

Wilson was one of two Assistant Secretaries working to W. McG. Eagar, still the Secretary-General of the National Institute. His starting salary was £250 a year which together with £150 interest on his investments was, he says in his diary, more than enough for his requirements. It paid for his accommodation and meals at the small hotel where he first lodged. He found Eagar a bit of a martinet in the office and rather pompous. But in general he greatly admired him and he was to benefit considerably from his experience, knowledge and assistance. The staff had been much depleted by the wartime call-up, so Wilson had many more opportunities than would normally have come his way, taking over as temporary head of various departments in turn.

It is said of the National Institute that at that time it was very Victorian in its approach to the problems of blindness, the general ethos being one of work, as a matter of charity, for the blind. Visually impaired people rightly criticize, indeed often resist, this approach, believing that the services they need should be received as a matter of right rather than charity. Wilson was in that camp, convinced that the thrust of the Institute's work must be to develop opportunities for blind people to participate in society and help themselves. This philosophy admirably suited the area where he was to develop particular expertise in the next few years – the employment of blind people in industry. There was a severe shortage of labour in military production which he believed could be redressed by training blind workers. He badly wanted to bury the notion that the inevitable lot of the blind was to take up 'bloody basket-making'. Germany and the United States had already shown that blind people could do a great variety of mechanized jobs. He perhaps established – certainly worked hard on – the Institute's wartime placement scheme. With other staff he visited war factories and assessed the tasks that could be carried out by blind people.

In June 1943, he wrote an article in *The Factory Manager* on 'The Blind – Their Place in Industry'. He marshalled the arguments and evidence for the employment of the blind, reinforcing these with a list of industrial processes now being competently performed by blind people and with photographs of them doing jobs that were not of the basket-making variety. He was already showing a good flair for presentation and publicity, as well as adopting the style and tone of a campaigner. By the end of the war some three thousand blind people were in proper employment.

In late 1944, he again wrote about the employment of visually impaired people, this time in the *New Beacon*, the Institute's periodical, to which he would contribute numerous pieces over the years. Entitled 'Towards Full Employment', this well-written and strongly felt article noted that many blind people were still engaged in traditional crafts whose economic justification was questionable even before the industrial revolution. He argued that blind workshops must modernize and mechanize for a future of greater opportunity, for otherwise no subsidy would save them. The new Disabled Persons (Employment) Act of 1944 offered unsubsidized employment in a wide range of enterprises. A constructive plan should be formulated. Wartime experience was showing that over a wide range of specialized factory operations 'the average blind man can equal, and in some cases surpass, the output of the seeing worker of similar general ability. Workshops should enter the light engineering, plastics and electrical industries, mechanizing production to the maximum.'

One of the Institute's main preoccupations at this time was to try to ensure that the work then proceeding in Britain on the creation of the welfare state made appropriate provision for blind people. The Beveridge Report, which proposed a comprehensive 'cradle to the grave' system of compulsory social insurance, had been published in 1942, and it became the basis for all detailed social planning and policy making for post-war Britain. Wilson noted in his diary that it received a good press except from the insurance companies and some members of the medical profession. He and others at the Institute had worked on a memorandum designed to counter the concept that work for blind people, which had a century or so of specialized development behind it, should simply be absorbed into a generic social service. They argued instead for specialized provision, using specialized institutions within a general framework. The memorandum, *Blind Welfare and Social Security*, was duly submitted to Sir William Beveridge's inter-departmental committee and Wilson later pronounced that the Institute's basic approach had been more or less accepted.

While at the Institute, John Wilson learned a good deal about the politics of blindness issues. A fellow member of staff was Ben Purse whom Wilson called 'my particular mentor'. Purse was a blind man with unrivalled knowledge of the personalities, policies and manoeuvrings of forty years' work for blind people. 'He conveyed to our generation the very real grass roots feel of the misery and passion which generated the first Blind Persons Act, when he marched with the blind on London in 1918, demanding bread before Braille.' Purse was one of the founders of the National League for the Blind and later the National Association of Blind Workers. These radical organizations disliked the whole idea of charity and disapproved of the National Institute. They believed that governmental rather than voluntary action was needed to improve the lot of visually impaired people, and that government would only be stirred to move by political pressure. The movement had some success, but by the end of the Second World War the National Association of Blind Workers was no longer effective and there were moves to dissolve it. Even Purse thought that radicalism had had its day. A new generation was emerging among blind people. Many now believed that progress would best be achieved by partnership between voluntary organizations and the state.

A little earlier, Wilson had formed the 'Worcester Study Group' at the National Institute, made up of people from Worcester College, the universities and blind people from the professions, to study contemporary issues in work for the blind, and especially to achieve better representation for blind people. A meeting was arranged between the Group and the National Association of Blind Workers which led in 1946 to the formation of the National Federation of the Blind. Wilson later became its second President, serving from 1955 to 1960. Today, the Federation's new headquarters, opened in Wakefield in 2002, is called 'John Wilson House'.

Since leaving Oxford Wilson had had one or two health problems. In September 1941, he had an operation to relieve 'traumatic glaucoma', a description which always puzzled him. He often felt pain in the areas around his eyes. That operation, whatever it was, did not solve the problem. In June 1942, he had an operation on his appendix at the National Temperance Hospital in London. Rowing friends who came to visit were amused by the venue and left empty beer bottles under his bed. But these medical interludes had little effect on his work, and it is noticeable from the diary that, after the rather introspective and dark tone of his last year in Oxford, the old sense of fun and optimism was returning. Involvement in interesting and useful work doubtless explains this in part. But there was a more important factor: Wilson was in love again.

Some time after his eye operation, he decided to move out of central London, not least because his parents were worried about the continued German bombing. Through his sister he found accommodation in a house in the (then) village of Eastcote, near Pinner in Middlesex, where a widow and her daughter lived. The daughter was Jean McDermid, then aged nineteen. She was studying history at Westfield College, a part of the University of London which had been evacuated to St Peter's Hall, Oxford, during the war.

By mid 1942, John and Jean were spending a lot of time together and John confided to his diary that he was acutely aware of the shy happiness between them, adding, 'How a blind man misses the visual content, the sign and half-sign, and how difficult this must all be for Jean. Fearing to break the precious, frail thread of intimacy, I am determined to do nothing which might seem to force the pace. Let us grow simply and naturally together. Yet I feel sure with a conviction I've never dared before that this can be the beginning of a momentous change, treading carefully into a new and holy land, so different from the importunity and ultimate disenchantment of earlier relationships.'

He invited Jean to spend two weeks of the summer holidays with his family at Buxton in August 1942. His father, George, the devotee of archaeology, knowing that Jean was a historian, put some skulls and other finds from his digs on the top of the wardrobe in her bedroom. On Jean's birthday George gave her a book with which, perhaps not with the greatest subtlety, he enclosed some lines from Housman:

'Now of your three score years and ten
Twenty will not come again.
And take from seventy years a score,
It only leaves you fifty more.'

On 28 August they walked to the Ramshaw Rocks. Let the diary
speak. 'A fine sunny day, warm amongst the rocks and the wild
bracken with a tingling scent of thyme and the honey scent of
heather, the air alive with the constant buzz and traffic of incense.'
And later, 'Evening came on. The warmth and the noise went out of
the air, leaving a cold breeze and complete silence.' John asked Jean
to marry him. She agreed to do so. 'Fog was coming on. We walked
rapidly along the road and I felt that we were shining together as we
walked.'

Back home at midnight, they told Wilson's parents, who were delighted. After Jean had gone to bed, George said, 'You've struck oil
there, lad.' A brother-in-law who met Jean told John, 'She is a real
English beauty. Blonde, honey hair. A marvellous figure. And those
straight eyes. You wouldn't want to try any nonsense with her. She
looks far too intelligent for my liking.'

When Jean returned to Oxford for her studies, John visited her at
weekends. They took long walks, spent time on the river, and went
to the theatre and to services in college chapels. Deeply in love,
Wilson composed a poem:

'No need for sign or half-sign
Let but our fingers touch
Our feet are off the earth
Here in the hollow of my two hands
Is the knowledge of you
Here in the corner of my mind
Is the secret stored
In the quick blood
And deep in the dull bone
Is the joy of my beloved
Above the substance and the image
Strive together the form and the idea
But here in the silence
Is the dark presence of my beloved
She is that one alone

That is no trespasser
Whose presence is as rain on soft grass falling
A silence dropping thro' the still air.'

Wilson's optimism was quite restored. 'How good it is that we share this incomparable city together.' And then a twinge of conscience: 'We are so easily happy, just enjoying this full life together, somewhat guiltily because so many people are just losing everything in this awful war.' They decided to postpone their wedding until Jean had finished her studies at Oxford, but they were beginning to regret this decision by the spring of 1944. They were eventually married on 4 July 1944 at Ruislip Parish Church. A marriage of fifty-five years lay ahead of them. It will be a constant thread running through the rest of this story. Each made a distinctive contribution, but together they formed a partnership which was crucial to Wilson's career and achievements across the world.

The main activities of the National Institute for the Blind were focused on the United Kingdom. But it had international interests as well, in which Wilson became involved. He was given some responsibility for international relations and re-building national organizations for blind people in Europe.

The war had revealed new facts about visual impairment in the British colonies in Africa and Asia. A large number of Africans, in particular, had been found unfit for military service because of defective eyesight. As military hospitals were established in some of the colonies to handle casualties on the battlefield, their medical staff became conscious of – and reported on – the health situation of the civilian populations in their areas. Then, when British troops returned from the colonies towards the end of the war, further reports were received about the status of blind people and the prevalence of blinding diseases in the tropics. The Institute collected and analysed this information and reconstituted its Empire and Colonial Sub-Committee, which had been disbanded at the outset of the war, with a mandate to keep the question of blind welfare in the colonies under review and to make recommendations. Wilson became its Secretary. This piece of bureaucracy became the unlikely springboard for a big leap forward in his life and career.

The Colonial Office – the department of government principally responsible for policy towards the colonies – was entering a period of considerable change. A series of events in recent years had led to much domestic and international criticism of economic and social conditions in the colonies. Earlier, colonial governments had largely been left to take decisions about development by themselves and to finance their plans with such funds as they could raise within their territories. Social services were not a priority, and few territories offered anything in this field. But it was now recognized in London that more initiative from the centre was required, and a certain amount of funding was provided by the 1940 Colonial Development and Welfare Act and its successors.

This was by no means entirely the product of undiluted idealism. British governments were increasingly preoccupied by the United Kingdom's grave economic and financial situation, induced by the heavy strains of the war. For many in Westminster and Whitehall the purpose of investment in the colonies was to make them more profitable and to ease Britain's own difficulties. But there were other views. Arthur Creech-Jones, who became Colonial Secretary in the new Labour government in 1946, had long been associated with African nationalism through the Fabian Society. He advocated a progressive colonial policy based on long-term economic, technological and educational development. Within the Colonial Office itself, which expanded rapidly through the 1940s to take on new tasks, there were some active reformers. Its Social Services Department had begun taking an interest in blind welfare and the prevention of blindness in the Colonies well before the end of the war.

The Colonial Office agreed to provide a Chairman for the resurrected Empire and Colonial Sub-Committee at the Institute and appointed to the job Sir Bernard Reilly, who had been Governor of Aden until 1940 and had since been working in London. The Institute asked the Colonial Office how they could help it to develop blind welfare in the Colonies and were told that the best course might be to send out an emissary to judge the size and nature of the problem, to stimulate interest and to create a nucleus of working machinery.

Discussion continued throughout the summer of 1945 and by September it was agreed that the government and the Institute would share the cost of a tour and that it should be undertaken by a team of three. Two of these should have a thorough knowledge of blind welfare. Ideally one should be a man and one a woman, the latter because in some of the territories to be visited it would be easier for a woman to deal with women and children. 'With regard to the sending of a blind man or woman,' the minutes state, 'it was thought that the all-important factor was that of suitability, knowledge and experience, which should override all other considerations.' The third member of the Mission was originally to have been a doctor, but it was later decided that a Colonial Office official was needed instead. Initially, the plan was to despatch the team in December 1945 but this proved impossible because air transport, priorities for which in the immediate post-war situation were still laid down by the Cabinet, could not be made available. So the tour was re-planned to begin in July 1946 at a total cost of about £5,000.

Although Wilson was seen as a candidate for the tour early on, Eagar was still saying in the autumn of 1946 that he was not sure Wilson could be made available because so far no replacement for him had been identified. If that view had prevailed, Wilson's whole life would have been radically different. But some solution must have been found because on 10 January 1946, the Committee approved the composition: Wilson, described by the Colonial Office as 'an expert in industrial training and placement of the blind'; Miss Mary Thomas, Information Officer at the Institute and an expert in the training of blind teachers and blind homeworkers; and Captain Douglas Heath, a former Administrative Officer in Nigeria, who had fought in the war, was now working in the Colonial Office and was said to have an established interest in the medical care of blind persons and the prevention of blindness – after the tour he was appointed Secretary of the Medical Department in Tanganyika. The purpose of the Mission was 'to advise on and stimulate interest in blind welfare and the prevention of blindness, and to report on facts relevant to future policy.' Prevention of blindness, as distinct from its cure and measures to assist blind people, was a new concept at this time, but it was to become a major theme of Wilson's life.

The task was distinctly ambitious, particularly for this group of people. Heath had some knowledge of Africa and India, and of colonial government. Mary Thomas had not travelled abroad widely, if at all. Sighted and in her late fifties, she was an early woman graduate of Cambridge. Wilson described her as an 'almost classic old maid, but very amusing and gallant'. She had taken a particular interest in him when he had arrived at the Institute and, according to a contemporary, gave him a lot of help. Wilson, aged twenty-seven, had never left Britain and never been on an aircraft.

(In 1947 only three per cent of Britons went abroad on holiday and forty-three per cent took no holiday at all.)

Sir Bernard Reilly was worried about how a blind man would cope with a nine-month tour of Africa and the Middle East and suggested to Eagar that Wilson would need to be accompanied by a manservant or by one of the Arab 'boys' he had brought back with him as household staff from Aden. Eagar dismissed this at once: 'I dare not suggest to Wilson that he must have a man to look after him. That is contrary to the whole ethos of the blind and of our work for and with them. The presence of a manservant to look after him because he is blind would negate the reasons for sending a blind man on the Mission.'

Wilson wrote to Reilly in late January 1946 asking for a list of books he should read, 'something which will give me an insight into the principles of administration which are being applied in the various areas we are to visit ... I want, if I can, to get a living picture of conditions and of the frame of mind of the individual African.'

He must have felt he was going into something of a void. In an address to the British Psychological Society in February he said, 'Contemplating a tour of tropical Africa which I plan to undertake this summer, I am completely unable to achieve any conception of the territory apart from specific situations such as myself in a mosquito net, myself listening to the buzz and chatter of an African market. A sighted person with a similar background to my own would probably have a workable conception of tropical Africa built up from films, pictures and visits to the zoo and tropical gardens.'

Looking back many years afterwards, he said that the Mission were unprepared for the trip, and that they received no briefing. This is not strictly true. Colonial Office files show that papers, somewhat scanty to be sure, were prepared on the problems of blindness in the colonies they were to visit. Moreover, the team would have absorbed a certain amount of information from discussion in the Sub-Committee. Its Chairman, Reilly, had explained at the outset the need for realism: the idea of the Mission had arisen because colonial administrations were too short of staff to investigate blindness themselves; this was not the moment for an extensive new venture, placing additional responsibilities upon colonial governments. But the fact is that it would have been impossible for a substantial briefing to have been provided because the Mission was novel. It was to examine an area where there was not much expertise available in London. It was largely uncharted territory. Moreover, the whole concept of the Mission was bold. At the beginning of the twenty-first century, when overseas travel is an unremarked part of ordinary life, it needs a considerable effort of the imagination to appreciate the scale of the task of travelling to and around rural Africa in the 1940s, especially for an unsighted person.

Some of the problems that might have arisen were mitigated by the fact that the tour took place under the umbrella of the Colonial Office. In pre-independence Africa the effectiveness of the team's investigations would necessarily depend heavily on the attitude of colonial administrations. Captain Heath had been appointed, essentially, to liaise between the Mission and colonial officials. The Colonial Office asked all the administrations in the colonies to be visited to prepare detailed itineraries. The Mission was often accompanied on the spot by colonial officials, usually those holding a welfare brief. Outfit allowances were provided, but it was agreed that the Institute's members of the party need not be rigidly bound by the 'inadequate' level of these. In a delightful piece of nannying the Sub-Committee minutes solemnly record that 'the essentiality that adequate rest be taken by the party was also emphasized.' It would become clear that 'rest' was not Wilson's top priority, now or ever.

Reflecting much later on the decision to despatch the Mission, Wilson said, 'I remember still with great clarity the extraordinary feeling that this was a turning point in my life. Another turning point, and something I must do, accompanied by the distress of leaving Jean to cope with the house we were adapting and also at the almost unthinkable idea of leaving for a while the joy, humour, grace and delight of our marriage.' But Jean was excited by the idea and they jointly agreed that he should go ahead.

There had been much discussion with the Colonial Office over the precise itinerary to be followed. But it was finally settled that it should be: Cyprus, Palestine, Aden, Kenya, Uganda, Tanganyika, Zanzibar, Northern Rhodesia (later Zambia), Nyasaland (Malawi), Nigeria, the Gold Coast (Ghana) and Sierra Leone. They would also visit Egypt, although it was not a colony, in view of the results already achieved there in the prevention and cure of blindness. The tour would take nine months from July 1946 until March 1947.

On 19 July, Wilson arrived at Staines airport (later Heathrow), which he found was still in a very temporary state. There were flapping marquees and primitive sanitary arrangements. The nine passengers waited interminably for loads to be balanced on the Dakota aircraft. They included Creech-Jones, the Colonial Secretary, and Andrew Cohen, the strongest advocate among Colonial Office officials of progressive colonial policies, who were leaving for a separate mission to East Africa.

As Wilson, who was to travel hundreds of thousands of miles in the future, had never flown before, a steward showed him how to use his seatbelt and to breathe deeply as the plane took off, holding his nose and blowing to equalize the pressure. They were prevented from landing at Bordeaux by a storm: 'A lurch, a sickening lift of the stomach and a staccato pattern of hail on the fuselage, the plane veering in every direction'. They reached Cairo the next day. Wilson spent a fascinating afternoon there with Taha Hussein, the celebrated Egyptian writer who, as a blind child, had begun his education in a Koranic school and had memorized much of the Koran by the age of ten. He told Wilson that by the time he had heard of Braille he was too busy to learn it. Wilson found him to be interested in the psychology and philosophy of blindness but not in blind welfare. By the end of August the Mission had also visited Cyprus, Palestine and Aden and were ready to move on to Africa where they would spend the remaining seven months or so of their allotted time.

At this point the information from Wilson's diary becomes much thinner, primarily because he lost two of the four Braille volumes which covered the period of the Mission's work. But by now the team were beginning to send back detailed interim reports on each country visited. In his only book written for a popular readership, *Travelling Blind* (Hutchinson, 1963), he would comment on this and other travels. It is a colourful, perceptive and witty account but so bereft of dates that it is by no means always clear which particular visit to which country is being discussed.

We shall come to the substance of the Mission's work shortly. But the experience was memorable for Wilson in many other ways. He had left behind the dismal atmosphere of post-war Britain with its inheritance of bombed cities, food shortages, rationing and political and social tension and he was about to miss the terribly cold, snow-bound winter of 1946-7. Instead, he was exposed for the first time to the exhilaration of foreign travel.

Crossing Lake Victoria in October he wrote to Jean of the 'regal

Lake eagles diving powerfully across the full length of the ship with their fearful, sobbing, heathen cry ... I stood for hours in the bows with the keen wind blowing through my hair, listening to the zip of water cut by the prow, and astern the sound of the screw is like a waterfall.'

In November he was in Zanzibar to which, he said in a later BBC broadcast, he gave his 'smell' prize: 'A mile offshore you get the first whiff of cloves and frangipani, but the full impact is in the alley-ways: warehouses stocked with perfumes, spices and abominable shark meat, shuttered courtyards where there is lemon blossom and the frail scent of moonflowers. There are misty little cubicles where Chinese herbalists sell cures for everything: seahorse for asthma, ginger oil for falling hair, a row of vile-smelling concoctions for backache. Zanzibar women wear a perfume called ylang ylang, distilled from a pure blossom.' The sounds and smells of the places he visited, and his sense of touch, always gave him the power to produce vivid passages of description.

He recorded, too, the impact made on him by the apparatus of Empire: 'The Colonies with their Governors and Pro-Consuls. Great Government Houses. Chief Justices and District Officers. The White Man's Burden is seen slightly as a joke, but in reality it is still there in many ways with rioting students and urgent clamour from intellectuals who want to become political leaders.' Few realized in 1946 how quickly political independence would come in Africa. It would be an important backdrop to much of Wilson's subsequent work in the continent.

Then there were the difficulties of travel. Neither now, nor when he was a frequent user of jet aircraft, did he suffer much from jet-lag. He wondered if jetlag was visually triggered because in his experience many blind people did not suffer from it. He would stay in countless unfamiliar houses and hotels though he of course had available to him the techniques which are well known to visually impaired people, and some of which he invented himself. A pipe-smoker at that time, he habitually tied a pipe-cleaner round the door knob of his hotel room so that he could readily distinguish it from all the other identical rooms. The problem of choosing a shirt and tie to match the colour of his suit was simply solved through the small tabs sewn into the lining of his clothes, each tab stamped in Braille to tell him the colour and the pattern.

Other problems were less easily dealt with. He commented on a cocktail party in Bathurst (now Banjul, Gambia): 'On such an occasion I am always grateful if there is an air-conditioner in the room. Apart from its advertised advantages, it provides a static piece of sound around which you can navigate like a sailor fixing his course by the North Pole. A fan, and particularly a large ceiling fan, has the reverse effect: it disperses the sounds and scents. You turn to face a voice and find you're in fact simply facing the draught. The gardenia perfume which you have identified as the bank manager's wife comes disconcertingly from the direction of the Salvation Army Captain.'

The results of the Mission's nine-month enquiry were described in the report produced on their return, which was published by the Government as an official document in 1948. Wilson says that he was responsible for writing it. Certainly, his style is apparent in many parts. Those who have had the not unalloyed pleasure of reading Whitehall documents may agree that few official reports begin quite so graphically as this one: 'We came across a blind lad of fifteen, strong, heavily built, half reclining on a bench in the sun. He was not apparently feeble-minded, but so far as we could see he was completely lethargic, and to all the remarks and questions addressed to him by the African village teacher, he did not once reply. Will the casual passer-by, in ten, twenty, forty, fifty years' time, still find him sitting there? Mere physical existence is, in itself, of little value and such a blind person, untaught and untrained, will almost certainly degenerate into a condition not far removed from mental deficiency...Is life, in such circumstances, worth very much?'

The Mission were greatly surprised by the amount of blindness they discovered. However, they found it much harder to produce statistics to illustrate this. While Cyprus, Palestine and Aden were able to provide figures for the total number of blind people in their populations, only two of the African territories visited, Nyasaland and the Gold Coast, could supply similar statistics. The dismal social status of blind people struck them with force: 'In the primitive conditions of a native village, a blind individual is at a grave disadvantage as compared with his European counterparts. Hazards, living and immediate, against which sight alone is a defence, restrict his freedom of movement and even his chance of survival. He has none of the gadgets, techniques and institutions which aid the blind in modern countries, and his rural economy provides fewer opportunities...But perhaps his greatest handicap is his own and his neighbour's attitude towards his disability. At all stages of life, blindness means total incapacity – the child is pampered and useless, the man is a dependent relative, the woman is unmarriage-able, with all this means in primitive society. Though accident or disease may be recognized as the cause of blindness, its under-lying cause is felt to be supernatural – the curse of a magician, the malice of a spirit, or some offence committed in a previous exist-ence...The attitude is one of fatalistic resignation into the place prescribed by custom for the blind.'

In general, family and tribe ensured that blind people had food, shelter and clothing. But this relief covered merely their animal necessities and left out of account the right of the blind individual to develop the faculties and interests of a normal human being. And, with de-tribalization and urbanization, the system was break-ing down anyway. There was emerging a class of blind beggar in many areas, that was often dependent on alms-giving. For the time being, the Mission recommended, blind children in the rural areas should be educated and trained for work among their own people in their home village, so that family and tribal structures were pre-served. But the long-term policy should be to create a new type of blind person through a sequence of schools, training centres and employment.

The Mission often heard from medical and other sources that seventy-five to eighty per cent of blindness in the colonies was pre-ventable. They considered they had ample proof of this fact. But the point was then academic, given the sparseness of the medical services available. Everywhere these were sub-optimal. With their limited resources the existing services were compelled to con-centrate more than they wished on the clinical rather than the pre-ventive and health aspects of medicine. Tanganyika (later, with Zanzibar, Tanzania) had only 2.87 doctors per 100,000 population (England had 50 per 100,000 at the time). In Nigeria 'the total expenditure of the Medical Department is literally only sufficient to supply one aspirin tablet to every person once a year.' There was in general little emphasis on the prevention and treatment of eye diseases. Medical officers concentrated on the 'killing diseases'; medical training did not devote much time to eyes and, in the circumstances of Africa in the 1940s, general medical practice was the first priority.

As to the specific causes of blindness, again little statistical information was available. Trachoma (an eye infection that causes scarring on the underside of the eyelid, which then turns inward so that the eyelashes painfully scratch the eyeball) was, the Mission believed, endemic over most of the continent. Cataract (which causes the lens of the eyes to become hazy, and eventually blinds) was prevalent among older blind people. Nutritional deficiency, smallpox and leprosy were also thought to cause eye problems. Then there was onchocersiasis (a blinding disease caused by a parasite: a worm, transmitted to humans by the bite of the black simulium fly) which was known to be particularly severe in parts of Uganda, Kenya and the Gold Coast.

The Mission were by no means the first people to comment on these problems. Since at least the eighteenth century travellers had remarked on the high prevalence of blindness and had recorded the existence of organized blind communities in such places as Kano in Northern Nigeria. Missionary organizations and voluntary societies had been providing education for blind people for some decades in some of the African and Middle Eastern colonies. But coverage was very thin and there were only a handful of institutions. Some provided vocational training but, Palestine apart, the Mission found none which offered a full training, employment and aftercare service. Indeed, they did not think voluntary organizations could be expected to provide such a service and took the view that positive action was needed from colonial governments. The team visited a wide selection of institutions, mostly schools for blind children, but found only one run by government.

So what should be done? The first essential, the Mission reported, was to devise two types of organization: *local*, to coordinate the activities of departments and agencies involved in work on blindness in the territory concerned; and *inter-territorial*, to supply services that were common to a group of adjacent territories and could not economically be provided by each colony separately. Detailed proposals were made as to how the local organizations should be structured. But most emphasis was placed on the need for the three 'dynamic' inter-territorial organizations proposed for East and Central Africa (together), West Africa, and the Mediterranean and the Near East (together). Elaborate structures were recommended. The first of the inter-territorial organizations, in Kampala, might be developed as a model and take the form of an independent corporation, sponsored by the Colonial Office and by each of the governments in the area. The overall task was to combine official and unofficial – including missionary – activity to produce the best blind welfare service that was obtainable in each territory. 'We emphatically hold the view that each government is primarily responsible for ensuring the best Blind Welfare Scheme which the Colony can afford.'

Money? The 'Imperial Treasury' should meet the main cost of initiating inter-territorial schemes. Colonial governments and local and native authorities should finance institutions and services in their own territories. The resources provided by the Colonial Development and Welfare Act should be used. Further detailed proposals were made for a scheme of registration for blind people and for the collection of statistics.

One of the largest chapters of the report was devoted to the *prevention* of blindness. Better education was needed to eradicate ignorance which was a leading cause of eye problems. Better sanitary services and water supplies were required. Vaccination against smallpox and simple personal measures such as the use of eye-drops should be promoted. As a policy matter, major emphasis should be placed on the widespread prevention of further disease rather than on elaborate hospital services for the probable cure of the few. Nevertheless, the clinical services for the treatment of eyes should be improved and extended. The ophthalmologist should not sit in the capital but should go on tour, especially in the rural areas. The travelling eye unit, a vehicle with personnel and equipment to deal with eye problems, which was already used in Egypt and India, should be introduced. African medical officers should be encouraged to take up eye work, and trained African opticians should relieve eye surgeons of refractive work (the provision of spectacles and other devices).

Only a minute proportion of blind children attended school. The education of the young blind should be part of the general education policy of each colony. Where there were not enough blind children to justify a special school, colonies should adopt, not the English system whereby the blind were educated in special schools, but the emerging American system, where 'Braille classes' were attached to schools for the sighted. Detailed proposals were made on teacher training and vocational training. Provision should be made for employing the blind as homeworkers, village craftsmen, employees in sheltered workshops, operatives in factories and clerks or professional staff. Finally, the Mission set out its ideas for developing the use of Braille in the colonies.

Wilson returned to England in April 1947. Later on he remembered 'the joy and delight of returning home and finding Jean so fit and well'. She had converted their house in West Hampstead into three flats, of which they occupied the bottom one. Jean was then working at an agency, teaching history to girls who were going on to university. For the next four months Wilson must have been preoccupied with writing the report I have described, which was a substantial document running to nearly a hundred pages.

The Empire and Colonial Sub-Committee reconvened in May with the three members of the Mission in attendance. But not until 17 October did it decide to send the report to the Colonial Office for printing. At that day's meeting, Reilly warned the Committee that colonial governments were working under pressure; some were short of money and all were short of staff. They were being pressed on every side to put in hand development and welfare projects as well as to extend their normal services. The Colonial Development and Welfare Fund, though large, was inadequate to meet all demands, and all sorts of schemes were being prepared and priorities re-cast. He added that the Committee should remember that colonial governments were constitutional bodies which, in varying degrees, controlled their own affairs and their own finances.

This was a good deal more than a hint that the Mission's report was not going to have an easy passage. It is not difficult to imagine how the young Wilson felt as the cold water of Whitehall began to be poured on the document which he had compiled (though all three members of the Mission had signed it). He was neither the first nor the last to present enthusiastic ideas to his superiors and to discover that they, unaccountably, did not altogether share the enthusiasm of their authors.

In April 1948 the report was sent to all colonial governments in the territories visited. Reilly contributed a foreword which showed how the wind was blowing. It was, he said, the hope of the Colonial Secretary that the recommendations would be carefully and sympathetically examined. Some would be expensive to implement but it was hoped that they would be largely adopted. 'A regional organization for the treatment of the problems of the blind in East and West Africa is one of the proposals ... which may be regarded with some hesitation. On the other hand, the Committee feels that it is a proposal which deserves careful consideration, and that it may prove to be a most fruitful suggestion.' The wording is balanced but no recipient of the report would have felt under serious pressure from London to adopt the always ambitious proposals for inter-territorial organizations which were central to the report.

Wilson had some other preoccupations. Around this time he worked with a number of colleagues on a draft constitution for a World Council for the Welfare of the Blind, later to be the World Blind Union. He was also active in work which was proceeding under UNESCO auspices to develop a world Braille code. But he was feeling frustrated. In May 1948, Eagar wrote to a Colonial Office official to say that Wilson was worrying a good deal about his future, 'not surprisingly as he is a good man who needs scope for his energy, ideas and practical ability.' Wilson, he continued, had had an offer of a job with the United Nations but as things had developed he would prefer to work in the colonial service, and particularly in Africa. The official agreed to see Wilson on 8 June. Wilson told him that he saw no immediate likelihood of a respon-sible job at the Institute and was anxious to improve his prospects. During his tour in Africa he had developed a keen interest in colonial problems and he therefore wondered whether there was any possibility of the Colonial Office employing him. He was especially interested in the report's proposal to establish inter-territorial organizations.

The official obtained the clear impression that what Wilson really wanted was the post of Director of Blind Welfare Services in East and Central Africa which the report had recommended. He recorded his view that Wilson was 'a thoroughly competent man with a gift for administration, who had achieved a remarkable degree of independence and ability to get about and lead a useful life in spite of his great affliction.' It was agreed that the East African authorities should be consulted. When they eventually replied they turned down the idea, not because of reservations about Wilson or his blindness but because they had no enthusiasm for creating the inter-territorial organization to which the post would be attached. It is significant that, following his first exposure to Africa, Wilson wanted so much to work there rather than con-tinue at the Institute. Perhaps he also wanted to smoke out the Colonial Office on their attitude to one of the Mission's most important proposals. In any event, the Colonial Service's loss was, in the long run, the world's gain, particularly the world of visually impaired people.

When Reilly's Committee met again in October 1948, Wilson, probably impatiently, urged the need for action before the interest created by the report had dissipated. He recommended that the Colonial Office, together with the Institute, should prepare a costed scheme for the establishment of an inter-territorial organization, the expenditure being met from Colonial Office funds. But the meeting saw 'certain difficulties' in this and set up an ad hoc committee to look into the matter. The meeting also noted that few replies had so far been received from colonial governments and that most of these had been disappointing. For example, Uganda and Tanganyika were reluctant to establish special measures for the education and training of the blind. The Colonial Office felt there was so much to be done in education in general that it was difficult to quarrel with this decision. Reilly urged realism. The Committee must not be disappointed by the delay. 'Governors of Colonies are hard pressed. Not only do they have to cope with local problems such as bad crops, floods, outbreaks of violence like the lion murders in Tanganyika and leopard murders in the Gold Coast and Nigeria, but they receive from the Colonial Office an ever increasing bulk of circular despatches on all sorts of matters.' There spoke a former Governor with a thoroughly realistic awareness of the circumstances in which colonial officials worked.

It was now clear that the main proposal in the report would not run. If colonial governments could not take up the main role on blindness issues, who would? The Colonial Office could not do it itself. The National Institute thought the task was well outside its essentially domestic mandate. Something else was needed. The ad hoc committee decided at its first meeting that *voluntary* action was necessary to dramatize the needs of the colonial blind and to induce government action. In January 1949, Wilson developed this idea in a memorandum. Surveying all the British colonies, he noted that some had schools and welfare societies for the blind but that these fell well short of what was required and there were large gaps, mainly in Africa and the Mediterranean. Only three governments had shown any willingness to adopt the welfare proposals in the Mission's report. 'The only way to arouse interest is to create institutions – schools, training centres, workshops, etc – which, by their results, demonstrate that Blind Welfare is practicable and worthwhile.' He proposed, therefore, that the Institute should establish an organization, named perhaps the British Empire Society for the Blind, either as a subsidiary company or as an independent body on which the Institute was prominently represented. It should be financed by appeals for funds. Colonial Office backing would be essential to give the new Society a footing and status in the colonies. Its financial support for approved local schemes would be the strongest inducement to official action. The Colonial Office should therefore be strongly represented on the governing body of the Society but in such a way as not to prevent the Society from putting legitimate pressure on governments that were for the time being opposed to the development of work for the blind.

There was now an embryonic notion of a future non-governmental organization working on the problems of blindness overseas. The Social Services Department of the Colonial Office, with the help of Wilson and others, re-worked these ideas in a memorandum of 27 January 1949. This recognized that reactions from colonial governments had killed off the proposal for inter-territorial organizations and recommended instead that a voluntary organization of the kind proposed by Wilson should be established but with the broader objective of promoting work not just for the welfare of the blind but also for the prevention and treatment of blindness. It should relate to the Colonial Empire as a whole, and not just Africa. The governing body should contain as a nucleus three members from the Colonial Office and three from the National Institute. Colonial governments should be invited to contribute a total of £10,000 over three years, and the Institute a similar sum, to get the Society started, after which it would be expected to become independent and self-supporting.

In May 1949 this proposal was approved by the Empire and Colonial Sub-Committee, which resolved to transfer its own functions to the new voluntary Society. Wilson was appointed as its Secretary and Chief Executive at a salary of £800 per year, a reasonable amount at the time, plus an expense allowance to be settled later. He wrote to Reilly to say that there was no work he would rather do. 'I shall do my utmost to build up the Society as an efficient and humane organization.' But two issues remained to be settled – finance and the name of the new body.

The financial issue then, as ever, stimulated more Whitehall minuting than any other aspect of the proposal. It turned on the question of whether, if colonial governments did not subscribe as much as the £10,000 required from government, the Colonial Office would make up the sum. By late July Lord Ismay, Chairman of the National Institute and Churchill's Chief of Staff during the war, was brought into the act. In the time-honoured way, Ismay had a word with a senior Colonial Office official at a Buckingham Palace garden party and then sent him a sharp letter. Eventually, in September, it was agreed that if there was a deficit to make up, the money would be found. The National Institute had been irritated by the delay, the Colonial Office embarrassed.

The issue of the name is more interesting. Discussion reflected the considerable confusion in peoples' minds in 1949 about the notion of Empire. What did that term now mean? India and Pakistan had become independent in 1947, Ceylon (later Sri Lanka) in 1948. Decolonization in Africa was fast approaching. Wilson wrote to Reilly in May 1949 arguing that the name chosen for the new organization must indicate its functions and stature reasonably exactly. But it must be a brief, distinctive and easily remembered form of words which caught peoples' imagination and induced their support. The wrong choice of words could cost thousands of pounds in fundraising.

Personally, he favoured the title 'British Empire Society for the Blind', even though it was rather too long. 'The phrase "British Empire" still has magic about it and has many emotional associations.' It was exact enough, especially given Prime Minister Attlee's recent distinction in Parliament between the 'Commonwealth' (meaning the dominions), the 'Empire' (meaning the colonies, protectorates, mandates, etc) and the 'Commonwealth and Empire' (meaning the whole of His Majesty's Territories). 'The difficulty you have in mind, I imagine, is that the phrase "British Empire" used to include India and Pakistan and still in some quarters is used to mean what the Prime Minister called the Commonwealth and Empire. "British Colonial Empire Society for the Blind" might be more exact but it would be bad from an appeals point of view as it is too long and somewhat pedantic, and because the intrusive word "Colonial" destroys the emotional impact of the phrase "British Empire".' Wilson's logic was right and he got his way. But for the majority of Britons and many foreigners, who were perplexed about the term 'Empire' as Britain's governing role overseas rapidly diminished, it was probably a rather bewildering title, despite the logic. It did not last long.

In October, with money and name settled, the Colonial Secretary wrote to all colonial governments to state that the proposal to set up the new Society had his complete approval and support. Voluntary action of this kind was desirable as an expression of communal altruism and a denial of the pure materialism which was sweeping parts of the world. Each colony was allocated a target for the sum it was hoped it would contribute to the £10,000 Colonial Office grant to the Society. In the event, nearly all the colonies contributed together just over this total. Creech-Jones also said in his letter that Wilson would be a very suitable choice of Secretary, experienced, capable, energetic and realistic.

Wilson's first mission to Africa had been a rich and fascinating experience. In some ways it is difficult to see how he and his colleagues came to produce their complex organizational recommendations, most of which were thoroughly unrealistic in the light of the tasks facing post-war colonial governments and which were quickly dismissed on their return to Britain. They had been warned time and time again that colonial governments would not take on expensive and time-consuming new burdens. I have little doubt that the organizational proposals came from Wilson himself, since throughout his working life he was fascinated by new administrative structures and put more faith in their capacity to solve problems than others would. But this kind of criticism is easy. It would be fairer to recognize how inexperienced the team were in matters of government and how novel the territory was into which they had entered. No one before them had tried to devise the means of a comprehensive attack on the problems of blindness overseas. Africa, in particular, with its poverty and lack of infrastructure, presented a huge challenge. In their assessment that the problems of blindness would in the end be effectively tackled only by governmental effort, the team were undoubtedly right, as Wilson's life and work would show.

Even if the report's principal recommendations were not adopted, Wilson had returned with a considerable basis of knowledge of the problems that needed to be addressed. Some of the ideas in the report would be taken up by the new Society and were to have a powerful influence. For example, the concept of training and employing blind people in their own community anticipated by several decades the concept of 'community-based rehabilitation' which is today a fundamental feature of work with disabled people. During his lengthy tour he had established a network of contacts, principally but not exclusively with colonial officials, which he would put to good use. But the most fertile consequence of these months overseas was their emotional and psychological impact on Wilson. Many years afterwards he was asked by Peter White in a radio interview whether, on this first visit to Africa, there was one thing that stunned him. 'Yes,' he replied, 'meeting blind and other disabled people at the bottom of the pyramid who had to struggle to survive.' He used to say in later life that this early experience of blindness in Africa had instilled in him an 'amateur red rage', a passion to relieve the misery that visual impairment brought to so many in the developing world.

He was now to build up and lead an organization that offered the prospect of real action. While he is often described as the founder of what became the Royal Commonwealth Society for the Blind, and later Sight Savers International, he himself said that it had many founders. This chapter has shown that much discussion and many minds contributed to the creation of the organization. But there is no doubt as to who then turned a paper concept into a living body and led it for thirty-four years.

Chapter 3

Focus on Africa

John Wilson began the year 1950 with a clear purpose. For nearly three years since his return from Africa there had been long, often frustrating, discussion of how to organize and finance a serious attack on the problems of blindness in the colonies. Now his energies were released to get on with it. Whether the new Society would succeed or fall by the wayside depended largely on him. His vision was that the Society should be 'strong enough to command attention and big enough to span continents, yet simple enough to do something meaningful against the realities of an African village.' But the immediate tasks were rather more mundane.

He needed a base. He leased a room in a building (since destroyed) at 53 Victoria Street, London, and hired a secretary. With Jean Wilson's assistance, they spent their first morning scrubbing out the dirty room and removing carpet nails from the floor, since a new carpet was due at noon. The telephone rang. A journalist asked to speak to the 'information officer'. The phone was passed to Wilson who gave what he hoped was a convincing account of the Society's plans for the future, profoundly grateful that the journalist could not see the base from which these plans were to be launched.

The Society came into existence officially on 5 January 1950. Wilson's flair for public relations was immediately evident. Press releases, distributed with Colonial Office help, earned good coverage for the new organization in the shape of a *Times* leader and reports in the *Mirror*, *Telegraph*, *Guardian*, *Scotsman*, *Glasgow Herald*, *Empire Sunday News* and some provincial newspapers.

On 13 January the Council of the Society met formally for the first time. Its president was Lord Halifax, the former Foreign Secretary. The vice-presidents were the Secretary of State for the Colonies and Dr Helen Keller, the remarkable American woman, then seventy years old, who became both deaf and blind at the age of nineteen months but lived a full and inspirational life. Sir Bernard Reilly, the former Governor of Aden, was the natural choice as chairman, given his involvement in the discussion that had led to the establishment of the Society. Eagar, Secretary General of the National Institute, was vice-chairman and General Sir Bernard Paget, Commander in Chief of the Middle East Force during the war, was co-opted to chair the important Appeals Council. It was an interesting group: strong representation from the Colonial Office and the unmistakable stamp of the 'great and good' but also the broader international purpose represented by Helen Keller, whom the Wilsons would get to know quite well. (The organization bearing her name, Helen Keller International, formerly the American Foundation for the Overseas Blind, would collaborate with the Society overseas into the twenty-first century.)

Planning of the Society's future activities was already well in hand. In March 1950, Wilson presented to the Council a programme of action which laid down four main objectives: the formation in each colonial territory of an effective organization of the blind, capable of starting at least one school and employment centre; the establishment of regional offices to coordinate national activities and to do things which could best be done on a regional basis; surveys to ascertain the extent and causes of blindness and to formulate practical action for its prevention; and an appeal strategy for raising funds not just in Britain but, with Colonial Office help, overseas as well.

These objectives, backed up by a good deal of detail in the programme of action, set the essential framework for Wilson's activity for the rest of the decade and beyond. But first there was an immediate priority. Fundraising, as for every charity then and since, was a vital activity. In the Society's case, grants from the Colonial Office and the National Institute would expire in 1953 when it would have to stand on its own feet. Contributions from colonial governments to future activities could not be taken for granted.

The Society decided from the outset that it would try to mobilize funds to finance the whole strategy rather than specific local projects. Its first aim was to raise £25,000 at once by appealing to selected firms, organizations and individuals in Britain for support in financing the initial part of the programme. This campaign was launched by a letter to *The Times* signed by the Colonial Secretary. But it did not produce anything like £25,000 which, in retrospect, Wilson thought was a naïve goal. It raised just enough money to keep the Society afloat. More substantial donations were to come in when Lord Halifax and General Paget began to beard company chairmen in their boardrooms and, later, when the Society established its own professional appeals organization. Meanwhile, it decided to launch a major appeal in 1951 in Britain, the dominions (i.e. the independent countries of the Commonwealth) and the colonies. The Society thought people would be motivated to contribute by 'religion, patriotism, responsibilities of Empire, commercial goodwill in native markets, humanitarian interest in backward peoples and interest in education and medicine.'

In late 1950, the Colonial Secretary wrote to colonial governments to seek their help: the Society's target, not to be made public, was £500,000. Ninety per cent of the money collected in each territory would be paid into a local fund for the blind. Ten per cent would go to a central fund which the Society would use to support local efforts in the colonies. It quickly became apparent that not much financial support was likely to come from the dominions, except perhaps Canada. The major effort would again have to be made in Britain. This was initially hampered by a rather heated turf war with the National Institute which feared the Society would make inroads into its own fundraising for blind people in Britain. A sensible agreement, dividing up the categories of potential supporters, was eventually reached.

This major appeal, the 'British Empire Campaign Against Blindness', was formally launched by Lord Halifax in May 1951. Reporting the event, *The Times* described the Society as 'less … a deserving charity than an inescapable obligation of Imperial honour'. The *Spectator* wrote, 'It would be hard to exaggerate the possible importance of the British Empire Society for the Blind (or) the immensity of the need.' It was 'an interesting and most hopeful piece of cooperation between a voluntary body and the Colonial Office.' In the Gold Coast, a newspaper announced: 'An Empire Blindness Appeal will be launched … Be prepared from now, from this very Cocoa Season, this Christmas-tide, to lay by something very substantial in response to this appeal.'

The target of £500,000 was extremely ambitious. Today's equivalent would probably be about £10,000,000. Fundraisers at modern charities like to set targets that have a realistic chance of being achieved, for the obvious reason that failure to reach a target is demotivating for the fundraisers. In 1953, two years after the appeal was launched, the Society's annual report recorded a total income of only just over £81,000 and stated: 'Our voluntary revenue ... is still gravely inadequate ... we need the help of every company trading in the Colonies, of every individual concerned with the wellbeing of Colonial peoples and of every newspaper and other agency which can bring the facts more forcibly to public attention.' Concerns about the mismatch of ambition and money would be with the Society for many years.

In his letter to colonial governments the Colonial Secretary had also set out the most authoritative description of the new Society's functions yet produced. 'This body would assist and coordinate the work of such unofficial organizations as are already in existence in their endeavours to prevent blindness and to aid the blind. It would also take and encourage action to prevent blindness and to bring education, employment and welfare to people who are already blind. It would, for example, in close consultation with the local health authorities, organize specific projects such as mobile units for surveys and research and generally, where applicable, amplify local medical resources. It would also promote sight-saving propaganda, found schools, training centres, workshops and welfare services of all kinds and take steps to adapt the Braille system to the languages spoken in Colonial Territories. At the same time the Society would stimulate interest in the United Kingdom in the circumstances of the blind throughout the Colonial Empire.'

Wilson, who would certainly have been consulted about, and probably drafted, this letter now had a clear and pretty formidable agenda for action. But he could not implement it by sitting in his London office. Much of his work for the Society would henceforth consist of frequent travelling around the world, organizing, activating, cajoling and inspiring others. But the Wilsons had also started a family.

Their first daughter, Claire, had been born in 1948. Their other daughter, Jane, would follow in 1953. Like many parents since, Wilson must have wondered at first how he would square the travel imperatives with child-care, especially since he and Jean wanted to travel together. But in 1955 Jean's mother, Chloe, moved into their new house in Roedean, near Brighton, where a granny-flat was constructed for her and where she would live until she died in 1985. Wilson then said, 'But for the secure house, the economic management, the happy environment which Chloe provided, it would not have been possible for Jean and me to travel over a million miles setting up the work of the Society.' The Wilsons' daughters were very fond of Chloe and her impish sense of humour and remember her with great affection.

Only the most important of Wilson's numerous travels will be noted in this book. But one of those was certainly his return journey to West Africa in the early autumn of 1950. It made a particularly strong impression on him and he would often refer to it in speeches long after the event. Leaving the two-year-old Claire in the care of Chloe, the Wilsons spent about six weeks travelling some ten thousand miles in Nigeria and the Gold Coast. Wilson's detailed and lucid report stated that interest in work for the blind had greatly increased since his last visit in 1947. It was no longer necessary to make a case for such work; governments now wanted from the Society expert advice, well-trained staff and active demonstration. The intention to set up a regional office in Accra was welcomed. An embryonic Society for the Blind was established in both Nigeria and the Gold Coast. Proposals for schools and training centres for the blind were advanced. Perhaps most important of all, an ophthalmic survey, which the Society was contemplating, to assess the prevalence and nature of blindness in the area, was planned in detail.

These were good results from a tour of a few weeks. But the event which made the deepest impression on Wilson, and on which he wrote a separate report, was a visit to a village called Nakong, on the east bank of the Sisile River in the Northern Gold Coast, where he and Jean lived in a mud hut for four days. He had heard of the 'country of the blind' on his first African trip and was determined to investigate it. The area was heavily affected by onchocersiasis (the blinding disease referred to earlier, that is transmitted to humans by the black simulium fly, which breeds in fast flowing streams and rivers). Although the cause of this disease had been discovered a few years previously, much about it was still unknown.

Wilson reported that 'Nakong is a place of horror. The people, a dying community, are losing the fight for survival against the tiny flies which multiply each breeding season in ideal conditions in the river. By contrast with the animated hubbub of the villages through which we had passed on the previous day, the silence of this village of invalids was startling and oppressive. At this season flies are everywhere, filling the air with sound like a distant dynamo.' Blindness was so prevalent that the necessary work of the village could be carried on only by enlisting the blind as well as the sighted. Years later Wilson was still referring in his speeches to the blind farmers who planted their grain along a straight bit of bamboo and the women who had a hemp rope to lead them to the well. He recorded his emotions, not in his report to the Society but in his diary: 'As we left those villages I felt sick and angry and was possessed with the urgent need to get something done about the situation.' When he returned to London he argued strongly and successfully for the launching by the Society of its first ophthalmic and entomological survey, despite the estimated cost of £40,000, which was barely affordable, and he personally made radio appeals for support.

He had been deeply moved by the plight of the 'country of the blind' but he well knew that his future work would uncover other places of horror and that personal reactions had to be controlled. In a letter of about this time he wrote: 'Unless you treat the subject of blindness in Africa lightly, it would break your heart.'

An incident occurred on this journey for which all lay readers of this book may be grateful. One evening the Wilsons' vehicle got stuck in a riverbed. As the driver went to get help they wound up the windows with the simulium flies pinging against them and Jean said, 'You know, it's no good calling this thing onchocersiasis. No one can pronounce it or spell it. You certainly can't raise funds for it. Let's call it "River Blindness".' That name is still widely used and it will be preferred from now on in this account.

Usually together with Jean, Wilson visited Africa twice more in the 1950s and six times in the 1960s. The political context of the Society's work changed dramatically in this period. By 1949 the 'Empire' was giving way to the 'Commonwealth of Nations', the eight independent states of Great Britain, Canada, Australia, New Zealand, South Africa, India, Pakistan and Ceylon. In that year, too, the British Government accepted publicly the aim of 'self-government within the British Commonwealth' as the realistic aim for the remaining colonies. Until about 1954 this was regarded as an educative process, against which some colonies were judged more mature, and thus more ripe for self-government, than others. But by the early 1960s any notion that Britain could carefully prepare the economic and social conditions in a territory before it was ripe for political independence was largely dead. The clamour for liberation had become too strong. In 1955 there were only four independent African states (Egypt, Ethiopia, Liberia and South Africa). By 1963 there were over thirty. Ghana, where so much of the Society's first effort was concentrated, celebrated its independence in 1957. In the next twenty-seven years, up to Wilson's retirement from the Society in 1984, twelve wars would be fought in Africa and thirteen African heads of state would be assassinated. The Society's success would in part depend on how sensitively it behaved in independent Africa and how robust its work on the problem of blindness proved to be as the political environment became more difficult.

Although the Society's name, the British Empire Society for the Blind, was quickly looking out of kilter with the times, its concept of its role was more in tune with them. The 1953 annual report stated that it was 'emphatically not a central organization charged with overall responsibility for the care of the blind throughout the Colonial Territories. It is a voluntary organization founded to initiate work for the blind and to supplement the activities of others.' The aim was to stimulate and guide action by governments and unofficial agencies to a point where local resources would be adequate to deal with the local problems. Wherever possible it would work with and through an existing organization, giving it technical and other assistance without impairing its autonomy.

Wilson worked hard to establish local organizations in colonies where they did not exist, that is to say in the big majority. The Colonial Office encouraged governors to help who, in their turn, typically induced well-known local personalities, mostly at this stage expatriates but including some Africans, to set up national societies for the blind. By 1955 Wilson recorded that twenty active organizations were in place in Aden, the Bahamas, Barbados, British Guyana (Guyana), Cyprus, Gibraltar, the Gold Coast, Jamaica, Kenya, the Leeward Islands (Antigua and St Kitts), Malaya, Mauritius, Northern Nigeria, Northern Rhodesia, Nyasaland, Sierra Leone, Singapore, Trinidad, Uganda and Zanzibar. In eight other territories there were embryonic committees but in a dozen or so there was as yet nothing. Two years later, in 1957, there were twenty-eight of these bodies, most of which had graduated from the status of branches of the Society to become independent, affiliated organizations. By 1971, when the Society's work had settled into an established pattern, it was working with affiliated national organizations in thirty-two Commonwealth countries ranging in size from a tiny body in Nevis to the Indian National Association for the Blind which itself had more than one hundred affiliates.

It was not all plain sailing. The energy and commitment of these national bodies would vary a good deal over the years. In the mid 1950s, for example, there were considerable difficulties over the Federal Nigerian Society for the Blind; the Governor General of Nigeria told the Society's regional representative that he was tired of 'the everlasting talk' of the local organization and thought the Society should just get on and do things by itself. But this was not the general experience. Some national bodies, for example those in Kenya and Sierra Leone, took early initiatives to raise money and finance projects from surveys to schools. The Society's sensible decision to foster their independence meant that they were well able to fit into a changing local political pattern. Interestingly, the branch in the Gold Coast was known as the 'Ghana' branch some eighteen months before the country officially chose that name.

Wilson became very adept at using this important network to promote action on the problems of blindness. He was to comment that it gave the Society 'the possibility of immediate, sensitive contact with every institution for the blind in the Commonwealth'.

The relationship between the Society and the Colonial Office inevitably weakened over time, as colonies became independent states and as the Society developed its own resources and expertise. Wilson came to value its voluntary status. 'Which government department,' he asked in 1959, 'could be affiliated on the same terms with the Antigua "Friends of the Blind" and the Central Blind Welfare Organisation in India? Which government department could accept responsibility for an overseas staff which works impartially in the Colonies and the Dominions and can on occasion even nip over into French territory to eliminate simulium flies?'

The overseas staff to which he referred were at this time a mere handful. But they were true pioneers. Several of them had been through the Second World War and had emerged, as many others did at that time, with the conviction that somehow, through whatever personal efforts could be made, the world had to become a better place. Recruited by Wilson, they were to be a winning team.

In 1951 Ronnie Babonau, a member of the Society's staff, was sent to Accra to set up the West African regional office. Babonau (a Huguenot family name) was then forty-one years old, the son of a doctor in the Indian Medical Service. He began to lose his sight in the 1930s. Despite that, he joined the Pioneer Corps during the war when a bomb blast further damaged his eyes. By the 1950s he was almost totally blind. For twenty-five years, accompanied by his wife, Norah, the daughter of a Governor of Borneo, he would be the Society's senior overseas administrator. His most important achievement was to pioneer rural employment and re-settlement schemes for blind people in Africa, Southern Asia and Malaya. At Ikeja, near Lagos in Nigeria, he created a rural centre which became famous throughout Africa for its training of blind villagers. Later, with the West African organizations flourishing under local management, he helped to set up, at Phansa, a hundred miles from Bombay, the first rural training scheme in the Indian sub-continent, and then other such schemes in Malaya, Sarawak and Sabah. When he died in 1984 Wilson stated that through his work 'thousands of blind people were given a way of independence within their own village communities and a new rural dimension was added to work for the blind.' From the Ikeja training farm Babonau once wrote, 'It's a case of the blind leading the blind. We have certainly fallen into the ditch but there is nothing in this farm which we cannot do.'

It was crucial to the success of such schemes that the trained farmers could live and work effectively when they went back to their village. Wilson appointed a number of after-care officers to supervise this process. One of these was Grace Ingham, 'a Lancashire girl with the tough, resilient spirit of the mill towns and with an expert's knowledge of work for the blind'. She would accompany each of the blind farmers back to their village and stay with him until he was capable of standing alone. This is easy enough to write. But here is a single woman in Africa in the 1950s. Her journeys through Nigeria and Cameroon were often long and difficult. If there was no rest house, she slept in her car or a tent and on one occasion spent the night in the wives' quarters of the house of one of the Cameroon chiefs.

On the other side of Africa, Alex MacKay, an Indian Army veteran, established an East African regional office in Kampala and subsequently became the full-time Executive Officer of the Kenya Society for the Blind until 1975. In about 1956 an international expert on work for the blind visited East Africa. Sir Clutha

MacKenzie, a New Zealander, had been blinded at Gallipoli in the First World War and had since devoted his life to blind welfare in many countries. As described in Wilson's book *Travelling Blind*, MacKenzie travelled extensively throughout East Africa, seeking out blind people who had not been content simply to accept the verdict of society but had made a life for themselves as peasant cultivators or craftsmen. This led him to help the Uganda Foundation for the Blind establish at Salama a training centre for blind village farmers, introducing new techniques of rehabilitation that were to be adopted by many other countries.

Another key pioneer was Geoffrey Salisbury who had been shot down when a pilot in the war, spent some time in a German prison and fought with the Maquis Resistance in the Ardennes. He met Wilson in 1952, joined the Society and worked in Africa, accompanied by his wife, Cathleen, for many years – later describing his experiences in *Yesterday's Safari* (Book Guild, 1990). He helped to found the first of the Society's schools for blind children in sixty acres of overgrown swamp in the Northern Rhodesian copper belt. Then, having visited the United States to study its experiments in 'open education' – the education of blind children in mainstream schools – he developed such a system in Central Africa, Tanzania and Uganda and most effectively in Northern Nigeria. In the early 1970s he moved on to work for blind people in Bangladesh.

Salisbury commented on this early group of Society appointees that 'Without realistic planning by John Wilson...the flair and initiative of the team he had collected around him would have been futile.' It was Wilson who organized and directed their work. Resilient characters though they doubtless were, they needed his encouragement from time to time. This was rural Africa of the 1950s, with all the physical and other difficulties that accompanied life and work. 'There were,' wrote Salisbury, 'no cosy inducements, no built-in subsidy benefits, certainly no air-conditioning or fridge.' But they were highly motivated. They were all experienced in work for blind people in the developed world, all of them initially chastened by the conditions in which blind people lived in Africa. But all, perhaps, would have shared Salisbury's view that they had 'the opportunity to create, to build something out of nothing for a humanity which, a few years earlier, was bent on destroying itself'.

All the members of this small group, like most others employed by the Society in the early years, came, as Wilson himself did, from a background of blind welfare. They had worked for organizations such as the National Institute that provided services for blind people, especially in the fields of education, training and employment. Not surprisingly, the Society's first programmes in Africa covered these areas. But they were innovatory and designed to fit the conditions of Africa.

At this time the Society spent more of its budget on training the blind for employment than anything else. This was not a new activity. The movement to organize work for blind people had begun in France at the end of the eighteenth century. By the mid twentieth century, in countries like Britain, the United States, the Soviet Union and Japan, considerable progress had been made. But these efforts had largely been directed at providing sheltered workshops in towns. There had been few attempts to organize *rural* occupations. Wilson quickly grasped that in Africa, where most people did not live in towns and where agriculture was the principal occupation, the emphasis must be on rural training. The Western system of teaching Braille and providing jobs in sheltered workshops, which missionary societies had tried to apply in Africa, could not effectively meet the needs of the villagers and tribesmen who constituted the overwhelming majority of blind people in Africa (and Asia, too).

A few isolated farm training schemes that had been started in Europe and America gave encouragement to the Society's efforts to establish realistic village training – to found a new rural pattern of work for the blind adapted to the realities of life in an African tribe or an Asian village. From 1955 onwards the Society helped to create and run rural training centres in Kenya, Uganda, Tanganyika, Northern Rhodesia, Nigeria and Nyasaland. By 1963, in its overall area of operations which covered, in addition to Africa, the Middle East, Asia and the Caribbean, there were twenty-three rural centres and sixty-one employment centres in all, training close to 1,500 blind people. Most, though not all, were established with the Society's help.

In Africa, this movement was highly original. It faced many obstacles, notably the prevailing culture which saw blind people as outcasts, naturally condemned to inactivity. Wilson, and especially his staff in the field, worked to remove this innate prejudice and to demonstrate by example and achievement that blind persons were trainable, that they were part and parcel of the community and that they had a right to live and work side by side with those who could see. Geoffrey Salisbury wrote later that 'the idea of building on the background, the culture, traditions and customs of the tribe with which we were working, rather than attempting to obliterate local culture, was the cardinal principle which led to the success' of the Society. Work was guided not by abstract notions of what blind people could do but by what blind villagers could do in the villages from which they came and to which they must return after training.

Mistakes were made. At the beginning, Wilson admitted later, there was a tendency to focus exclusively on agricultural training and virtually to ignore other aspects of village life. Agricultural work was often merely seasonal and thus some supplementary training was necessary. Early examples were carpentry, rural tanning, brick-making and the production of chain-link fencing and fishing tackle. But agriculture was at the heart of the training and at the Ikeja Farmcraft Centre in Nigeria a visitor would see a remarkable range of activity: 'Blind men were building the compost heaps, watering the crops, staking the beans, weeding a plot of pineapple, sifting earth into seed boxes, laying a new path with pegs and a rope line to mark the boundary, and digging and ridging a difficult piece of new land. At one place, ten feet up on a bamboo construction, blind men were fixing the roofing thatch on a typical village hut with dried mud walls.'

The Society had made good, internationally recognized, progress in rural training and would continue to develop such schemes. In *Travelling Blind* Wilson wrote that four-fifths of the world's 10,000,000 blind belonged to rural communities where for lack of a realistic system of rehabilitation they were usually condemned to a life of misery and want. He believed that the solutions adopted at Ikeja and similar places 'could open a new horizon of opportunity to millions of blind people in Africa, Asia and Latin America.' While his mind was focused on Africa at this time, he was always alert to the global implications of what the Society was doing. But exploiting that opportunity was far beyond the resources of the Society. The task, it felt, would need to be taken up by governments as well as organizations for the blind. Unless that was done 'this enterprise with its immense possibilities will prove abortive.' The inadequacy of governmental effort in work on problems of blindness was a theme that would outlast John Wilson and is still with us.

Many of the issues in blind welfare have an apparently timeless quality. The *Economist* of 14 February 2004 carried an article about special schools for disabled children, remarking that some saw them as a form of educational apartheid and wanted them abolished, while others thought them vital. It is an old debate, which Wilson and the Society had to confront as they addressed the issue of education of blind people in the countries where they were working in the 1950s.

In 1958 the Wilsons visited the United States. While there, Jean took an interest in American systems for educating blind children. In Britain a network of special schools was firmly established. But in the United States some forty per cent of such children were being co-educated with seeing children in ordinary schools. There were arguments in favour of both systems. On behalf of special schools it was contended that there were certain subjects in which blind children could be efficiently instructed only by specially trained people, and that there were certain skills, such as the capacity for walking about confidently without the aid of sight, which also needed special teaching. On the other hand, advocates of what was known in America as 'integrated education' saw educational and psychological advantage in educating blind and seeing children together and believed, above all, that co-education was the best way to establish equality of rights for disabled persons, and to maximize their chances of having a flourishing life later on.

But the United Kingdom and America were one thing, and most of the territories where the Society was working quite another. In a few of these, notably Singapore, Hong Kong, Trinidad and Malta, practically all known blind children were in schools of one sort or another. There was some, albeit very inadequate, provision in the Indian sub-continent. In Africa south of the Sahara, only about 1,600 out of an estimated 120,000 blind children were being educated in only thirty-three schools, many of them new, and many of them run by missionaries. It was perfectly clear, in the context of Africa at the time, that governments that were doing their best with limited resources to satisfy the fast-growing African demand for greatly increased ordinary education facilities would not be able to provide an extensive network for special schools for blind children. So another approach was needed.

In late 1959 Geoffrey Salisbury visited America to carry out a more detailed examination of 'integrated' education. Shortly afterwards the Society decided to experiment with this kind of education in Africa. They preferred the term 'open education' since 'integration' could have political overtones. But the basic concept of co-education of blind and seeing children remained. It was agreed with the government of Northern Nigeria that fourteen schools in Katsina Province would be used for the experiment. Blind children in the area would attend ordinary primary schools while an itinerant body of specially trained teachers would be built up to supplement the normal teaching staff by regularly visiting the schools, usually by bicycle. Small groups of blind children were gradually assimilated into classes of sighted children in such a way as not to upset the normal balance of work. With a policy of gradual assimilation and skilful guidance, it was hoped that the blind children would not be regarded as oddities. Their particular needs were met by Braille books and equipment, trained teachers or visiting tutors. Where necessary, separate residential annexes or 'resource centres' were built for them in the school grounds.

The Katsina experiment was so successful that the Society's help was sought in extending it to all three regions of Nigeria. It was agreed to spend £25,000 on this project over a period of three years. Wilson encouraged other governments, in and outside Africa, to consider the results of this experiment. He recorded in 1971 that Ministers of Education in eleven Commonwealth countries had adopted the system, while the Society had built some thirty-one 'resource centres' and helped many existing schools. It had also started programmes of further education for blind people.

The achievement was considerable. It had been demonstrated that an adequate education system for blind people could be provided within the ordinary education system in Africa and Asia. But problems had also surfaced. The Society had difficulty in tracing blind children and then convincing their parents that schooling was practicable for them. It was proving hard to recruit the right kind of teacher. Local governments were all too inclined to leave the whole task to the Society. The number of blind children in schools in the countries where the Society operated was still pitifully small, no more than a few thousand at best. The question, as in the case of the rural training and employment schemes described earlier, was whether governments would have the necessary political will and resources to implement a co-education policy on a large scale. Once again, practical results would fall far short of Wilson's vision. When he retired from the Society in 1984 it was estimated that ninety-five per cent of blind children in developing countries still did not receive any kind of formal education. But one of Wilson's greatest qualities was his resilience, his utter refusal to abandon his efforts in the face of daunting statistics such as these. In a speech in Bangkok in July 1992, to the International Council for Education of the Visually Handicapped, he said that he hoped the world had now outgrown the controversy between residential and mainstream education. 'We must use every strategy, every option: residential schools, annexes, integration, specialist teachers, itinerant teachers and multi-purpose teachers... All these methods take their place.' But, he added, 'It is in the mainstream of a country's education that equality is most likely to be achieved.'

A striking feature of these early attempts to bring blind welfare services to Africa is the care the Society took to adapt Western techniques to African realities. I have little doubt that it was Wilson personally who developed and insisted on this policy, drawing on his experience of Africa since his 1946 visit and his close contact with Colonial Service officers and others who specialized in Africa. Wilson's sensitivity to foreign cultures was a strong feature of his personality. Throughout his life, people from other countries warmed to him and were inspired by him.

A remarkable instance of his acceptability occurred in Ghana. The country became independent in 1957. John Wilson had visited its first President, Kwame Nkrumah, in prison before independence and called on him after that event. In 1960 the Ghanaian government asked Wilson to chair a committee on the education, training and employment of disabled persons. After only eight weeks' work, he sent his report to President Nkrumah with a foreword setting out its main conclusions, which, he says, were later endorsed by the legislature. There were, he wrote, at least a hundred thousand permanently disabled people in Ghana. Many could be restored to economic and social independence. They should not be treated as a segregated group but as people able to join effectively in normal occupations of town and country. Handicapped children should be brought into the general education system. In the towns the disabled should not be confined to sheltered employment but helped to find jobs in offices and factories. In villages, they should train as farmers and craftsmen.

The Society's annual report for 1960-1 positively purred: 'It is particularly gratifying that an Englishman, who is himself blind, should have been asked to preside over a Cabinet Committee appointed to frame a domestic policy for a newly independent nation.' They were right to be pleased, but the appointment must have owed something to the fact that in 1959 the Society had acquired a new chairman in the shape of Sir Charles Arden-Clarke who had been Governor of the Gold Coast from 1949 until it became independent as Ghana and whose relationship with Nkrumah was regarded by some in the Colonial Office as distinctly over-friendly.

The Society's early concentration on rehabilitation projects was natural enough, given the background of most of its staff. As they became more and more conscious of the number of blind Africans in the developing countries their reaction was, inevitably, to consider how their experience of services to blind people in the developed world could be applied. But John Wilson reflected later that, 'This was starting at the wrong end. There was, above all, a need for prevention. Preventive measures up until then had been sporadic and confined mostly to the town. We were keen to concentrate on the rural areas.' This practical concern was to lead to a revolution in the approach to world blindness.

It might seem obvious enough that preventing people becoming blind in the first place should be the top priority. But that was not the conventional view. There was a good deal of discussion in the Society's Council, with some, notably the National Institute's representatives, arguing that the work of providing services to people who were already blind was a sufficient task and that the organization should not dissipate its resources in the largely uncharted field of prevention. Encouraged by Helen Keller, one of the vice presidents, who believed that the cost of prevention would be a fraction of the cost of support, and persuaded by his own analysis, Wilson put his weight solidly behind the concept of prevention. This would become one of the great themes of his life and would produce perhaps his greatest achievement.

Prevention could not be effective unless and until a much clearer picture of the nature and scale of the problem became available. With the advice of its Medical Advisory Panel, which included Dr Harold Ridley, a pioneer ophthalmologist who had already worked on river blindness, the Society finally decided in 1952 to launch the survey of that disease in West Africa that Wilson had so strongly advocated. It was to be conducted by two teams. The first was led by Dr Freddie Rodger, a Scottish eye surgeon who had served as a Medical Officer in the Burma Campaign. Accompanied by his wife, Jess, he spent four years on the project and wrote a definitive work on river blindness (*Blindness in West Africa*. H. K. Lewis and Co, 1959). Long before his death in 2002, his work on eye diseases was recognized internationally. The second team was led by an entomologist, Dr Geoffrey Crisp, who had also fought in the war and who died young, possibly as a result of illness contracted in Africa on a subsequent project. His book on *Simulium and Onchocerciasis in the Northern Territories of the Gold Coast* was published in 1956 (also H. K. Lewis and Co).

The Society's decision was bold. The £40,000 that the survey was predicted to cost was simply not available in its budget. It decided to go ahead regardless, the Treasurer commenting, 'If this is where we go bankrupt, at least it will be in a good cause.' In the event the whole cost was met by British firms and individuals, moved by the story of the 'country of the blind' which Wilson so often told with passion.

In East Africa the Kenya branch of the Society launched, from its own resources and with much help from the colonial medical authorities, an ophthalmic survey of the country under Dr R. D. Calcott. He and his other colleagues travelled widely and bravely at the height of the Mau Mau emergency to examine the prevalence of blindness and its causes.

In Zambia, Dr Malcolm Phillips made a special study of the Luapala Valley, otherwise known as the 'Valley of the Blind', and reached the conclusion that much of the widespread visual disability he encountered was due to the indiscriminate use of native medicine. 'If you believe, as these people did, that eye trouble is not caused by a virus but by the influence of a spirit or the malice of a wizard, then you go first to a witch doctor.' Two surveys were also conducted in Aden.

In his diary Wilson describes how, as the results of the West Africa survey came in, they were recorded on a map in the London office. It was a grim picture. 'Among the 1,000,000 inhabitants of Northern Ghana, it was estimated that 600,000 were affected by river blindness and that 30,000 were blind. There was a similar picture in Northern Nigeria.' Some of the survey's findings were challenged but, as Wilson wrote, 'The controversy had the effect of arousing international interest and of mobilizing the big battalions, which was what we had been trying to do from the start.'

The teams, Wilson states in *Travelling Blind*, had shown that the problems of eye disease in West Africa affected vast territories and whole communities. They had demonstrated not only that most of this blindness was unnecessary but also that practical measures could be taken to reduce it. In particular, he says, they had brought onchocersiasis out of its obscurity as an unpronounceable medical curiosity, had described it with textbook precision and had formulated a method of control in Northern Ghana. Well, up to a point. The problem of controlling river blindness was much bigger than Wilson or others realized at this time. The geographical extent of the disease was also much greater than they appreciated. Control was going to require an extensive programme of international action, to which we shall return. But the Society's work had certainly paved the way for, and contributed to, that later international programme.

Taken together, the surveys conducted at this time revealed unprecedented levels of blindness. They produced the firmest basis yet available for future action, although it would be many years before anything approaching accurate statistics of world blindness was available. They had shown that, in addition to river blindness, problems of trachoma and cataract were present everywhere, and also that one cause of blindness was malnutrition. Perhaps the most significant conclusion was that around eighty per cent of the blindness surveyed was preventable or curable, i.e. that it was unnecessary. This conclusion has stood the test of time and further research and holds broadly true today. The surveys had another consequence – action. As someone said at the time, 'It is not enough to count eyes; it costs very little more to cure them.'

The survey teams, professional as they were, were often distressed by the condition of the blind people they met. One specialist reported: 'Five miles out, after leaving the village, we passed a lonely compound. I got out of the car, and walked across to two figures under a tree. They were a man and wife – and behind the tree a small child. The woman was blind and the man had incipient cataracts. The child's eyelids were swollen and infected. We gave such immediate relief as was possible and I told the old man about the Society. To my great distress, he offered me, from his pathetic remnant of food, one of his fowls; this was for the good work.

I made a sudden goodbye, leaving him sitting under the tree with the blind woman, who had uttered no word during my visit, utterly still, utterly resigned. That is how I left them in the deserted village in the bush, sitting under the dawadawah tree, waiting only for death.'

Dr Rodger and his colleagues in the West Africa Survey were, the Society's annual report stated, 'deeply moved by the spectacle of blind men and women who, given the time and the material means, could have been healed or helped, vainly seeking relief from their sufferings, and being bitterly disappointed in the expectations aroused by the survey team, which was compelled to move on, turning away hundreds of deserving cases.'

Inevitably, what had begun as epidemiological surveys rapidly developed into treatment programmes as well, using for the first time, for ophthalmic purposes in Africa, mobile clinics staffed both by ophthalmic surgeons and trained African auxiliaries. A mobile clinic in its simplest form was a vehicle, perhaps a Landrover, carrying operating equipment and other medical supplies plus camping equipment, which enabled an eye surgeon and his staff to bring treatment to at least some of the rural areas where no static hospital or clinic existed (which, of course, was the case in most of Africa at this time). Later, a fully equipped mobile unit might consist of two vehicles, a medical officer in his own car and assistant staff in a long wheel-base Landrover with the necessary equipment. Between 1959 and 1964, the Society provided eleven mobile clinics to six African countries and South Arabia, with the understanding that the clinics must operate in the context of a national medical plan and that government should provide continuity once the clinics had demonstrated what could be done. These clinics carried out about 200,000 eye treatments annually.

Another innovative device promoted by the Society was the use of trained medical auxiliaries. Wilson would campaign long and hard, in more than one continent, for the use of such people. It was easy to show that they could treat many eye conditions that would normally be left to a few overworked specialists. But this proposition would be controversial for many more years, not least because ophthalmologists sought to protect their vested interests, often from the comparative comfort of urban living. But in time the use of 'paramedics' would become an essential element in the fight against blindness. Wilson liked to cite the case of the Kenyan,

Richard Amiani, previously a village health-worker, whom the Society trained and equipped with a second-hand motorbike, fitted with steel panniers to carry his drugs and other equipment. In one year he examined 6,796 patients and treated 5,513 for trachoma and other infections.

By the 1960s there had been a decisive shift in the Society's approach – from rehabilitation to prevention and from social to medical work. As it stated in its 1961-2 report (and the language must be Wilson's): 'It is a reproach that blind people should be obliged to live as beggars when they could be trained to be self-supporting citizens, but it is an even graver reproach that large numbers of people should go blind needlessly every year or be condemned to permanent blindness when their sight could be restored.' For the first time, a major organization for the blind had adopted the dual role of welfare and prevention.

Others were moving in that direction. For a time Wilson chaired the Prevention of Blindness Committee of the World Council for the Welfare of the Blind, on which national blind welfare organizations from forty-six countries were represented and which was recognized as the international focus for blind welfare. In America, the International Eye Foundation was established in 1962 with a mandate to prevent and cure blindness worldwide. But prevention was a massive task, the scale of which was probably not fully appreciated in the 1960s. It would certainly require many decades of action by governments and international agencies if it was to be successful. Significantly, Wilson persuaded the World Health Organization in 1962 to make the theme of its annual World Health Day 'Prevention of Blindness', and Jean Wilson helped to design the publicity material. But it would be another decade before international action began to become effective, a story we shall take up. Suffice it to say here that many of the leading figures still working in this field firmly attribute to John Wilson the achievement of making the concept of prevention central to international work on problems of visual impairment.

As we have seen, in all the areas where the Society was working – education, training and employment of the blind, and prevention and cure of blindness – it insisted that its role was to demonstrate what could be achieved but that substantial progress would need action by governments and international agencies. Yet these had their own priorities and problems, and it was always unlikely that they would commit the resources and effort to problems of visual impairment that Wilson and the Society believed to be necessary. Wilson nevertheless mounted one form of pressure after another in his attempt to bring about a decisive response to the problems of blindness.

It was the age of 'plans' and faith in planning. In 1964 the Labour government in Britain had set up a Department of Economic Affairs to develop strategic economic policy and in 1965 a National Economic Plan was published. It was rapidly pushed aside by reality and the vogue for such instruments passed. Wilson saw in the plan concept a possible method of moving governments into action. As we shall see in the next chapter, he had proposed an Asian Plan for the Blind in 1963. The next year he worked up an idea for an African Plan and a conference to discuss it.

In January 1966, the First African Conference on Work for the Blind was held in Lagos. It was a curious affair. Ostensibly concerned with thirty-two countries of tropical and equatorial Africa, only eleven of these participated. Sixteen of the thirty-four delegates from African countries came from the host country, Nigeria, which also supplied nineteen of the twenty-four observers. Many absentees were probably put off by the political situation. The meeting coincided with a military coup d'état in Lagos. John Wilson woke on the first morning to hear shouting and gunfire. 'Rather inanely, I got inside the bath to provide another layer between me and bullets.' Another delegate was put in a room from which the military had just dragged away the previous occupant for execution. The Provisional Government said they wished to go ahead with the Conference to give an appearance of normality. But many minds must have been on things other than the Conference proceedings.

Wilson presented a paper on 'Blindness in Africa'. He estimated that there were 1,400,000 blind persons in the thirty-two countries concerned, including 100,000 blind children. He forecast that in the next thirty-five years the population of the area would treble; and that, unless the blindness rate was reduced by two-thirds, there would, by the year 2000, be more blind people in Africa than there were at the time of the Conference. 'We must gallop if we are to stand still.' Two-thirds of this blindness was preventable. The question was whether it could be prevented fast enough to keep pace with population growth. 'The opportunity is spectacular but whether it can be grasped will depend on the priority which African governments give to the task.'

In a keynote speech, he proposed the adoption of an African Plan for the Blind, aimed at trebling the number of blind children in school from 2,000 to 6,000 in five years; increasing to 3,000 the number of blind persons trained and settled annually in rural occupations; and providing in each country at least one efficient centre for training for urban employment. But, he insisted, none of this made any sense without resolute action to *prevent* blindness. The Society would gladly help. International organizations had become adept at ventriloquizing calls for aid 'but there is no substitute for the real voice of Africa.' There must be greater involvement of African governments who should draw up their own five-year plans in this field.

In a flashback to the report of his 1946 Mission to Africa he proposed the formation of Regional Action Committees. The ultimate aim might be a Pan-African Organization for the Blind. As can be the way with international conferences, confronted by one determined speaker and organizer, most of these proposals were endorsed in a series of resolutions, one of which recorded thanks 'to the Society and its Director, Mr J. F. Wilson CBE without whose long and extensive knowledge and interest in pursuing the welfare of the blind no conference of this nature in Africa could be as complete or as far-reaching in its ultimate results.' (This was the hey-day of anti-colonialism. At this time I used to attend United Nations conferences in New York, which admittedly were not strictly comparable, but where such praise of a citizen of one of the leading colonial powers was pretty well unthinkable.)

How much influence the Plan had on real life is very questionable. Given the fragile political situation in Nigeria, the Society set up a new regional office in Freetown, Sierra Leone, to pursue implementation of the Plan in West Africa. But it soon became clear that political conditions made it impossible to proceed. There were a few encouraging moves in East and Central Africa, but references to the Plan soon disappeared from the Society's annual reports.

The political situation in several countries where the Society worked was becoming more unstable. The military coup that co-incided with the Lagos conference was the first of several coups that marked many years of political uncertainty in Nigeria. During the

Biafran Civil War from 1967 to 1970 the rural training scheme at Ikeja was directly affected when all the trainees and staff from the Eastern region of Nigeria were deported. Later, the Society would have to contemplate moving the centre entirely because so much of its land had been appropriated by the armed forces for married quarters. In Uganda, the depredations of the Idi Amin regime were to lead to a substantial breakdown of medical and social services. The Salama Rural Training Centre, once perhaps the finest rehabilitation centre in Africa, became derelict. In South Arabia, as 129 years of British rule approached its end in 1967, security conditions gave the Society anxious moments about the safety of its staff there. In 1966, the two women concerned, with their mobile units reinforced to give some protection against land-mines, travelled unarmed and unmolested through five thousand miles of desert villages to treat eye conditions. But in the summer of 1967 they had to leave.

The main effect of the many political upheavals in the Society's area of operation, and the economic decline which so often accompanied them, was to postpone even further the day when governments would focus seriously on social development and the problems of blindness. The direct effect on the Society's work was, however, more limited than one might expect. Projects for blind people encountered political difficulties only rarely. Wilson asked his West African Regional Officer, F. H. Butcher, to report in 1967 on what effect the events in Nigeria in 1966 had had on the work originally inspired by the Society. Apart from the case of Ikeja, referred to above, he concluded that not only was the work still being carried on in West Africa but that it was steadily increasing in most places. The system of 'open education' had largely survived and blind children attended more than a hundred schools. The fact that work for blind people and on blindness continued as successfully as it did may well owe much to that wise decision, taken at the outset in Africa, to foster the growth of autonomous local organizations for the blind rather than attempt to centralize activity on the Society itself; for the latter approach would surely have made it a target in times of political tension.

Throughout this story of John Wilson's life, however many plans 'failed' or projects faltered, however much ambition was frustrated, the following points must be emphasized. All the time the lives of many thousands of people were being transformed by the restoration of their sight. Because of the work on prevention, many more thousands who would have become blind retained their sight. Further, large numbers of irreversibly blind people were rehabilitated to allow them to live their lives more fully. All the time governments and communities were being made more aware of the problems of blindness and the growing opportunity to solve them. The last person to be deterred by setbacks and frustration was Wilson himself. He would constantly turn to new ideas, new areas of work, new schemes to promote what he would more and more describe as a great humanitarian cause.

Wilson had long asked himself whether something dramatic could be done to destroy the image of the blind person in Africa as a useless member of society. He had, for example, toyed with the idea of a trans-Sahara expedition by a group of visually impaired people. In 1964, a young Kenyan, Tom Wijenjie, who was on a course in Britain, suggested to him instead that a group should climb Mount Kilimanjaro in Kenya. The idea matured in Wilson's mind and he discussed it, on a visit to Kenya, with the warden of the East African Mountain School in Nairobi. In early 1968, Wilson told Geoffrey Salisbury that the climb would take place in February 1969 and gave Salisbury the main task of organizing it and taking part. The Society sponsored the climb in collaboration with the Outward Bound Trust, the East African Mountaineering School and organizations for the blind in Kenya, Tanzania and Uganda. The cost, some £1,200, was met by contributions from schools in Britain. A principal aim of the project was to demonstrate to parents across Africa that, far from regarding their blind children as useless to society, they should send them to school. If blind people could climb Kilimanjaro they could go to school and do much else.

Nine blind African men, mostly around twenty-five years old, were selected from a large number of applicants. One rather older member of the group had to give up early in the climb. Another had to abandon it at 16,000 feet. This left seven, together with three instructors (including Salisbury) and a few porters, to start for the summit at dawn on 20 February. By 11.30 they were in real trouble. Many were violently sick and even the instructors had headaches (symptoms of altitude sickness familiar to those who have gone to these heights). The last four hundred feet took an hour but they reached the summit at 19,340 feet at 12.20. The descent was rather a nightmare with all but two of the climbers suffering from severe cold and sickness. They spent the night in a cave at 15,000 feet, but the next day, feeling a good deal better, walked for eleven hours back to base.

The Queen sent a telegram: 'Please convey to the seven blind climbers who reached the summit of Kilimanjaro my warm congratulations on their splendid achievement.' Lord Hunt, who had famously conquered Mount Everest, and who had been consulted about this expedition, also sent his congratulations. But it was the words of Andikati, one of the blind climbers, as he reached the end of the trek, that stayed in the memory of those involved: 'We were blind, we are now new men. We have met fear. We have conquered it. Though we still cannot see, we have walked through the gardens of the Gods and they were not angry...It has been a fearsome and beautiful experience, has it not my brothers?' (translated from the Samburu language).

The story was front-page news in most African papers. There was a good deal of international interest and the Society's switchboard back in Britain was deluged with calls. Geoffrey Salisbury, from whom this account is taken, wrote later: 'It was a magnificent achievement, the climax of years of preparation, an exercise to show Africa and the world that, given the chance, fortitude, tenacity and courage are an integral part of the character of blind and handicapped people. It staked a claim that contemporary Africa could not ignore. It registered a triumph in the story of man's ability to overcome adversity.' And more blind children *did* go to school as a result.

Kilimanjaro, now much climbed, has been a powerful symbol for the Society ever since. In 1999, to mark its fiftieth anniversary, six blind British teenagers joined six blind East African teenagers and, with sighted guides, attempted the mountain, some nine of the twelve getting to the top. In 2003, four of the Society's trustees climbed Kilimanjaro and returned to tell their tales.

The main focus of John Wilson's work in the 1950s and much of the 1960s was Africa, as we have seen. But he was also active in the other areas covered by the Society's original mandate which embraced all the then colonial territories.

In 1954 the Wilsons toured the West Indies and produced for the Society its first detailed picture of the extent of blindness in that region and of the work and needs of the local organizations involved. The Society decided that it could make an important contribution by supplying expatriate help to build a modern system of blind welfare, in association with the Canadian Institute for the Blind which was already active in the area. A British West Indies Campaign against Blindness was launched and an educational adviser and employment adviser appointed.

Wilson visited the area again in 1961 and offered to collaborate in producing a Caribbean Plan for the Blind, but this became impracticable when the Federation of the West Indies was dissolved for political reasons.

He returned in 1966, taking his elder daughter, Claire, with him for the first time, on a ten-week tour of the Caribbean, Canada and the United States. He noted in his diary that she was by far the most attractive young female on the boat that took them to the Caribbean and 'created quite a sensation, as she did in the West Indies.' More seriously, this was the beginning of a long working relationship between Claire and her father. She was employed by the Society for some years from 1979 and came to be a key figure in the establishment and running of Impact (see Chapter Six).

In 1967, Wilson was back in the area again, this time to attend a Caribbean Conference on Work for the Blind in Port of Spain. He addressed participants on how the methods that were being used to assist blind people in other parts of the world might be applied to the Caribbean. The Conference led to the establishment of a Caribbean Council for the Blind and a regional plan to assist the blind of the area. The estimated number of blind persons in the Caribbean Commonwealth countries was about 10,000, small compared to other regions, and there was by now a fairly comprehensive network of organizations and facilities for blind people, much of these pre-dating the Society's entry into the field. The various forms of expert assistance provided by the Society were no doubt welcome and effective but the Caribbean was bound to be lower on the list of priorities than other regions where the problems of blindness were so much more acute.

Wilson's exhaustive travels in other continents did not permit him to return very often to the Caribbean, but his diaries contain a vivid description of a later visit to Barbados when a volcano on the nearby island of St Vincent erupted. He followed events closely on his radio and became worried that among the stream of people who were having to move away from the area of the eruption the particular plight of disabled people might be forgotten. Through the Chief Justice's Office he made a call to the Central Emergency Control. He soon heard the radio disc jockey, who was advising his audience on the crisis, say: 'Look folks, watch out for the disabled – the blind, deaf, crippled. Give them a lift along the road.' As Wilson followed the radio broadcast through the night he was captivated by the variety of West Indian accents: 'Guyanese sounding like Irishmen, Trinidadians like Welshmen, Barbadians a sort of curdled Cornish, the Indian civil servants like speeded up Oxford dons.'

One method of assessing the effectiveness of Wilson's work is to study the projects of one kind and another launched by the Society and other organizations he built up and calculate the number of people who benefited from their measures to prevent and cure blindness and from schemes of rehabilitation. I shall attempt such assessments further on in this book. But there is another method – less tangible but perhaps equally important. Wilson met and influenced many people in many lands who were encouraged, as a result of their interaction with him, to begin or increase work on the problems of blindness. How far the effectiveness of their own efforts can then be attributed to Wilson is of course largely a matter of speculation, but there are plenty of cases where his contribution was obviously important.

In the summer of 2003, Sam Campbell, the blind principal of the Milton Margai School for the Blind of Sierra Leone, was touring Britain with the school choir which gave a series of concerts at the Methodist Central Hall, Westminster, the Shrivenham Defence Academy and Eden Court, Inverness, among other places. Sam Campbell interrupted a busy programme to talk to me on his mobile phone from a Welsh valley where the choir were to perform. What, I wanted to know, was his connection with Wilson? This is the story.

In 1951 Wilson visited Sierra Leone, met the Prime Minister, Milton Margai, and suggested that his government should start a programme of measures for the blind. A Sierra Leone Society for the Blind was established with help from Ronnie Babonau. Wilson returned in 1953, met the young Sam Campbell and advised the Sierra Leone Government to send him to school in Ghana. In 1955, while in Ghana, Wilson met this school's headmaster and proposed that Sam be trained as a teacher because there was a need to start a school for the blind in Sierra Leone. In 1961 Sam Campbell became principal of the Milton Margai School for the Blind, a post he has held for more than forty years. He saw little of Wilson in subsequent years. Many hundreds of blind children have passed through his hands. Many have doubtless gone on to help others with sight problems.

Wilson invited Campbell to take part in the 1962 All-African Conference for the Blind in Lagos which was described earlier. He became in effect not just a school principal but also a spokesman for blind people. In 1971 he visited the Gambia to take part in the inauguration of the new Gambia Society for the Blind. In his speech, a copy of which is in the Society's archives, he said:

'The blind people of yesterday, and the day before yesterday, had little choice but to accept the tragic view that blindness is a disaster. Their horizons were limited to the bounty of charity and their world was bounded in sheltered workhouses in Europe and America, etc, where they earned their living; as for our unfortunate blind African folks, they earned their living by begging. At every turn they were coaxed into immobility and dependency. It is no wonder that they fulfilled the prophecy of disaster; believing it themselves they made it come true.

'But that was another time, another era, another world. The blind people of today have carried out a revolution and have won their independence. Thanks to societies for the blind and societies of the blind. We have won it by finding our own voice, we have won it by finding our own direction and we have won it by finding our own doctrine. That doctrine may be simply stated: it is that the blind are normal people who cannot see; it is that blindness is not a "dying" but a challenge to make a new life...

'Up to now it has not been possible for blind children to go to school in Gambia; it has not been possible for them to read and write; it has not been possible for the blind to work and earn their living; it has not been possible for the blind to participate in social activities. Thanks to the Government of the Republic of the Gambia, the Gambia Society for the Blind and the Royal Commonwealth Society for the Blind (the new name for the British Empire Society), these things can now become possible and the Gambian blind people will soon take their rightful places in society as useful citizens.'

Sam Campbell's contribution to the welfare of blind people over four decades has been striking. Wilson's own influence on that story is clear if unmeasurable. There will be other telling examples.

The Society's work in Africa and the Caribbean would continue throughout Wilson's life, and it persists today. But by the 1960s Wilson's main focus had shifted to Asia. This continent brought new challenges and, above all, exciting new opportunities.

Chapter 4

The Eyes of Asia

Asia, and especially the Indian sub-continent, occupied much of the Wilsons' energy for nearly four decades, from the late 1950s until the late 1990s. In this region they registered some of their most important achievements. Today, the Wilson name is still recalled with respect, admiration and affection in many parts of the area. But none of this was inevitable. It grew out of an initial political problem, the solution to which presented an opportunity. Wilson seized it with the vision and energy that we have already seen at work in Africa.

The march of African and Asian colonies towards independence in the 1950s made the Society's original name and mandate – covering British colonies, protectorates, protected states and trust territories – increasingly anomalous. The problem was more than one of words. When a territory such as the Gold Coast became independent in 1957, as Ghana, what was the Society supposed to do? Stop working there? It had only just begun. It naturally wanted to continue. How were newly independent states supposed to relate to a 'British Empire Society for the Blind'? One Indian told Wilson that that name was an 'eyesore' for countries such as his. Another said that if the Society wished to work in independent India, it had better change its name.

The Society debated the problem in 1957 and amended its constitution to give itself the power, in addition to working for blind people in the remaining colonies, to 'foster collaboration between organizations for the blind and for the prevention of blindness throughout the Commonwealth and to promote activities for the benefit of such organizations'. The Society was re-named the Commonwealth Society for the Blind and was later granted the prefix 'Royal' – much more quickly than usual because Lord Halifax made a special plea to the Home Secretary, Rab Butler, who 'put it through'. This is just one of many examples of how the Society benefited from the presence on its Council of prominent members of the establishment.

It was all very well for the Society to give itself a Commonwealth-wide mandate but how would other members of the Common-wealth, who had not been consulted, react? It was decided that the Wilsons should embark on a major tour in 1958 to explain the purpose of the constitutional change and attempt to develop new relationships and affiliations. Although Wilson often referred to this expedition as a 'world tour' it was in fact a journey to the Asia-Pacific region and North America, covering, in order, Pakistan, India, Ceylon (Sri Lanka), Singapore, Malaya, Sarawak, Brunei, North Borneo, Hong Kong, Australia, New Zealand, Fiji, Canada and the United States. The latter was included because Wilson hoped that American organizations for the blind would cooperate in work in developing countries.

The Wilsons spent some four and a half months on the journey and travelled about fifty thousand miles at a cost of £1,550 (prob-ably about £20,000 in today's money). The journey entailed both a very long absence from headquarters and considerable expense. But the Society's Council recognized that Wilson's role as a travelling ambassador was invaluable to its plans and had therefore given his deputy director new responsibilities for running the headquarters office from now on, in order to relieve Wilson from detailed office administration (though there is not much evidence that he ever really surrendered such work). The results of the 1958 tour far exceeded its original objectives.

In his by now customary fashion, Wilson recorded his general impressions of the countries he visited in his diary. But he also described the professional, substantive content of his travels in a long series of individual reports on those countries, always with practical recommendations for action. While the diary suggests an interesting, colourful piece of extended tourism, the voluminous but clear and forceful reporting shows that he and Jean Wilson worked extremely hard.

Air travel had developed fast since that first flight that John Wilson had taken to Africa in 1946. He continued to be fascinated and somewhat repelled by the experience. At Tehran in January 1958, in transit to Karachi, he referred in his diary to his Air France aircraft: 'There is something indecently lavish about this plane and its amenities. In the first place, "Super-Constellation". Could anybody think of something bigger and better that they could possibly call it? Then the food: a seven-course dinner last night with a choice of twenty-two liqueurs. Today, for lunch, I have *not* eaten caviar. All you need is a paper hat and it would be a Christmas party. This sort of orgiastic display, to which no doubt the airlines are driven by competition, is indecent and slightly impious when travelling through the stratosphere at five miles a minute. Something more simple, even bread and water, would be psychologically more appropriate to an experience which is still mysterious and almost sacramental.'

The Wilsons were visiting Asia for the first time. Although the problems of blindness were very substantial, especially in the Indian sub-continent, the landscape was nothing like so bare of organizations working for blind people as Africa had been on his first visit there. An eye infirmary had been opened in Madras as early as 1819. The first school for the blind in India had been founded by a blind Christian missionary in 1887. In 1944 the Indian government published a report on blindness in India. The Indian National Association for the Blind was set up in 1952. Helen Keller paid an 'electrifying visit' to the country in 1955 and laid the foundation stone of India's first modern sheltered workshop. By the time the Wilsons set foot in the country, there were probably around a hundred schools and organizations for blind people scattered over its vast area. Other activities, some involving the Society, some not, were in train in other Asian countries.

In Pakistan, their first stop, the Wilsons visited Karachi, Lahore and Rawalpindi. The National Federation for the Blind of Pakistan said they wanted to be affiliated to the Society. Wilson cordially welcomed this proposal and made a number of practical suggestions for the development of its work.

After an intensive stay in India which took in Delhi, Dehra Dun, Calcutta, Bombay and Madras, he reflected in his diary that 'India is altogether too massive, too complex, too turbulent for the casual tourist. You must fix your gaze on some single thing and what interested me particularly was the Indian attitude, in retrospect, to British rule.' He found this, as many have since done, to be ambivalent. But what struck him with force was the scale of everything. 'Nationalism is a continental hysteria; progress and for that matter retrogression are on such a big scale ... the squalor and overcrowding in the cities are indescribable ... mental turbulence, clamour, incredible progress in literacy and village betterment, unthinkable corruption, all assail you at every street corner. Yet it is a thrilling experience to go to India. One parliament functions over the whole country, surely the biggest single triumph of democracy.'

If the diary reflections were rather rambling in character his reports to headquarters were certainly not. He found the blind schools and workshops in India and Pakistan, with very few exceptions, to be unbelievably bad. He visited the Indian Government's Central Training Institute for the Blind at Dehra Dun and put forward suggestions for its re-organization. He studied the Indian National Association for the Blind and recommended acceptance of its request for affiliation to the Society. He reached the view that India urgently needed a realistic programme of rural training for the blind in the framework of its spectacular 'Community Development Programme'.

Pregnant with implications for the future was a note he wrote about 'eye camps'. These were rural diagnostic and operating clinics, set up in any suitable accommodation available. Empty schools, halls and private buildings were transformed temporarily into operating rooms, outpatient departments and wards to accommodate patients. Essentially, these 'camps' provided a means of eye treatment in rural areas that were out of the reach of established hospitals or clinics. But they were controversial. Wilson listened to the Indian arguments. The protagonists saw the camps as the best way of dealing with eye problems, especially cataract, on a large scale. The opponents argued that the camps were responsible for a good deal of indifferent treatment by unskilled practitioners. Wilson noted that the balance of opinion was that, 'Under proper control, and with adequate staff, time and preparation, the eye camp can be remarkably effective.' He would later become enthusiastic about the possibilities.

In Ceylon, which he found relaxing after the turmoil of India, he produced a report on the status of work for blind people and also recorded a conversation with a Buddhist priest about the doctrine of karma. Wilson always took a considerable interest in faiths other than his own, as we shall see in Chapter Seven.

In Singapore he found the Association for the Blind anxious for the Society's help in establishing a workshop for blind people. During a lengthy visit to Malaya he met the Prime Minister, Tunku Abdul Rahman. He produced a report for the Malayan Government and the Association for the Blind, which the Society had helped to establish some years earlier, on the present state of work for blind people, and made proposals for help from the Society. He took similar action in Sarawak and Brunei, fell temporarily ill with dengue fever in North Borneo, where Jean Wilson stood in for him, and then reached Hong Kong. Here he found 'the condition of the blind, many of whom are sleeping in the streets or in indescribable slum conditions...the worst I have ever seen.' He advised the Government and the Hong Kong Society for the Blind to set about improving the two 'pathetically inadequate' schools for the blind, start a really modern workshop and organize a proper blind welfare system. He found no one in Hong Kong who knew how to go about this and proposed that the Society should second someone. Which they did. Today's officials of the Hong Kong Society for the Blind, which I visited in January 2004, freely recognize that this assistance was crucial to its development from those early days to the impressive organization it now is.

After Fiji, where there was a disturbingly high blindness rate and where he again advanced practical proposals, the next steps of his tour took him to the different environment of the dominions of Australia, New Zealand and Canada which he hoped to enlist in a Commonwealth effort. In Australia, the Wilsons went just to the main cities: 'Darwin, hot and bustling; Sydney, money-conscious, turbulent, full of the noise of motor engines; Melbourne, quieter and more traditional but still something of a metropolis; Adelaide, like a sleepy, satisfactory English cathedral town, with the parks full of birdsong; Hobart, raining when we arrived and more English than any English town of the twentieth century manages to be; Perth, oddly different and conscious of its separation from the rest of the country; Brisbane, with its sunny ways and almost embarrassing hospitality.' 'This,' wrote Wilson 'is a land where men are men, and women carry their own suitcases.'

John and Jean travelled over eight thousand miles in Australia and visited every institution for the blind in the country. Wilson gave twenty radio broadcasts and two television talks. He found that the organizations *of* the blind were violently opposed to the organizations *for* the blind (Wilson was well attuned to this traditional contest from his days at the National Institute and later) and that work for the blind was also impeded by the typically Australian inter-state disputes which arise from the nature of the Australian federal system. The institutions for the blind were 'Dickensian, the workshops (with a few exceptions) appalling and the schools not much better'. He made proposals for improving things and found, in particular, that his suggestion that Australia should take action to help blind people in Borneo, Brunei, Sarawak, Malaya and Hong Kong was well received.

He seems to have derived particular pleasure from his visits in New Zealand to Auckland, Hamilton and Wellington. He reached agreement with the New Zealand Foundation for the Blind to set up a joint committee with the Society to undertake a shared pro-gramme of work for blind people in Commonwealth territories of the South-West Pacific. Then he proceeded to Canada (Vancouver, Calgary, Edmonton, Winnipeg and Toronto) where the Canadian National Institute for the Blind offered to seek authority to make available one per cent (perhaps £10,000) of their annual income for work in the least developed Commonwealth countries. Canada was emerging as the leading supporter of the Society among the dominions. The president of the Canadian National Institute for the Blind became one of the Society's vice-presidents and practical co-operation grew. Wilson wrote to headquarters: 'I really am begin-ning to feel pleased with the results of this tour. Not only will we obtain substantial additional funds, something more than £15,000 annually, but we can claim that all the major Dominions are now coming into our movement in the most practical manner.'

During his visit to New York, the last stopping point on this very long journey, he called on American organizations for the blind and held some fairly routine talks at the United Nations. But Wilson's sense of fun always ensured that he got pleasure out of a visit to America. At Idlewild airport in New York, an American immi-gration official asked the then routine questions about communist affiliations. 'He next enquired: "Do you have any communicable diseases?" Here he read out a list of suggestions which seemed to cover everything from bubonic plague to dandruff. When he came to disabilities he said, "Maybe we got a problem here; I'll have to check." Soon he came back. "Okay buddy, yours doesn't count, you're through".'

Wilson once speculated on what was the most difficult problem for a blind person when travelling. He concluded that the most con-fusing experience was 'one of those vast impersonal sky-scraping hotels in New York'. On this occasion the Wilsons went to a hotel with two thousand rooms on forty storeys. 'The first problem was to get into the hotel, through the revolving door spinning at supersonic velocity. I stood for a while, admiring the aplomb with which the New York women charge in butt-end first and emerge none the worse for the experience. I tested the speed of the door from time to time with my stick and during a lull made my entrance with nothing worse than a slight abrasion on the back of my skull.' And then: 'The bedroom was a miracle of concentrated amenity. There was a television set, a radio, a telephone, a control panel for the air-conditioning unit, a row of call buttons and a locker containing a Bible presented by the Gideons. I have learned to approach this gadgetry with caution, as, on one occasion in just such a bedroom, an apparently orthodox chair turned out to be an electrically operated vibrating machine for people with a tendency to thrombosis' (from *Travelling Blind*).

He wrote elsewhere that the first time he stayed in such a hotel, there was a strip of paper tightly stretched across the toilet seat. 'In Europe that would have meant that the plumbing was out of order, or that the contraption was dangerous or possibly that Marie Antoinette had slept there. I treated it with respect for some time until I discovered that all it said was "This seat has been sanitized for your protection".'

By any standards this extensive and hardworking tour had been productive, and well worth its expense. The constant flow of practical proposals, both to headquarters and often to governments and institutions in the countries visited, was impressive. Fundraising in the dominions and cooperation with them in third countries had made a promising start. As a result of the tour the Society now felt able to begin planning a number of activities on a Commonwealth scale.

This seed, the concept of Commonwealth action on blindness, was to grow and flourish in Wilson's mind. The Society's Planning Committee noted in 1959 that there were at least 2,300,000 blind in India, Pakistan and Ceylon (almost certainly a serious underestimate) and expressed the view that the organization should move gradually into a larger role as coordinator of a Commonwealth movement for the blind. This would involve 'imaginative projection of the idea of Commonwealth partnership in its application to the blind, readiness to take on new commitments (particularly in Asia) and the possibility of substantial new support from the older

Dominions'. The Society hoped to develop a Commonwealth con-science towards blindness. The movement would draw its strength from the combined activities of organizations working on problems of visual impairment in more than thirty countries. Each of those organizations was fully independent, but they were associated with the Society and with each other by a link of common purpose, by ties of close friendship and by the practical requirements of an enterprise that would have been impossible without cooperation and mutual confidence. 'Such a relationship could not readily exist in any setting other than the Commonwealth.'

Some years afterwards, in January 1968, *The Times* noted that in three years' time Britain would have withdrawn its troops from East of Suez. To date, Britain had been central to the Commonwealth, but its position was being eroded. If the Commonwealth was to continue, the paper argued, it must be given new meaning. The next day Wilson wrote to *The Times*: 'At the broad ground level of every day collaboration, the continuation of a British military presence is not the decisive factor in survival. This is true for those Common-wealth organizations which are not working at the pinnacle of political and strategic power. They exist to serve practical needs ... They form an essential part of the new Commonwealth... The Royal Commonwealth Society for the Blind serves 4,000,000 blind people. To many of them, and particularly to the 10,000 whose sight it restored last year, it *is* the Commonwealth.'

To emphasize the concept of a modern, Commonwealth-wide operation, the Society abandoned the distinction in its mandate between two areas of operation – the remaining colonies and the independent countries – and allotted to itself a single area of oper-ation defined as the whole Commonwealth other than the United Kingdom, Canada, Australia and New Zealand.

Following his first visit to Asia, Wilson thought long and hard about the problems of blindness in that continent. A number of the detailed proposals evolved in the course of his tour were im-plemented. But, as so often, he was mentally grasping for a bigger idea which might have substantial impact on the massive problems which the journey had brought to his attention. He concluded that the only action that offered a real chance of progress would be a concerted effort undertaken by the international organizations con-cerned with blindness and its prevention in Asia. The Society reached agreement with the American Foundation for the Overseas

Blind (now Helen Keller International), the World Council for the Welfare of the Blind and the Malayan Association for the Blind to promote an Asian conference in Kuala Lumpur in May 1963 with the specific purpose of adopting an Asian Plan for the Blind. The Wilsons then organized a further tour to prepare the conference and persuade the governments and institutions concerned of the merits of the Plan. In April 1963 they left for Aden, Pakistan, India, Ceylon, Singapore, Malaya, Borneo, Hong Kong, Canada and the United States.

Together with Eric Boulter, former President of the American Foundation for the Overseas Blind, and with Jean's help, Wilson drafted a document which set out three objectives for the next five years: to double the number of school places for Asian blind children; to increase rural training facilities to the point at which at least one thousand rural blind workers would be trained and re-settled annually as farmers and village craftsmen; and, in at least fifty industrial centres, to make arrangements for blind people to work in ordinary factories and to establish modern, sheltered work-shops.

In his speech to the conference Wilson described the scale of eye problems in Asia and said, 'It is evident that no single government and no single international agency can effectively tackle a problem of this magnitude. To make an impact, a concerted effort would be required, mobilizing all available resources, both nationally and internationally, of governments and unofficial enterprises. Such an effort, imaginatively planned and projected, might change the whole situation but it would need to be organized not as a routine operation (at which level it has conspicuously failed in the past) but with something of the flair and momentum of an international cause.' This is perhaps the earliest statement of Wilson's vision of a truly international campaign to deal with problems of blindness.

Seventeen countries participated in the conference. They adopted the Asian Plan unanimously, not altogether surprisingly after all the preparation and given the content, which it would have been hard to vote against. In 1964, the United Nations commended it to its specialized agencies and both the United Nations Children's Fund (UNICEF) and UNESCO urged governments to take comprehensive measures for the education of handicapped children. Some of the countries present in Kuala Lumpur took initial steps to implement the Plan. In India, the Society and OXFAM agreed to help with a scheme to promote the enrolment of 4,300 blind children in 500 primary schools. But, according to Wilson, political conditions in India made it impossible to go ahead. In the event, much of the Asian Plan for the Blind was set back by political change and economic recession. One prominent Indian ophthalmologist, who was active at the time, told me in 2003 that he could not remember the Plan at all. But it did help the Society consolidate its relationships in Asia, and it was one of the factors that led it to expand its work in India during the 1970s, to establish programmes in Pakistan and what became Bangladesh and to set up regional offices in India and Malaysia.

In 1965 the Society was fifteen years old. In that year it produced its second five-year plan for the period 1965 to 1970, entitled 'Commonwealth in Action'. This set out a series of policies and intentions on education, training and employment and noted, significantly in view of what was to come, that research into the link between malnutrition and blindness should be supported. As to the cure and prevention of blindness, the Society was still finding its way. The value of mobile clinics had been proved and they would be increased in the period of the new plan. While noting that 'there must be hundreds of thousands of blind people whose sight could be restored with competent surgery,' the plan recommended no more than that specialists and surgical teams should undertake visits for this purpose. But a more dramatic approach to the reduction of unnecessary blindness was now not far away.

The Society still had only about twenty overseas staff. The headquarters staff, now housed in new offices at 48 Victoria Street in London, was also lean. But its superstructure was distinctly plump. Since the death of Lord Halifax in 1959 Princess Alexandra of Kent had been president (as she is today). There were five vice-presidents. Two of them, the Commonwealth and Colonial Secretaries, held these honorary appointments for historical reasons only. The other three were Dr Helen Keller, Sir Bernard Reilly, the Society's first Chairman, and the President of the Canadian National Institute for the Blind. The Chairman for the next four years, Sir Peter Runge, presided over a Council of thirty people, large by modern standards and surely very unwieldy even then. There was a panel of medical advisers and five regional committees and some twenty-four committees had been established in individual cities or areas of Britain, largely connected with fundraising.

The worry, as so often in the life of charities, was money. The authors of the new five-year plan were optimistic. Income in the last five years had increased by 180% to £143,000 (though the calculation appears to omit the effects of inflation). It should be possible to reach £260,000 by 1970. That turned out once again to be a vain hope. When the plan was published the Chairman added a postscript stating that the Society, like many others in Britain at the time, had suffered a severe drop in revenue, owing to economic conditions. 1967, for example, produced just under £140,000 against the plan's predicted figure of £200,000.

In that year, interestingly, Jean Wilson was for the first time given a formal appointment at the Society as National Appeals Secretary. She was of course already deeply involved in the organization's work through her partnership with John on his overseas travels and in many other ways (which I shall explore in more detail in Chapter Seven). She had also, for many years, made a specific contribution: she was an excellent photographer and many of the photographs she had taken, especially overseas, were used to illustrate the annual reports and other publications. Now, with the children in their teens, she was able to accept a formal appointment. She was to develop a flair for fundraising, from which the Society would benefit substantially over the years. She studied the direct marketing techniques which were beginning to be adopted in the United States and applied them, ahead of most comparable charities, in Britain. Also, despite the reservations of her husband and others, she quickly developed the concept of 'productizing' (for which there should be a more beautiful word), inviting donors, for example, to provide £2 for an eye operation or £130 to finance an eye camp. Wilson's next grand scheme would provide excellent opportunities for the use of this fundraising technique.

As we have seen, during his visit to India in 1958 Wilson had noted the arguments put forward by both the protagonists and the opponents of eye camps. These camps, a means of providing mass treatment and cure of eye problems, especially cataract, in rural areas, had already had a long history in India. Eye surgeons, Indian and Western, had been running them for some fifty years. One of the most famous was Sir Henry Holland, an early member of the Society's Council, who had gone to Quetta in what is now Pakistan in 1900 and helped to establish a hospital which, in Wilson's words, 'would outlast the Raj and in the minds of so many ragged patients

1 John Wilson using a Braille typewriter, 1950
(A. Whittington; copyright John Bull)

2A John Wilson aged nine, 1928

2C Reading in the garden, 1945

2B At Worcester College for the Blind, c.1935 (John Wilson on the right)

2D Studying a Braille map of Africa, with Jean Wilson and their daughter Claire, 1950 (A. Whittington; copyright John Bull)

3A John Wilson on safari in West Africa

3B Showing a Braille newspaper to the Emir of Kano, Nigeria, 1950

3C 'Blindness was so prevalent that the necessary work of the village could be carried on only by enlisting the blind as well as the sighted.' West Africa

4 A blind African farmer with John Wilson, c.1968

5A John Wilson showing his tape recorder to a blind African

5B The simulium fly, the cause of river blindness (photograph by E.B. Ogun, London)

5C The blind climbers and their guides on top of Mount Kilimanjaro, 1969

ABOVE
6A A mobile eye unit in
India, c.1967

TOP RIGHT
6B Girl Guides with the
gift of a Landrover to be
used overseas

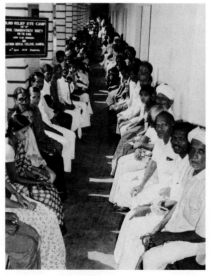

6C A young eye patient at Harare
hospital, Zimbabwe, 1969
(copyright *The Herald*, *The Sunday
Mail* and Kwayedza; photograph by
A.W. Gray)

6D Patients waiting at an eye camp
in India, c.1974

7A John Wilson received by Indira Gandhi, Prime Minister of India

7B Jibon Tari floating hospital, the Boat of Life, Bangladesh

8A John Wilson
addressing the
World Health
Assembly, 1980

8B With
Dr Venkataswamy
at an IAPB
conference

would remain the most cherished and characteristic memory of Imperial India.' In 1935 an earthquake destroyed the hospital. Two-thirds of its patients were among the 25,000 people estimated to have been killed in the area. Holland rebuilt it and re-established it as a base for mass treatment of cataract. He is said to have carried out more than 100,000 cataract operations personally before he re-tired. He was succeeded by his son, Ronnie Holland who, with his wife, Joan, disabled by polio, carried on the work and was for a time a member of the Society's staff.

During his visit to India in 1963, Wilson had become further impressed with the possibilities of eye camps. On his return he initiated a systematic study which resulted in the formation of a code of practice for their organization and operation and led to the Society extending some assistance to a few 'model camps' in the Indian sub-continent. On his next visit to India, in 1969, he went to Sitapur where Dr Mehrey, an Indian eye surgeon, conducted such camps. The Sitapur hospital, with its capacity for 750 in-patients and a vast outpatient capacity, and its links to a complex of some thirty eye-hospitals in Northern India, was probably the largest eye hospital in the world at the time. Wilson found it startling that it was situated in a comparatively small town in rural India. Dis-cussion with Dr Mehrey seems to have convinced Wilson that the eye camp technique provided a valid and realistic way of tackling cataract and other problems on a massive scale. On the same trip, he spoke at a conference of the World Council for the Welfare of the Blind in Delhi where he outlined the objectives of what by now had become the Society's programme of support for eye camps. He urged international backing for the programme and strongly ad-vocated the whole concept of prevention of blindness as a necessary adjunct to the conference's main interests of rehabilitation and edu-cation.

Returning home at the end of 1969, Wilson outlined to the Society a new project, the 'Eyes of India' Campaign. His motivation was clear. 'It was...the possibility of immediate, inexpensive restoration of sight on a massive scale rather than the long and un-certain prospects of prevention...which led the Society to make its contribution to this work in India.' He recalled that during the year it had already been helping selected hospitals in order to gain ex-perience of the possibilities and limitations of mobile clinics, mobile hospitals and eye camps as a means of tackling blindness in rural areas in Asia. By using modern drugs, improved transport and more trained eye specialists, the potential of the camps could be greatly increased and the risks formerly associated with them reduced to negligible proportions. In 1969, in six regions of India and one region of Pakistan, medical teams supported by the Society had treated 107,000 patients, performed 6,386 operations for the restoration of sight and conducted 2,704 further operations for the prevention of imminent blindness. The average cost of each operation was about £2 and of each eye camp between £130 and £170.

It was on the basis of this experience that he proposed that the Society should launch the 'Eyes of India' Campaign in 1970, aiming, in a single year, to finance in rural areas at least 20,000 operations for the restoration of sight or for preventing imminent blindness, and to treat at least 200,000 outpatients. If it succeeded, the effort would continue into the future. Each institution carrying out the practical work would have to meet rigid conditions covering the professional qualifications of surgeons, the proximity of base hospitals and the adequacy of nursing staff, after-care and follow-up. Satisfactory arrangements for financial and administrative control would also have to be in place. The Society would routinely check that the conditions were being met.

He further proposed that the Society should make the Campaign a special feature of its fundraising in 1970 and should set up a regional office in Bombay to coordinate expansion of its activities in South Asia, with, as its head, a visually impaired Indian called Rajendra Vyas, henceforth a prominent figure in the Society's work in Asia. It was planned that in that year, too, the Society should double its expenditure in Asia. For the first time in its history the amount spent on the prevention and cure of blindness would exceed that spent on rehabilitation and welfare. The scheme went ahead as proposed.

The Society itself did not *run* eye camps. This was a matter for local administrators and eye surgeons. Depending on the needs of particular camps in particular parts of the sub-continent, the Society might provide vehicles, medical equipment, eye surgeons or simply financial aid. The money was often raised by special appeals to particular organizations or individuals in the United Kingdom who were invited to sponsor a camp or a specific number of operations.

It was an exciting new venture for it guaranteed practical results and it would bring relief to hundreds of thousands. It also presented new fundraising possibilities. Two influential international organizations, Rotary and the Lions, became an important source of funding for the Society at this time, contributing something like 20% of its income. Both were keen supporters of eye camps. Indeed, their local branches often ran camps, for example in India. Wilson's talent for presenting a cause to potential donors was demonstrated in a series of speeches he made to Rotary and the Lions at home and abroad.

Addressing the Lions International Convention in Tokyo later, he said: 'Let me take you in imagination to one of those camps. You drive along the dirty, bush road. You pass blind people on creaking bullock carts, clinging perilously to the pillions of motorcycles or ferried in cars. You come to the townships where Lions Club members have been making preparations. The schoolhouse, smelling improbably of carbolic soap, has become a temporary hospital. Lion wives are cooking rice meals. A Lion electrician has constructed a dangerous-looking contraption to sterilize the instruments. To that township have come two thousand people with eye trouble and every home has offered hospitality to provide a bed space.

'Eye doctors arrive in a white mobile clinic. Each doctor works on three tables, leading his team with mass production precision. In a single day, that team can perform 250 cataract operations at the average cost of $5.

'But, stay a few days until the bandages are removed. Then you will see the extraordinary miracle of sight restored. A mother sees her child again. An old man looks out on the hills. A child is startled by the first shock of light.'

The images are crystal clear. The sentences move crisply toward the climax of the last paragraph. I and many others who have seen an operation to restore sight, perhaps in a mud hut in Gambia or a small hospital in rural India or in a London hospital, have felt, however many times we see it, that there is a miraculous quality to the event. Wilson could convey this with a wonderful lucidity. There is pathos in his description, too. For he himself could not benefit from that miracle. But he could with the greatest authority convey to his listeners what the restoration of sight meant to an individual. He did so, as in the speech quoted above, without crude exploitation of the emotions involved. But the appeal of his precise account of what is involved in dealing with blindness is to my mind irresistible. It must have been hard not to contribute to such a cause when you had heard this man expound it.

In 1974, he was to make a speech to Rotary in Bournemouth which was long remembered. It ended with the words 'Wouldn't it be wonderful if every Rotarian club could sponsor an eye camp?' The response from Rotary was overwhelming. Many Rotary clubs came forward to finance camps and the Society took on a special member of staff, a Rotarian, to supervise this connection.

The Society's public appeal for the Campaign raised £65,000, a substantial sum in today's terms. Specific donations in later years would increase that figure substantially. The need was massive. The backlog of cataract cases in India at that time was estimated at roughly 5,000,000. From now on, the Society's annual reports would record with some excitement the number of people whose sight had been restored or who had been otherwise treated. Wilson once said that 'Annual Reports, like Mozart heroines, are usually either faithful or beautiful, seldom both.' True. Even his own reports have to be read with some caution. In 1983, he would claim that in the last ten years the Society had restored sight to over 1,000,000 blind people in the sub-continent. The shorthand is misleading. It was rarely the Society's direct employees who had restored sight. But the operations it had supported had had that result. That was a remarkable achievement and it owed a great deal to Wilson's vision and energy.

The Indian sub-continent was also the theatre for another Wilson campaign, that against blinding malnutrition in children, caused by vitamin A deficiency in the form of xerophthalmia. Nowadays leading experts in the field believe that this form of deficiency is hardly anywhere a threat to sight at the public health level. But that was certainly not the case during Wilson's time with the Society. It had been shown to be the single most common cause of blindness in pre-school-age children worldwide.

The first account of the disease on a large scale had appeared as long ago as 1904. But it did not figure prominently in the Society's early thinking about blindness. Indeed, Professor Donald McLaren, one of the recognized world authorities on the disease, recalls meeting Wilson in the 1950s to try to persuade him of the severity and likely magnitude of the problem. But he was at that time so preoccupied with river blindness in West Africa that he appeared indifferent to the argument. If one of Wilson's great strengths was his capacity to focus on a single objective and drive or inspire people towards that target, one of his weaknesses was the obverse of that strength, a failure to realize that his single-mindedness might distort priorities and cause serious problems to be overlooked. To do him justice he would often say subsequently, and publicly, that he had made a mistake in not recognizing earlier the importance of blinding malnutrition. Moreover, it has to be remembered that in the 1950s the Society was a small organization with a small budget and there was a practical limit to the number of tasks it could undertake. In any case, at that time there was similar indifference on the part of governments and global organizations such as the World Health Organization and the United Nations Children's Fund.

A survey in the Luapula Valley in Zambia in the early 1960s indicated that malnutrition was indeed a major contributory cause of blindness. The Society then began to focus on the problem more clearly. In the late 1960s, it helped to raise funds for the establishment of the Ophthalmic Research Centre in Oxford whose Director, Dr Antoinette Pirie, had a particular interest in nutrition. But the turning point for Wilson was his attendance at a conference of the World Council for the Welfare of the Blind in New Delhi in October 1969, where, as we saw earlier, he spoke of the Society's new programme of support for eye camps. At that meeting one of the most remarkable personalities in world ophthalmic practice, Dr Gorindappa Venkataswamy, spoke, and presented a paper on child blindness caused by malnutrition. Wilson, typically, was moved to pretty well instant action. At his prompting, Dr Pirie went to India and met Dr Venkataswamy, with the result that a unique rehabilitation centre for xerophthalmia was set up in Madurai in the Southern Indian state of Tamil Nadu, Dr Venkataswamy's base. The Society helped to fund the centre for many years and Dr Pirie provided key consultancy advice. The underlying concept of the centre was that mothers should be admitted with their malnourished children and receive training in every aspect of nutrition and childcare. When they left the centre, there were regular follow-up visits by staff of the centre to their homes.

Between 1971 and 1980, some 2,000 children with xerophthalmia were treated at this centre. Jean Wilson, through the Associated Country Women of the World, simultaneously promoted the 'Forty-Six Villages Scheme' in Tamil Nadu, in which mothers in selected villages were taught in basic childcare centres to improve the diet of their children by adding vitamin-rich vegetables. The scheme was later extended to a further one hundred villages.

The Madurai project was the prototype for subsequent projects established by the Society in the Indian states of Gujarat and Uttar Pradesh and it led to an Indian national programme against xerophthalmia. It was not all plain sailing. Dietary deficiency is often the result of traditional ways of life, especially in the poorest communities, and habits can be hard to change. But, again, the Wilsons' energy and clarity of purpose had shown what could be done. 'It was the vision of John Wilson which made me start this project,' says Dr Venkataswamy.

In April 1971, Wilson, speaking on behalf of several blindness organizations, addressed the Executive Board of the United Nations Children's Fund (UNICEF). He spoke powerfully of the 'massive and growing problem' of infants who go blind for lack of vitamin A in the critical months immediately after weaning. The number of irremediably blind children was increasing to the point where, unless decisive action was taken, special educational and rehabilitation services would face a problem of unprecedented size. Not just South Asia, but South-East Asia, the Middle East, tropical Africa and extensive areas of South America were involved. The number of children at risk was to be counted in scores of millions. Programmes were needed to ensure that children in the vulnerable areas received sufficient quantities of vitamin A. Only governments and the international agencies could take action on an adequate scale. He made proposals for practical action, especially by UNICEF, and ended: 'There are at least 15,000,000 blind people in the world. Those of us who are in this community think that 15,000,000 is more than enough. We will do everything in our power to collaborate in international efforts to reduce needless blindness and to offer to every handicapped child a chance of fulfilment.'

At a seminar on the prevention of blindness in Jerusalem later in the same year a 'Xerophthalmia Club' of experts in this field was formed. This was not really a club in any organized sense but it did lead to the production of the *Xerophthalmia Club Bulletin*, for which the Society provided the funds and Wilson wrote the first foreword. The *Bulletin* lasted until 1999, the year of Wilson's death, when it merged with another publication.

The gravity of the problem that Wilson had addressed in his

speech to UNICEF was dramatically illustrated – more quickly than he or anyone else expected. Following a destructive civil war between the two halves of Pakistan in 1971, East Pakistan became independent as Bangladesh in 1972. For the new country, always so prone to natural disasters, that year was one of floods, hurricanes and widespread famine. Alarmed by the reports of large numbers (perhaps 100,000) of Bangladeshi children going blind through famine, and at the request of the Bangladesh government, the Wilsons flew to the scene. They travelled extensively through the villages. They would long remember 'those blind babies and their bewildered parents' and the 'thin, bitter smell' of hunger. It was clear to them that many more children would go blind unless action was taken. Wilson and the local UNICEF representative worked out a plan for a national programme aimed at dealing with vitamin A deficiency in the villages. John called on the Prime Minister, Sheikh Mujibur Rahman, who agreed to a nationwide distribution of vitamin A capsules. In three months, by Wilson's account, 8,000,000 children under five years of age had been covered and, by the end of 1973, a further 7,000,000 had received this treatment.

As usual, there were critics. They argued that before action was taken a survey of the prevalence of blindness in the country should have been conducted. Wilson thought, rightly in my view, that in the prevailing conditions of famine and disorganization, that would have been a time-wasting impossibility (it is worth noting that the first-ever survey of blindness prevalence in Bangladesh was not in fact completed until 2002). The better view, to which most observers subscribed, is that the intervention of UNICEF and Wilson probably saved the sight of several hundred thousand babies.

In the following year, 1973, the Wilsons returned to the subcontinent. In Bangladesh John Wilson inaugurated the first eye camp of the Bangladesh National Society for the Blind, which he had helped to found, and supplied two mobile clinics for its eye-camp programme. He also met another sub-continental pioneer in eye medicine, Dr Rabiul Hussein, and established a relationship which would help and encourage Hussein as he developed, from small beginnings, what is today a major eye hospital and training complex in Chittagong in the south of Bangladesh.

As before, the main focus of this visit was India. Wilson had been invited to speak to a meeting of the All-India Ophthalmic Society in Bangalore in January, 1973. He decided to use the occasion to try to convince this powerful, professional group that it should back his concept of modernizing eye camps to provide reliable mass treatment in rural areas. Certain in his own mind that the problems were soluble, he set out to persuade. He was well aware that there would be opposition. Some argued that mass treatment would mean second-class surgery. And, as Wilson noted, there had undoubtedly been some deplorable eye camps in which 'quacks had got into the business.'

He referred to a stone elephant outside the conference building: 'That elephant is immensely impressive but it never gets off its pedestal, just like a specialist who never moves from his city hospital though he has in his hands a skill which could save thousands of people from blindness in the villages.' Rajendra Vyas, the Society's Regional Director, who was there, tells me that the speech was 'electrifying', that the critics were disarmed and many of them came forward afterwards to undertake eye camps in rural areas. How many resented the lecture and declined to join this movement is not recorded.

But the most important event of this journey to India was a meeting with the country's Prime Minister, Indira Gandhi, in February 1973. Following the successful 'Eyes of India' Campaign and the growing work on childhood blindness, Wilson now strongly hoped that India would formulate and implement a national programme for the control of blindness. He had maintained for years that only when governments engaged with the problem and tackled it methodically could real progress be made. If India could give a lead, other developing countries might well follow, and Western donors would be encouraged to provide additional resources. An appointment was arranged through Dr Mehrey of Sitapur, whom we met earlier, and who had considerable influence in Indian political circles.

John and Jean spent many hours in careful preparation at their base in the Ashok Hotel, Delhi. They compiled a detailed memorandum covering the number of blind in India (estimated to be a minimum of 4,500,000), the development of mass cataract treatment and the work on malnutrition. In a covering letter to Mrs Gandhi, Wilson suggested that India might give 'the essential international leadership' by advocating at the United Nations a decade of concerted international action and promoting in India a nationwide programme designed to halve in ten years the cataract backlog and eliminate child blindness caused by vitamin deficiency. Costs would be modest. 'A sight-restoring operation in a village eye camp need not cost more than fifty rupees. A cupful of green vegetables daily can protect an infant's eyes from vitamin deficiency. It costs less to save a child's sight than to provide his first Braille frame at a blind school.'

The arguments were well prepared and the papers made a clear case. But at meetings with heads of government, who may well not have had the time or even the inclination to read the papers, what matters is what is said and the personal impact made by the advocate. John, Jean, Dr Mehrey and Rajendra Vyas sat down with Mrs Gandhi. Wilson's presentation was brief but very persuasive, say those who were there. Mrs Gandhi leant across the table and said, 'Yes, John, we will have the National Programme for the Control of Blindness.' This was a rare moment in international diplomacy, an immediate commitment from a head of government. Mrs Gandhi was not easily impressed by foreign visitors, but I have it from a good source that she took a liking to John Wilson.

After the necessary detailed work by Indian government departments and others had been completed, the Indian National Programme was eventually launched in 1976 with the overriding goal of reducing in twenty years the amount of preventable blindness by two-thirds. The plan was adopted by Government and Parliament, national funds were committed and international resources were obtained, especially from Denmark.

It was a good start. But it will come as no surprise to those who have been involved with such projects that various problems emerged in later years. Indeed, in 1980 Wilson had a second meeting with Mrs Gandhi, when he had the difficult task of presenting to her the problems which had arisen and seeking her agreement to solutions, delicately indicating the need for the replacement of the Director of the National Programme and also requesting her endorsement of a major programme to attack blinding malnutrition. These aims were broadly achieved although Mrs Gandhi stated that there would be no increased funding from central Government. She was to include 'Prevention of Blindness' as one of the items in her twenty-point programme of national reconstruction. She also often spoke publicly about childhood blindness and her government issued a pamphlet: *A Handful of Leaves Can Prevent Children Going Blind*. In 1981 the Society launched a formal campaign against blinding malnutrition in India with the objective, over five years, of saving the sight of 60,000 children at risk of blindness.

As I have suggested before, a proper estimate of Wilson's work cannot depend alone on how far formal plans, programmes or projects succeeded or did not succeed. He was one of those rare people who genuinely inspired in others a long-lasting commitment to action. The future achievements of those who had been so inspired certainly owed something to his inspiration but that something cannot be measured. A powerful example is that of Dr Venkataswamy, already referred to in this chapter.

In March 2003, I went to Madurai in Tamil Nadu to meet Dr V, as he is familiarly referred to by his Western friends. He is now about eighty-six years old and has a remarkable story to tell. He was born in a small village of South India. As a young man he followed the teachings of Mahatmah Gandhi and trained to be a doctor. He wanted to become an obstetrician because three of his cousins had died in the last months of their pregnancies and he wanted to prevent such deaths. But rheumatoid arthritis made it impossible for him to cope with the degree of physical activity involved in obstetrics and he took up ophthalmology instead, obtaining a degree from Madras University in 1955. He practised as a government ophthalmologist for twenty years until 1976 when Indian Government rules obliged him to retire at the age of fifty-eight.

Dr V then asked his three brothers and two sisters to join him in setting up a trust to fund and run an eye hospital. This opened in 1978 with eleven beds. Twenty-five years later, when I visited him, he was actively presiding over a huge conglomerate called 'The Aravind Eye Care System'. This consists of a base eye hospital at Madurai, four satellite hospitals, a laboratory for manufacturing medical equipment, an institute for training in community ophthalmology, a research foundation, an eye bank and a centre for women's, children's and community health. The complex provides 2,800 beds for eye patients, seventy per cent of which are reserved for patients who cannot afford to pay for treatment. It receives virtually no money from government but finances activities from income from those who can afford to pay. In 2003 it handled nearly 1,500,000 outpatients and conducted in total more than 2,000,000 surgical operations.

Everyone who visits Aravind seems, unfailingly, to be impressed by the achievement. It is a true centre of excellence, measured by any standards. The British National Health Service would be glad to have this weapon in its armoury. It remains a family concern, with many members of the family working in the hospitals as eye surgeons or in other capacities. The surgeons, all highly qualified, work very long days and many, on their 'day off', conduct eye camps in rural areas.

But there is more. The inspiration for the whole enterprise is spiritual. Aravind is named after Sri Aurobindo, an Indian spiritual leader and philosopher who was prominent in the early Indian opposition to British rule. It is from this source that Dr V derives his own philosophy: 'With a firm belief in approaching work from a spiritual perspective, I have striven to be open to the divine force. Doing this, one can accomplish things far greater than imagined … As we focused our energy into the growth of this Institute, it was as if somewhere along the line a force took over, helping us to overcome all obstacles and grow.' This quiet spiritual outlook is perfectly evident to any present-day visitor to Aravind.

The remarkable hospital complex is the result of the faith, work and ability of Dr V, his family and his Indian friends and helpers. International organizations have given various forms of assistance over the years. It would be quite wrong to attribute a large part of the achievement to John Wilson, but I was interested to hear what Dr V would say on the point.

Behind him, in the small office where he still goes to work every day, there is a portrait of his spiritual guide, Sri Aurobindo. Underneath it is a photograph of John Wilson. Dr V first met Wilson in 1965. 'In a way he has been a mentor to me right from the start. It was the beginning of a beautiful friendship. He was a constant source of encouragement. His support, both personal and professional, was invaluable to Aravind's beginning.' Through the years that followed this first meeting the two were constantly in touch by letter, telegram or telephone. Dr V was more than once surprised and pleased, when something positive had happened in the eye treatment field in India, to hear Wilson's voice on the telephone congratulating him.

The Society provided practical assistance. It supported eye camps in the area, donated vehicles and equipment and helped (as we have seen) to establish the nutrition rehabilitation centre and launch the project for childcare in forty-six villages. It also financed part of the building of the first hospital and later supported the free cataract operation service. Support of various kinds has continued until today.

Valuable as this material assistance was, especially in the early years, the relationship with John Wilson was worth a good deal more to Dr V. He found Wilson different to other Britons he had known in pre- and post-independent India. 'They all kept their distance. John was different. He put you at your ease and created a sort of bonding. You could communicate easily with him.' Any meeting with him was to be welcomed: 'He lifts you up. Gives you self-confidence. He always encouraged me to take on more responsibilities. He would communicate his passion to you. It did not feel like pressurizing.'

When Dr V visited England he often went to stay with the Wilsons at their home. 'Every time he used to take me upstairs to the guest room and show me how to operate the electric blanket and the cold and hot water taps and other details. We used to sit on the veranda of his house, facing the sea, and talk, sometimes for hours, about my work. In this way he has mentored me in my career considerably.'

In some ways this was an unlikely friendship, between an Oxford-educated, much travelled Englishman who rather relished the trappings of the old Empire and the quiet eye doctor from the south of India whose own spiritual mentors had opposed British rule in India. But Dr V is by no means the only person of Wilson's acquaintance who recalls the ease with which he crossed barriers, scarcely recognizing that they were there. He had an outstanding ability to get on with the widest range of people. Then, their mutual passion to get rid of unnecessary blindness united them. I suspect, too, that Wilson was drawn by the spirituality of Aravind. Dr V's strong sense of being guided by a divine force recalls similar words which Wilson used of his own life from time to time.

The Indian's description of his approach to his work would have evoked a ready response from the Englishman: 'Intelligence and capability are not enough. There must also be the joy of doing something beautiful. Being of service to God and humanity means going well beyond the sophistication of the best technology to the humble demonstration of courtesy and compassion to each patient.'

In 2003 a booklet, *Promises to Keep*, was published to commemorate twenty-five years of work at Aravind. In his foreword

Dr V notes that many people from within and outside India had helped the enterprise. But he mentions by name only one person: 'I would like to place on record my indebtedness to a very special friend and mentor, Sir John Wilson, Founder, Royal Commonwealth Society for the Blind, who was a consistent source of support and inspiration.'

Dr V, whose concern for the visually impaired extends well beyond the borders of his own country, told me that he greatly admired John Wilson's ability to think globally, to see the international implications of work being carried out in a particular country or region, to grasp how international efforts and resources could be marshalled to tackle a particular problem. He had the sense that Wilson kept abreast of all the work on blindness, in whatever region it was happening, and gave constant encouragement and advice to those involved. He ended our conversation of many hours with the wistful words: 'There is no one like him now.'

Chapter 5

Vision International

By the early 1970s John Wilson had led the Society for some twenty years. He had travelled the world as extensively as nearly anyone of his generation. He knew virtually everyone who was significantly engaged in work on problems of visual impairment. He had acquired a rich knowledge of many foreign countries, based not on casual tourism but on an unremitting effort over many years to understand foreign cultures and absorb information. He had a strong appetite for facts and statistics (one of his staff speaks of his 'compulsive numerology'). But his enquiring mind led him to try to penetrate beyond the material facts and investigate the intellectual and spiritual foundations of other cultures.

Most people who have travelled extensively have built up a stock of visual images, whether in the form of photographs or mind-pictures. That resource was not directly available to Wilson, of course, but his travelling partner, Jean, was adept at describing his surroundings to him so that some passages in the diaries come close to portraying visual images. For Wilson, however, there was an alternative. Where seeing people see landscapes, he heard what he called 'soundscapes'. He described some in a BBC radio interview in 1966:

'The Victoria Falls span the whole spectrum of imaginable sound from the hissing treble which pierces your ears to the profoundest bass, which is a vibration in the pit of your stomach. In Northern India during the monsoon, thunder bellows through the valleys until the hills stand in a silhouette of sound and a great slow echo booms back from the Himalayas. At Kyoto in Japan, the temple trees are festooned with a multitude of prayer gongs, and when a soft wind blows you can follow its passage through the gardens by the chime and tinkle of bells. No less impressive is the complete absence of sound. Sometimes in the desert the silence is absolute without a whisper of movement and you notice a pulse in the air which is the beating of your heart.'

The senses of hearing and of smell (discussed earlier) were powerful aids to Wilson's acquisition of knowledge as was the sense of touch. He was delighted when visiting the Getty Museum in California that the staff agreed to his request to turn off the alarm system 'so that I could feel the exquisite Greek and Roman sculptures.' He was aware of the hazards, too. Asked why he stood to attention in lifts, he explained that hands could be troublesome if you could not see. 'If you touch someone in the wrong place in a lift you may be misunderstood. There is another thing one must never do and that is to move forward with one's hands held out to protect oneself. Walking into a woman could cause embarrassment.'

His wide experience and knowledge of the world and his network of contacts were now to be put to a serious purpose. For years he had dreamt of an international movement to attack the problems of blindness. In the next decade the promotion of coordinated international action was the dominant theme of his life. He brought to it his well-developed skills of oratory and negotiation and his restless pursuit of effective action. His work in Africa, Asia and the Caribbean continued but his main stage now was that of international institutions, with their jargon and acronyms, their stimulus and frustration. The prize – coordinated, adequately resourced and properly directed action – was great in prospect. But its acquisition, if it *could* be acquired, would need all his energy and will-power.

The path for the creation of a global movement, Wilson reflected later, had been prepared by conceptual changes in the 1960s. The notion of prevention had become more firmly established. Research work, in at least some areas, had demonstrated the practicability of preventive measures. International ophthalmology had broadened in outlook. It was increasingly accepted that, if ophthalmologists were to realize their potential in eye-care work, they should be prepared, both in training and in practice, to extend their activities beyond the hospital and research laboratory and promote mass-treatment programmes in underdeveloped countries. Even those organizations whose primary purpose was to provide rehabilitation and education for blind people were now coming to recognize that the prevention of blindness was an essential accompaniment to international action in their fields. Then the American Foundation for the Overseas Blind (now Helen Keller International) had taken a strategic decision to become involved in medical activities. Also in the United States, the research work of the National Eye Institute and the international prevention and cure activities of the new International Eye Foundation were making an impact.

Most important of all, the World Health Organization (WHO) had made the prevention of blindness one of the themes of its work. The WHO is one of the so-called 'specialized agencies' of the United Nations. It is the main organization that brings together representatives of the world's governments to discuss and act upon health problems. It seeks to improve health standards, control communicable diseases and promote health education, training and research. Created in 1948, it had long been involved in health projects in the developing world. In the 1950s, for example, it was supporting schemes to control river blindness in Africa. Yet in the 1960s its work on the problems of blindness was still very limited in scope and was mainly centred on a trachoma control programme, of which Wilson thought highly, especially in respect of its work in the Middle East. In 1962, on a proposal from Wilson, the WHO had made the prevention of blindness the theme of its annual World Health Day, and the Society had worked with organizations in many countries to help produce extensive publicity for the event. But the most decisive step was taken in Boston in 1969 when the annual meeting of the World Health Assembly, the WHO's most important inter-governmental forum, requested its Director-General to undertake a study of the causes of blindness.

The device of a study has been used hundreds of times since the foundation of the United Nations. It is sometimes employed as a way of avoiding real action, and sometimes as a means of achieving minimal consensus when a bolder proposal for action would simply produce disagreement. But sometimes, as in this case, it is the essential basis for proceeding. The facts have to be established before governments will commit expenditure. After all the years since Wilson had begun work in the 1940s, the factual basis for work on blindness was still weak. Statistics of the prevalence of blindness were unsound. Knowledge of causes was patchy. The WHO Director-General did what he or she often does in response to a request for a study – and sent a questionnaire to governments. The replies constituted the first international account of the global extent and causes of blindness: still inadequate but a beginning.

The story of Wilson's creation of an international movement

plays out in many of the world's cities. The next venue for action was Jerusalem. In August 1971, the Israel Academy of Science brought together some three hundred experts, mostly ophthalmic surgeons, from twenty-one countries to discuss blindness prevention. John Wilson was, it seems, the only non-surgeon and the only blind person present. Invited to make a keynote speech, he was introduced as a 'man who had restored more sight than anyone else.' He argued the case that 'We now had most of the elements necessary for a global strategy against the major causes of blindness in developing countries.' This notion was included in the seminar's final communiqué which also proposed the establishment of an international organization to coordinate action. The concept of a global programme was now alive. Many of those present were to be involved in the actual creation and execution of that programme. But for the moment it was little more than words in a seminar communiqué – and we all know how quickly those can collect dust.

Some months later, in 1972, the World Health Assembly adopted its first ever resolution on the prevention of blindness. It noted that the data so far collected resulted in an estimate of ten to fifteen million blind people worldwide. But it believed the data to be fragmentary and the figures an underestimate. It warned that, with increasing population and life expectancy, the number of blind would rise. Unless active measures were taken, the total would reach thirty million by the year 2000. So the Assembly asked the WHO Secretariat to obtain additional data, to help member states in educational programmes and to intensify technical assistance to help the control of trachoma, river blindness and blinding malnutrition.

John Wilson seems to have been involved in drafting this resolution. It would have been unlike him not to have been. He was a past-master at that essential technique for success in international meetings – knowing clearly in advance what you want to get out of the event and ensuring, as best you can, that the final document enshrines that objective. The resolution also set up a WHO Study Group, another common UN device. Wilson became a member of its secretariat. The Group formulated definitions of blindness and visual impairment, drew up a classification of eye diseases and stated firmly that 'the case for the elimination of unnecessary blindness is justified not only on humanitarian terms but also by its social and economic consequences. In terms of economic loss, blindness is the most expensive of all causes of serious disablement. The magnitude of this problem is only now being fully appreciated and constitutes a compelling justification for more practical action both by international agencies and by member governments.'

The Group also proposed – and Wilson's hand was certainly active here – that mechanisms should be established to coordinate action both within the WHO and between non-governmental organizations like the Society. The idea of creating a mechanism *within* the WHO soon had to be abandoned for constitutional reasons. But the second thought was to carry Wilson into an important new phase of his life.

The WHO Secretariat began to consult all the relevant people about the idea, which had been born at the Jerusalem seminar and refined in later discussion, that a new organization should be established to coordinate the action of non-governmental organizations in the blindness field and to mobilize resources. In 1974, two WHO officials came to see Wilson at the Society's headquarters and asked him to try to devise a basis for such an organization. I am tempted to wonder whether he put the request in their mouths but in any case only one answer to that request was possible. He had long wanted such a body to be created. He loved new initiatives and was always fascinated by new structures. But it was not a straight-forward task. Vested interests were involved. First, there were still a few voices that argued that dealing with blindness was a privilege of ophthalmologists and that others should not be involved. Then there was a myriad of organizations involved in the field that would have to be persuaded either to join the new one or have a positive relationship with it if they were not to work against it in the future. One in particular, the International Association for the Prevention of Blindness, seemed by its very name to be carrying out the pro-posed role already. But, according to a well-informed source, it was 'basically a bunch of professors that met occasionally and produced nothing'. Wilson thought that what was needed, by contrast, was a pro-active agency, always present on the scene. He set to work to per-suade others and drafted a constitution for the new organization.

The key event in his negotiation was a seminar in Paris in July 1974 of the International Congress of Ophthalmology. As usual, he knew what he wanted while, according to some present, others simply did not realize what was happening. He was elected presi-dent of the moribund International Association for the Prevention of Blindness and was given authority to re-organize it 'into an effective instrument for attacking the problems of blindness on an international level'. But it was plain, at least to those who were awake, that re-organization would effectively involve its disappearance for, by a second decision, Wilson was also made president-designate of the new Agency which was to be created. His negotiation had been skilful. Key to it was his insistence throughout that the Royal Commonwealth Society for the Blind would have no pride of place in the new organization. It would be on a par with other similar bodies which joined. Some members of the Society were not exactly thrilled by this approach but it was clearly right. Any suggestion that the Society should be pre-eminent among the non-governmental organizations would have killed the idea at birth.

A principal target was the German non-governmental organization, Christoffel-Blindenmission, which was becoming one of the largest charities in the field. Founded in 1908 by a German pastor, Ernest J. Christoffe, to provide a worldwide ministry to the blind and handicapped, it had a strong Christian ethos. By the 1970s it was helping to maintain several hundred projects in Asia, Africa and Latin America. Initially, it wished to keep its distinctive role and not be part of a global movement but Wilson persuaded it to come into the tent.

The new organization was named the International Agency for the Prevention of Blindness (IAPB). Originally it was hoped that it would become known popularly as 'Vision International' but that name never caught on, partly because it was already used by another organisation. Essentially, the new Agency was an agglomeration of international non-governmental bodies such as the Society and organizations concerned with ophthalmology, and organizations of and for the blind. It also brought on board people to represent scientific disciplines other than ophthalmology and assembled another group of distinguished individuals who, it was judged, would make significant personal contributions to the Agency's work. Many of those first elected were of course experts with whom Wilson had long worked and corresponded in various regions of the world. Importantly, the Agency had an official relationship with the WHO that would enable Wilson, as President, to address the World Health Assembly and WHO Executive Board from time to time. He now had a post that would carry him virtually automatically onto the principal platforms at meetings where blindness was discussed. More often than not, he would be invited to make the keynote speech. He took up all the opportunities it offered with zest.

In November 1974, for example, he spoke in Cairo to an international conference on the prevention of blindness, advocating the merits of the new movement. From the time of the Pyramids, he said, cataract had been a scourge of the Middle East, and even today the areas of worst prevalence were within the boundaries of Islam. Trachoma was also endemic in the region. If Middle Eastern ophthalmologists and scientists could eliminate this disease they would make a unique contribution to the prevention of blindness throughout the world. Perhaps the splendid Islamic tradition of giving alms to the blind man at the mosque could find a new dimension in national and regional plans for preventing blindness, and also in a collective initiative, through the United Nations, to sponsor world action against trachoma and associated diseases. 'I invite you as individuals to join the new Agency and to give it your professional commitment. I hope that, as representatives of ophthalmic and health organizations, as representatives of governments, you will establish national and regional organizations as components of the new Agency.'

The IAPB began work in January 1975 on the very day of the Society's twenty-fifth anniversary. And where? At temporary offices in the Society's own headquarters (now, since 1971, at Haywards Heath in West Sussex). Wilson, anxious as ever to get on with things, offered this accommodation to the Agency's secretariat plus some financial help so that the new enterprise did not waste time. It was convenient for him as its President that it was in the same building as the Society – he could just walk down the corridor to visit the Agency instead of travelling to some foreign venue.

He well knew by now that in the end, if the problems which were his life's concern were to be properly tackled, only the United Nations and the governments of the world could marshal the required resources. But the UN and its Agencies could only act in response to requests from national governments and in a sympathetic climate of opinion. For that reason, he believed that an effective international non-governmental agency, such as the IAPB, had an indispensable role 'to coordinate action on a world scale. It could be the catalyst, the framework, the lever which might move the mass of public opinion and of international funds.'

In May 1975, he addressed governments at the World Health Assembly, speaking for the first time on behalf of all the non-governmental organizations that were concerned internationally with blindness and its prevention. Indeed, he claimed to speak also as a representative of the world's 16,000,000 blind people. The prospect of 30,000,000 blind by the end of the century was, he said, 'totally unacceptable...a grotesque anachronism'. Most of the blindness, he continued, was preventable or curable. In economic terms it was a disaster. The world already spent a billion dollars each year on rehabilitation of, and provision for, the blind. The aim of the IAPB was 'to break the link between blindness and population growth, to alert and arouse international opinion, to mobilize resources'. There were times, he said, in the history of world health when, politically and scientifically, the opportunity presented itself to make a great move forward. It had been done with smallpox and yaws (a contagious tropical skin disease). There was now a similar opportunity with blindness.

'All life is meeting,' said the Christian philosopher Dietrich Bonhoeffer. 'All life is meetings,' a weary civil servant (not me) improvised later. Wilson was now, and would remain, fully exposed to the international circuit, the remorseless round of UN and other conferences. He told the parishioners of his local church in Rottingdean during a sermon that 'In the last few years I have sat through interminable international meetings, drinking interminable cups of United Nations coffee, reading, or more often pretending I have read, all that monstrous multi-lingual documentation.'

Never far from his mind was the contrast between the comfortable conference facilities and the realities of life in the poorest developing countries. 'We speak so glibly of the Third World,' he told a Rotary conference, 'an abstract term for that part of our One World which is underprivileged, underfed, clamouring for status and resources, striving with crazily increasing populations against disease, illiteracy, natural and man-made disasters. In air-conditioned halls, drinking gallons of UN coffee, experts formulate elegant strategies. But only in such meetings can our modern world fumble towards a new framework of ideas.'

For a man always bent on action the bureaucracy, the time-wasting, the strutting of would-be but often third-rate orators, and the cynicism that are inescapably attached to the conference circuit were bound to be frustrating. But he saw clearly that his passionate desire for collective international action could not be achieved without the UN system. And in truth I think his enjoyment of the process outweighed the frustration. Those who worked with him at this period of his life were in no doubt that he loved being on the international stage. He relished all the personal contacts, the abundant opportunities to perform before potentially influential audiences and the new prospect of advancing the cause. He knew perfectly well that the process was necessary if there was to be any chance of mobilizing international opinion in the direction he wanted.

Jean Wilson was appointed coordinator of the Agency's campaign executive, whose task was to promote international publicity and to support national fundraising efforts. She brought to the job the experience and skills from which the Society itself had long benefited. She helped to organize a major publicity campaign for World Health Day in April 1976, working with the WHO and with the forty-four national committees on prevention of blindness which by then had been constituted to support the Agency.

Over 100,000 copies of a special prevention of blindness edition of the magazine *World Health* were distributed. A tailor-made film, *Focus on Sight*, was sent to seventy television outlets throughout the world. On the Day itself the prevention of blindness theme was celebrated in most of the 130 member states of the United Nations. There was a festival of light in Japan, church-bell ringing in North American cities, a helicopter dropping pamphlets over Ghanaian villages, the ceremonial lighting of candles in Hindu and Buddhist temples, a national song competition in South Korea and the broadcasting of a special calypso in Trinidad. The communist regimes of the Soviet Union, Poland, East Germany and China organized publicity as only they knew how.

The main disappointment was Britain. The British National Committee for the Prevention of Blindness held a press conference on 5 April, the eve of the Day, but its efforts were eclipsed by the announcement of a new Prime Minister and the next day's budget. That may not have been the whole story. Jean Wilson told the Society's Council that it was a matter of real concern that both the new Agency and the Society generally seemed to receive negligible attention from the British media. She quoted a remark made by Lord Halifax when he was chairman of the Society: 'The evil that men do makes better headlines than the good which is interred with their bones.' I suspect that the Society, which in its earlier days received excellent publicity in Britain, now suffered from the fact that the media viewed it as an 'old story'. Nor was there much enthusiasm in the British readership for stories about new international institutions.

Fundraising was to be mainly a matter for national committees of the Agency. But Jean gave the new organization the benefit of her advice. The aim should be not single, once-for-all contributions but a continuing and regular source of income, to make possible planning on a long-term basis. Nowadays, fundraising had to be specific. If the objective was to finance 500,000 cataract operations in Asia, the approach should be, not an emphasis on the total sum required, but requests to 500,000 people to provide individually the unit cost of five to ten dollars. If the aim was to build fifty eye hospitals, the target must be broken down into the unit cost per bed which, at $2,000 in an African base hospital, was a project which most organizations could afford. Then there must be a positive link between the donor and the recipient, a reliable administration that followed every dollar to its destination, and a proper feedback of information. All her points were good. If they sound commonplace to modern fundraisers, they would not have done to their predecessors thirty years ago.

But publicity and fundraising were not the only needs. There were professional and intellectual arguments to be addressed. In late March 1976, the WHO had convened in Baghdad an inter-regional conference on blindness prevention. Wilson, as president of the Agency, gave the introductory address. The Agency's motivation was, he said, simple: the misery and waste of millions of needlessly blind people; the fact that blindness on this scale was as costly as a major war; and the prediction that, unless effective action was taken, the number of the world's blind would double by the end of the century. There were many causes of blindness 'but we agree with the World Health Organization that the priority target in any global strategy must be the Four Giants – trachoma, river blindness, cataract and blinding malnutrition. Control these, and we can break the link between blindness and population growth. Neglect them, and twenty-five years from now, the whole rehabilitation system of the world will be inadequate to accommodate the multitude of blind people.'

An adequate technology existed for such control, he continued.

What was lacking was political will, economic resources and the adjustments required in the operative ideas of whole professions. The great ophthalmic institutions had an essential role. 'But behind the bricks and mortar, behind the elegant departmental structures, there must be services big enough, mobile and flexible enough, to cover whole communities and to offer eye care to millions.' The prevention of blindness was not just an ophthalmic sideshow. It was the sum of all the disciplines having any bearing on eye care and delivery, the coordination of all action necessary to prevent blindness in the community, the nation and the world. He concluded, 'There is a time for professional reservation, for bureaucratic caution, for political compromise; but also there is a time when the greater need is for vision of the objective, for a flash of purpose and action. If that could come from this meeting, it could electrify the whole situation and shine into millions of lives.'

Some participants at Baghdad recall the conference mainly for a professional dispute about the validity of the proposed strategy linking together the Four Giants to which Wilson had referred. A certain section of expert opinion disagreed fundamentally with this approach. To begin with, it was in their view a mistake to include cataract, which cannot be prevented (but can generally be cured), and which requires treatment by ophthalmologists, in a strategy which also contained three other diseases requiring, by contrast, a public health approach. Worse, they argued, the four diseases had little in common beyond the fact that they affected the eye. There was no more reason to link them together in action programmes than there was for linking, say, pulmonary tuberculosis, emphysema and pneumonia, just because they all affect the lung.

Professor Donald McLaren, a renowned authority on blinding malnutrition, with a background in general medicine, clinical nutrition and biochemistry, was a leading critic. He penned a verse:

'Four uneasy bedfellows came to Baghdad
Xero, Oncho, Trachoma and Cataract
They proved incompatible – too bad
All they had in common was to blind
Good for jerking tears and raising money
For prevention planning, no way to find.'

The Professor recognizes that as poetry this may fall short of the highest standard but he stands by the argument which, he says, came as a shock to most delegates. He and some others continue to argue the case today. They point to the fact that the Four Giants have very different aetiologies, risk groups and global occurrence and therefore require very different approaches. They think it neither logical nor cost-effective to hive off the relevant measures from the mainstream of primary healthcare just because these dissimilar diseases have the same target organ. They note, too, that nowadays non-governmental agencies dedicated to preventing blindness are increasingly supporting general healthcare, which suggests, to these critics, that the penny has dropped.

It is not clear how thoroughly the critics' arguments were addressed at Baghdad. Not very, I would guess, given the general enthusiasm to proclaim an active strategy. In an article the following year, Wilson argued somewhat defensively that a factor common to all the four diseases was the need for health education and, further, that there was a role for the ophthalmologist in all four programmes provided he was prepared to function within an interdisciplinary setting. Looking back later at 'the considerable swell of opposition at Baghdad,' he dealt brusquely with the 'purists' who argued that cataract, not being preventable, should not be part of a preventive strategy. 'Such pedantry,' he wrote, 'was soon swept away by the flood of statistics.' Similarly, the reservation that blinding malnutrition should be addressed through primary healthcare rather than by the new strategy was, he claimed, overcome by the Bangladesh famine of 1972 and the appalling prospect of thousands of infants being blinded. Leaving aside the fact that the Bangladesh famine preceded the Baghdad conference by four years and clearly *did not* cause the critics to abandon their reservations, these answers by Wilson to the opposition seem to me less than substantial.

A prominent authority of today tells me that, in his opinion, McLaren and his supporters were right from a medical point of view, certainly in the sense that cataract needed ophthalmologists where the other three diseases did not. But he believes that from the standpoint of eye-care services for a community in a developing country, it was right to pursue a strategy embracing all four. The Baghdad outcome was 'bio-medically wrong, perhaps, but developmentally right.'

In any event the dispute was not central to the conference.

The overwhelming view at Baghdad was that the strategy linking the Four Giants was right. It was adopted by the WHO and became the unifying concept for international action on blindness prevention. The communiqué issued by the conference made no reference to the controversy. It was a more sober document, containing detailed suggestions on the main diseases and on broader subjects such as manpower requirements, eye-health education and the development of eye-health services. It ended with a key set of guidelines and more general recommendations that in effect constituted a strategy for all the organizations concerned. It was plainly stated that the WHO was committed to the prevention of blindness and that a large proportion of that blindness was preventable and curable. The economic benefits of prevention were emphasized. While continuous efforts to improve technology were laudable, there was already enough technical knowledge for the delivery of eye-health services ('hear, hear!' Wilson must have murmured to himself for he had been arguing this for years). Eye-health services and manpower in many countries were inadequate. Priority should be given to the creation of community-oriented basic services for eye health. Projects should be drawn up to secure assistance from donors through voluntary agencies in association with the WHO and the Agency. It was recommended that each government should formulate a national policy and a national plan of action. Wilson thought it particularly important that the Conference had endorsed the concept of public-health ophthalmology, linking ophthalmic services to community action and primary healthcare.

The Baghdad meeting's conclusions were a significant outcome for the work of the new Agency. They gave it a jump-start by outlining for the first time a strategy for the prevention of blindness in developing countries. Its own role, and that of the non-governmental organizations who made up its membership, were now relatively clear. But governments were still only marginally engaged. Their fuller commitment would largely depend on the effectiveness of the WHO in carrying forward the Baghdad conclusions.

The impact of the Baghdad meeting, and the publicity surrounding the 1976 World Health Day's theme, 'Foresight Prevents Blindness', led in 1978 to the initiation of the WHO's Prevention of Blindness Programme, in large part because of Wilson's advocacy. The first director of the Programme was Mario Tarizzo, whom

Wilson knew well from his work on trachoma. After Tarizzo's un-expected death in 1980, it was led by Bjorn Thylefors, a Swedish ophthalmologist who had worked on trachoma in Algeria in the early 1970s and then spent six years assisting a new river-blindness programme in West Africa. As more funding was secured he built up a staff of a dozen or so people. A Programme Advisory Group was established as a forum through which the WHO could consult the IAPB and the non-governmental organizations. Wilson attended the early meetings.

Thylefors' first task was the old, uncompleted one – to define the magnitude and various causes of blindness. A taskforce was set up to address these issues and it produced the first epidemiologically sound estimate of 28,000,000 blind persons worldwide, where blindness is defined as less than 3/60 vision, or 42,000,000 on the stricter criterion of 6/60 vision. The first target given to the new Programme was to reduce blindness in all countries to less than 0.5 per cent of the population, with less than 1 per cent in any one community. The logic of the target was that, if it was achieved, avoidable (i.e. preventable and curable) blindness in the countries concerned would be eliminated. Since that time the WHO has regularly updated its data. Towards the end of this story we shall see how much progress has been achieved.

The key strategic element in the WHO Programme was the de-velopment of primary eye care as a specific component of primary health care. This concept was to be translated and adapted to many different settings all over the world and became universally accepted. The Programme also aimed to establish national com-mittees, plans and programmes in all countries where there was a need. Progress was made but it was many years before that target was reached.

Thylefors, who directed the Programme until 2000, describes John Wilson as *the* most important figure in action against blind-ness, especially in the early years. 'He had the charisma and vision.' He was the lobbyist and advocate. He was a frequent visitor to the WHO in Geneva and had his key contacts in Africa and India whom he would use to promote the WHO's objectives. 'The WHO Programme would not have existed without him,' says Thylefors who, of all people, should know.

Even in his headier moments of enthusiasm about the work of the Society and now the IAPB, Wilson always saw that their work was essentially demonstrative and catalytic. For a major assault on any of the Four Giants (or, indeed, other blinding diseases), the resources and power of governments were needed. River blindness, the horrors of which had struck him so forcibly in the 1940s, was a good example. Three decades had passed without effective preventive action. But in 1974 a coalition of the WHO, the World Bank, the United Nations Development Programme and the Food and Agriculture Organization, supported by more than twenty donor countries and agencies, sponsored the Onchocerciasis Control Programme in seven countries of West Africa and later extended it to four more. Its main method of control was to destroy the larvae of the black fly by aerial spraying of insecticide on breeding sites in fast-flowing rivers. Subsequently, it began to distribute to populations in affected areas the drug Ivermectin (Mectizan TM) which kills the larval worms that cause blindness in humans.

When the Programme was launched in 1974, more than 1,000,000 people in the eleven countries concerned suffered from river blindness. Of these, 100,000 had serious eye problems and 35,000 of them were blind. Today, the number of people suffering from river blindness in the original area is virtually nil. At the same time, the Programme probably saved some 300,000 people from going blind. There were profound economic effects as well. Large areas of fertile land became cultivable because the potential labour force was no longer debilitated by the disease. The success of the Onchocerciasis Control Programme led in 1995 to a much larger programme, the African Programme of Onchocerciasis Control in the other nineteen countries of Africa, where a further 15,000,000 people were at risk.

On their visits to Africa in the 1970s and 1980s the Wilsons were delighted to see the progress made in controlling this scourge which had left such a sharp impression on their own minds decades earlier. It had been a long, slow business, but the research and experiments in control carried out by the Society and others in the earlier years had been valuable. Wilson was particularly pleased to be told by a representative of the firm Merck & Co Inc, which since 1987 has donated the drug Mectizan free, that the research they had undertaken to find such a drug was largely stimulated by those early reports. His advocacy had certainly raised awareness internationally about river blindness. He had addressed large numbers of audiences on the subject, speaking movingly of the consequences of river blindness for men, women and children, especially in remote rural Africa.

Wilson's campaign to create, organize and stimulate an international movement against blindness was intensely serious. But as the panorama of endless conferences, resolutions and bureaucratic devices unfolds, it is well to remember that the man at the heart of it had not changed. His zest for life and fun was undiminished. A priceless asset for overcoming the tedium of the international conference circuit is a sense of humour. It is good for your own morale but for that of others too, because everyone shares the tedium except perhaps the speaker of the moment. Wilson's taste for the amusing was never far below the surface. No one was more passionately committed to relieving the hardship and advancing the rights of blind people, but he also enjoyed jokes involving them. He sometimes recalled an occasion when, in a town in southern Britain, a scented garden for the blind was to be opened. The town clerk warned the lady mayoress to be careful about her language, for example not to refer to 'the blind'. What the poor lady actually said, recalls Wilson, was 'You know, our visually impaired citizens are wonderful, sensitive people. They can't see but they really do smell.'

He used to tell another story of a blind friend, a street beggar in Trinidad, who reckoned that he could tell nationality by footsteps. One day when Wilson met him he was carrying two collecting tins, one held in front and the other at an angle behind him. 'Man,' said the beggar, 'there are so many Americans about today, I decided to open a branch.'

Wilson was President of the IAPB for eight years, from 1974 until 1982. Initially, he was mainly concerned to establish national committees for the prevention of blindness, some of them formed on the nucleus of former branches of the International Association which the Agency had replaced but more of them based on collaboration between groups of ophthalmologists, organizations for the blind and governments. He and Jean travelled extensively to stimulate the establishment of these committees, as did Dr John Holmes, Vice-President of the Association.

In July 1978, the Agency convened its first General Assembly at the Sheldonian Theatre in Oxford. By then, national committees, including the British Prevention of Blindness Committee, had been founded in fifty-four countries. Delegates from forty-four of these and representatives of international and regional organizations attended. Wilson prepared notes for Lord Home of the Hirsel, the former British Prime Minister and Foreign Secretary, who opened the Conference.

As president, John Wilson also spoke at the opening session. His words were heady stuff for such gatherings: 'Our demand is for action now.' He brought Africa into the conference room. 'In those river blindness villages of West Africa, Ghana, Volta, Chad, Mali, it will be morning now. The blind farmers will be making their way to the fields, in villages where blindness, not sight, is the normal expectation.' He emphasized how the problems of river blindness in Africa, trachoma in the Middle East, cataract in India and blinding malnutrition were being overcome. He insisted that 'We have to break through the anaesthetizing abstraction of a Third World of generalized poverty (and) separate the causes of that poverty into its components, one of which is blindness.' The objective of the Agency was to break the link between blindness and population growth: 'We must do this before the end of this century.' There was 'an unprecedented opportunity to promote, with our world partners, a decade of systematic action, thrusting through all the arguments and politics and bureaucratic clutter to achieve a single, massive realisable goal... And the justification is this: freedom from needless blindness is not just a question of privilege but of human rights.'

The main proceedings of the Conference were brought together in a publication *World Blindness and its Prevention* (OUP, 1980) which was edited by the Agency under Wilson's direction. It summarized the state of work on the six main causes of blindness (glaucoma and ocular trauma, i.e. blinding accidents, being added to the familiar four), described policies and strategies and gave a detailed account of activity in each of the world's regions.

Wilson himself contributed a feisty foreword, taking up the themes in his opening speech. Characteristically, he again related the Conference discussions, held in the heady intellectual atmosphere of Oxford, to the realities. 'Blinding malnutrition is not an abstraction. It is a blind village girl in Bangladesh – hungry, frightened, frail, utterly weary, with a demanding baby at her breast. Onchocerciasis is not just a disease category. It is a West African village where blind farmers plant grain along a straight piece of bamboo and a hemp rope leads blind women to the wells. Cataract surgery is not just a programme. It is an Indian eye camp where, after an operation costing $5, an old man looks out on the hills and a child is startled by the first shock of light.' His use of words was as skilful as ever, the passion unmistakable.

But neither a conference under Wilson's chairmanship nor a book of which he was editor were likely to be limited to description. The main outcome was a strong statement on the need for action. The Agency must, the statement said, continue to speak to the world's conscience and create the will to act. International co-operation was the key to breaking the logjam by achieving a decade of intensive attack on the problems in those communities with the greatest need. The developed countries had obvious contributions to make by way of technical knowledge, training, financial resources and equipment. But in the developing countries, with appropriate organization and community education it should be practicable to mobilize enormous resources of work-power at simple levels, for example by training part-time village health workers.

While encouraging contributions to the WHO's Voluntary Fund for Health Promotion, which had a special prevention of blindness account, the Agency should develop its own role as a clearing-house to facilitate contact between donors and potential recipient countries, and also to disseminate information about the many organizations concerned with prevention of blindness. It was also stated, gently because there were still sensitivities, that the Agency could play a useful role in coordinating the efforts of these bodies at a non-governmental level.

Then, looking to individual countries, the Agency should co-operate with national committees to promote the teaching of preventive ophthalmology, and also 'to bring legitimate pressure to bear on governments, to create and maintain awareness of avoidable blindness and to achieve governmental determination to act.' The recommendations of the Conference ended with a 'General outline of action and managerial sequence required to ensure elimination of avoidable blindness.' This was a sixteen-point blueprint, starting from the moment when a government became aware of an 'over-burden' of potentially avoidable blindness and continuing through the conducting of surveys, the construction of an outline plan of action, the allocation of resources and the provision of training to an *attack phase* of initial intensive intervention, a *consolidation phase* where the action is incorporated into primary-health-care development and a *surveillance phase* where data is collected to indicate success or failure and what further activity is necessary.

These workmanlike, forward-looking conclusions obviously drew heavily on the long experience of Wilson and the Society as well as that of the WHO and the other leading organizations in the field. There was not much more to say about what needed to be done. But the perennial questions remained. Could the resources be found? Could governments be moved to give adequate priority to these problems? It was certain that the Wilsons would not stop trying to mobilize governments and resources.

In November 1978, John Wilson took part in the WHO Task Force on Blindness Data, meeting in Geneva. Early in 1979, he was corresponding with Judith Hart, the British Minister for Overseas Development, about blinding malnutrition. In the next few months he visited the Federal Republic of Germany, where he addressed that country's national committee on the prevention of blindness, as well as Miami, Washington, New York and Jamaica. In April he was back in India, examining eye-camp work. In June he travelled to Rome to address the Rotary International Convention. Day in, day out he was campaigning for the new international movement.

He returned to Africa in early 1980, and later in the year visited India for his continuing work on blinding malnutrition and mass cataract and his meeting with Prime Minister Gandhi, discussed earlier. The next year was as full as ever with a round of activities related to disability in general which we shall come to. 1981 was a key date also for another project Wilson strongly supported, and which was to be of long-lasting significance. Plans to establish in London a centre of preventive ophthalmology had been under discussion for some years. Wilson had recognized their significance at once. The world had no such centre, though plans to set one up were already well advanced in America. Its foundation would, argued Wilson, be an important step forward in the practical implementation of 'the new and exciting international strategy for the prevention of blindness.' He persuaded the Society to grant up to £30,000 per annum for at least three years towards the recurrent costs of the new centre and arranged for its staff to act as honorary advisers to the Society, and to train suitably qualified students recommended by the Society. He encouraged and supported Professor Barrie Jones, one of the world's leading clinical ophthalmologists and research workers, who was perhaps the principal advocate of the centre and became its first director. With support from a wide variety of sources, the International Centre for Eye Health was opened in September 1981. Its declared aims were 'to recruit interest, train personnel at all levels and provide facilities for research on the major problems of world blindness.' It was designated by the WHO as a Collaborating Centre for the Prevention of Blindness. It later moved to the London School of Hygiene and Tropical Medicine and is today one of the leading players in the international prevention of blindness movement.

So by the time the General Assembly of the Agency met again, in Bethesda, Maryland, USA in October 1982, Wilson had vigorously advanced his world campaign. It was the second and last Assembly over which he presided. As he assessed the gathering he must have felt—and would, in my view, have been justified in feeling—that the international movement to deal with eye problems was now really on the map. Nearly 180 people participated from nearly 60 countries, a roll-call of virtually all the key names at work on the prevention of blindness, many of them long-standing colleagues and friends, and in sum a formidable body of expertise and commitment. The geographical coverage of the Agency extended way beyond the Society's traditional area of activity. There were regional chairmen for Africa, Latin America, North America, the Middle East, South-East Asia, Southern Asia, the Western Pacific, Western Europe and Eastern Europe.

The key international non-governmental organizations in the field, all affiliated to the Agency, were there in force: the Asian Foundation for the Prevention of Blindness, started with Wilson's help in Hong Kong in 1981 and actively involved in blindness prevention programmes in Bangladesh, China, India, Indonesia and Korea; the Christoffel-Blindenmission, now operating in ninety countries in Asia, Africa, Latin America and Oceania; Foresight, an Australian organization, working on prevention projects in Bangladesh, Papua New Guinea and the South Pacific; Helen Keller International, active in the Pacific, Asia, Africa and Latin America; the American International Eye Foundation, twenty-one years old and working in a large range of countries worldwide; the International Glaucoma Foundation, established in 1974 and based in London; Operation Eyesight Universal, a Canadian body dating from 1963, with programmes in sixteen of the world's developing countries; the Seva Foundation, which concentrated at that time particularly on

Nepal and India; and of course the Society itself. The list was a powerful demonstration of the potential for action if the multifarious activities could be coordinated and directed towards clear objectives.

In an impressive keynote address, Dr Robert Muller, Assistant Secretary General of the United Nations, set the new movement in a strategic perspective. He recalled that around the year 1970 it had become apparent to the UN that there were about 350,000,000 handicapped people on the planet and that there was a need to embark on a campaign to prevent disability in general. But the creation of the IAPB meant that for at least one component of the world's handicapped, namely the blind, the world community was already organizing itself for prevention. This task needed a systematic world strategy with an intensification of research and technology in the developing countries. He was delighted that the WHO was involved in setting up collaborating centres for the prevention of blindness, in order to have a coordinated system of research on specific diseases and their prevention.

He regarded prevention as the most important activity the international community could undertake. The IAPB could be a model for what might be done in many other fields. It would receive every possible help from the United Nations system. He continued more colourfully. The world was, in one sense, spending hugely on vision – on enlarging the infinitely small with conventional microscopes, electronic microscopes and now picoscopes; on inspecting particles and sub-particles by using immense cyclotrons; and on extending vision into the outer reaches of space with ever more sophisticated telescopes. It was staggering that we spent so much more in order to see particles and sub-particles, and to look at far-away planets and galaxies, than we spent on 'the few millions of our brothers and sisters' who did not even have normal vision. ('Few' was a major understatement; there were over forty million.)

Following the conference, a second volume of *World Blindness and its Prevention* was published, again under Wilson's general editorial direction (OUP, 1984). As before, it summarized in convenient form the main deliberations of the conference. It began with a disturbing look at the future. Certain eye diseases would assume greater importance over the years. They included cataract, glaucoma and other diseases associated with ageing. With life expectancy rising in both the developed and developing countries, the incidence of these ageing-related disorders was also increasing. In the United States, as an example, the prevalence of cataract, glaucoma and senile macular degeneration among people of fifty-five and older was expected to increase by 150% in the next half-century. Demographic trends suggested a similar surge in ageing-related eye disease in developing countries. So unless new methods of prevention were found, a massive, worldwide increase in several blinding diseases could be expected. 'While the world's vision researchers seek the needed preventive measures, the IAPB and its national blindness prevention committees must attempt to ensure that health care systems are prepared to deal with the projected upsurge in ageing-related eye disease if it occurs.'

The book then surveyed the present state of knowledge on trachoma, blinding malnutrition, river blindness, cataract, glaucoma and ocular trauma, and set out in each case a strategy agreed by the conference for national committees to use in promoting prevention of blindness programmes in their own countries.

The chairpersons of the Assembly's nine regional committees reported on the progress achieved in their regions since the Oxford Assembly of 1978. There were wide disparities. The gloomy report from Africa stated that, with the possible exception of Kenya, no African country yet operated an identifiable blindness prevention programme. By contrast, in South Asia (the Indian sub-continent and surrounding countries) every country except Bhutan had formulated a national action plan and implementation was in progress. Reports from Eastern Europe, South-East Asia, the Western Pacific and Latin America were relatively encouraging, and, as one might expect, those from North America and Western Europe showed both that there were sophisticated mechanisms for dealing with the problems in their areas and that those problems were a good deal less serious than elsewhere.

Wilson is quoted as observing that it was no coincidence that in practically every country where a national programme was in operation, the preliminary action had been taken by a national committee for the prevention of blindness. The fact that such committees, linked to the Agency, now existed in over fifty countries should, he believed, provide a strong base for growth in the future. He urged those present whose countries did not yet have an effective national committee to make the formation or strengthening of one a personal commitment and obligation. You did not leave a meeting chaired by Wilson feeling satisfied with just voting for a flabby resolution. He expected you to go back home and get something done.

A series of papers were presented to the conference, and summarized in the book, which described from the authors' own experiences various aspects of setting up and running national programmes. The Assembly distilled these experiences into a set of recommendations. The Agency should encourage every country to examine the prevalence of blindness and its own eye services. Each should be stimulated to set goals for blindness reduction and implement programmes to achieve these goals. Given the large disparity in many countries between the needs of basic eye care and the number of available ophthalmologists, the Assembly applauded any attempt to bring innovative approaches to eye treatment. Each country with a significant prevalence of avoidable blindness should be encouraged to increase the content of ophthalmology in the undergraduate medical curriculum, with the emphasis on community ophthalmology. The Agency should itself collect and distribute information on the personnel needed and available for blindness prevention programmes and the techniques needed and available for use in those programmes.

A number of experts, including Jean Wilson, presented their views and advice on how to mobilize resources for the cause. Again the Assembly made recommendations. Prevention of blindness programmes must be fully integrated into the primary-health-care systems of each country, so that full use could be made of existing health-care resources and activities. In this way the expense of blindness prevention could be kept to a minimum and blindness prevention activities could be better justified to cost-conscious governments and other possible contributors of resources. The cost-effectiveness of programmes should be documented, so that official and private donors could be assured that these would yield economic as well as humanitarian benefit. Various ideas for improving the Agency's communications and publicity efforts were listed. And, in a last, rather schoolmasterly flourish, the Agency was asked to maintain a roster of ophthalmologists willing to work for a year or more in developing countries and put the individuals in touch with those needing their services.

Conferences dealing with serious and intractable problems can leave delegates feeling pretty dispirited. At some point morale has to be raised and people re-energized to pursue the cause. Wilson was good at this. As the outgoing president, he noted that there had been a number of encouraging developments. There were now national committees on the prevention of blindness in fifty-six countries. More important, national programmes were operating in twenty-four countries and the expectation was that such programmes would be established in some sixty developing countries in the next five years. Non-governmental organizations which were members of the Agency were now spending over $20,000,000 annually on prevention of blindness activities. The WHO had established a special voluntary account for blindness prevention to which governments had contributed substantial resources.

Then, the WHO's Programme Advisory Group had met annually since 1978. It was a convincing demonstration of effective cooperation between UN agencies, governments and non-governmental interests. It had given the whole movement a definition and precision which could not have been achieved in any other way. The prevention of blindness had been increasingly recognized as a new and essential international dimension in ophthalmology. Community eye care had become a priority of health policy and, with a distinct strategy and multi-disciplinary staff, was almost acquiring the status of a separate discipline.

The new President, Dr Carl Kupfer, who succeeded Wilson in 1982 and from then on provided a base for the Agency at the American National Eye Institute, rounded off the proceedings with a reference to the evident collegial spirit among those who had taken up the cause of preventing blindness. 'More than anyone else,' he said, 'Sir John Wilson has been responsible for fostering that spirit. He has been the inspiration for the Agency and we are indebted to him for guiding it into its activist role. In his eight years as Agency President, he has alerted leaders of countries, officials of the WHO and decision-makers in the private and non-governmental sectors to the vast needs and opportunities that exist in the field of blindness prevention. Also, he has focused their attention on the need to make prevention of blindness programmes an integral part of all health care programmes. In all the undertakings of the Agency, we must continue what John has begun.' This was more than conventional praise. The main practitioners in this field then and now state unreservedly that the Agency was John Wilson's creation, and that he was the chief inspiration for its work.

The Wilsons had come a long way from that small office in Victoria Street, London, where they had set up the Society in 1950. They and the Society had made a major impact on the handling of eye diseases in large areas of the developing world. They had inspired a succession of other men and women to begin and intensify work themselves on these problems. Now they had established and nurtured an international structure to lead a coordinated attack on the scourges they had witnessed for themselves in deserts and jungles, in urban slums and rural backwaters, especially among the poorest communities in the developing world.

But, the sceptics may ask, so what? Had they done more than add yet further expensive pieces to the massive jigsaw of international bureaucracy? Who nowadays is impressed by the accumulation of UN resolutions, declarations and recommendations when most of their predecessors languish somewhere in filing cabinets, unread and unimplemented? Wherever you look there are agencies, conferences, committees helping to consume the world's wealth. Do real people seriously benefit? Good questions. In the last chapter of this book I shall try to assess Wilson's legacy. The present effectiveness and achievements of the organizations he founded will be an important part of that assessment; but before we reach that point, there is one more phase in the life of this restless, inventive visionary – a new, or almost new, field of endeavour.

Chapter 6

To Move, To Hear, To See

Anyone involved in the effort to prevent and cure blindness and other problems of visual impairment knows well enough that there are potentially competing causes. Why devote resources and effort to blindness in particular, when there are many other forms of impairment and, indeed, many other health problems, some of which have the capacity to kill? John Wilson never claimed that there was a hierarchy of diseases, with those of the eye pre-eminent. He argued instead that it was right to tackle the problems of visual impairment, not just because it was an obvious way to reduce human suffering, but because most of these problems, unlike many others in the health field, were in general demonstrably soluble. You *could* prevent countless numbers of people going blind and you *could* cure countless numbers of people who were already blind. This was an area where success was eminently achievable. That achievement would give enormous encouragement to efforts to solve other problems in world health where success, at least for the time being, seemed a more remote possibility.

If, like Wilson, you had spent a lifetime dealing with eye problems, you were necessarily conscious of other forms of disability. Problems of hearing and movement were often found in the same places as visual problems, and typically in the world's poorest communities in developing countries, though of course they were very much present in the industrialized countries as well. Moreover, in the 1980s, as his own hearing ability began to deteriorate, he had a strong personal incentive to think about that particular form of disability.

But his interest in the general problem was of long standing. In 1960, as we saw in Chapter Three, he had chaired a Ghanaian government committee which addressed problems of disability in the round. He later proposed a comprehensive programme on similar lines for Guyana. But in those days the world was not ready for a general approach to disability. At any particular time a good litmus test of the international community's awareness of, and willingness to tackle, particular health problems is the degree of activity devoted to it by the World Health Organization. In the 1950s and again in the 1960s the WHO had convened expert committees on the rehabilitation of the disabled. But in the early 1970s a fresh conceptual framework developed. There was a wholly new emphasis on the *prevention* of disability and a shift from traditional institutional care and rehabilitation to community-level action. In 1976 the WHO published a policy and strategies on 'Disability Prevention and Rehabilitation' and developed programmes and projects to match.

In 1976, too, the United Nations General Assembly proclaimed that 1981 would be the International Year of Disabled Persons. This UN habit of designating particular years for particular causes has become very common. Barely a year is allowed to pass nowadays without a special label being attached to it. It is a safe bet that at any given time the mass of people in the world are not conscious of which UN year they are in. The slogan passes them by. A good deal of cynicism about the value of such Years co-exists with a good deal of enthusiasm from those who are already working on, or are affected by, the designated subject. The main value of the device is to raise awareness, to improve the prospects of support from governments and the public for action and to persuade people of imagination to take the lead in proposing new activities and new solutions. At the most basic level, it is difficult for governments, at any rate those in democracies, to do nothing about these Years. They will soon be asked by their parliaments or their media what they are doing. The cause is usually such that it is politically impossible to do nothing. Depending on public interest, a Year can sometimes stimulate quite extensive programmes in individual countries.

It would have been quite unlike Wilson not to be spurred into fresh action by the prospect of the International Year of Disabled Persons. To begin with, he was a recognized leader in the effort to help one section of disabled people, the visually impaired. For more than thirty years he had actively sought solutions to their problems. Earlier than most, he had come to believe that the emphasis must be placed on prevention and cure. Since 1974, he had been president of the world's leading organization in the field, the International Agency for the Prevention of Blindness. He had become increasingly convinced that his experience in preventing blindness could be applied to other forms of disability. His mind was searching for the kind of overall vision on disability that had so inspired work on blindness. Could a similar world movement be created? What structures would it need? How could governmental and public support be mobilized?

The context, however, was different. When he had begun his work on blindness, there was very little organized international interest in the subject and the concept of preventing blindness was undeveloped. The field was pretty much unploughed. But in 1981 a considerable international effort was already being devoted to disability issues. For example, in the twelve months from October 1980 the WHO arranged more than eighty meetings across the world on various aspects of disability. One of that organization's most important preventive instruments, the Expanded Programme of Immunization, had been active since 1977. It sought to reduce morbidity and mortality by providing immunization against six major killers of children in the developing world: diphtheria, whooping cough, tetanus, measles, poliomyelitis and tuberculosis. These diseases were estimated to kill some 5,000,000 children annually, but also to disable 5,000,000 more with paralysis, blindness, deafness or mental retardation.

In 1980 the UN General Assembly adopted a Plan of Action for the International Year. A report was prepared on the 'World Situation of Disabled Persons'. This analysed the efforts in the disability field of all the relevant United Nations bodies but concluded both that the UN lacked strategies, policies and coherent programmes, and that its member states did not yet pay sufficient attention to the needs of the disabled. There were, said the report, some 500,000,000 disabled people in the world. 400,000,000 of these lived in developing countries, nearly all of them in rural areas. 'The plight of the disabled in rural areas is, after famine, and often because of it, one of the disgraces of our time.' The UN was spending only $1.50 per disabled person per year. The number of disabled was likely to reach 900,000,000 by the year 2000. A number of suggestions for future action were put forward and a world symposium of experts was convened in Vienna in October 1981 to consider the problem.

The International Year was conceived in terms of human rights – the right of every individual to move, to hear, to see. Wilson was quick to apply the lessons and language of his work on blindness to the broader target. At a conference on rehabilitation of the disabled in Gothenburg, Sweden, in May 1981 he stated: 'We affirm the right of all the disabled to education, rehabilitation and employment. Yet throughout the developing world nine out of ten disabled children are not at school and not one disabled in a hundred has a satisfactory job. In the international perspective, the rehabilitated, self-supporting, participating, disabled man is a minute exception. The norm, in massive, depressing majorities is mendicant, illiterate, destitute.' He knew. He had seen it for years across the world. Now that his mind was focusing on the nature and consequences of global disability he was unlikely to be satisfied by speech making.

Leeds Castle in Kent has a long and colourful history, beginning in the year 857 when a Saxon thane built a wooden fort on an island in a lake as a refuge against sudden attack by the Vikings. Later on it was replaced by a fully-fledged castle, which was greatly enlarged by Henry VIII and, much nearer to our time, restored and re-dedicated to the service of the nation. The trustees of the Leeds Castle Foundation now administer it as a charity and, among other things, provide first-class conference facilities in a beautiful setting. As the International Year approached, two members of the sister Leeds Castle Foundation in the United States proposed to those running Leeds Castle that they invite the Wilsons for a weekend. While there, John expressed the view that an event should be held to mark the Year, and there and then worked up a scheme for a conference.

Prompted by Wilson, the trustees secured the support of the British government for the holding of a seminar at Leeds Castle in November 1981. Financial support was provided by the Department of Health and Social Security and by private donors. In the preceding months there had been a good deal of international activity but little of it had been devoted to the issue of *preventing* disablement. Wilson wanted the seminar to concentrate precisely on that notion. Twenty-five scientists, clinicians, Ministers of Health and UN administrators, many of them leading men and women in their field, devoted five days to the topic. The Prince of Wales paid a working visit to the seminar. Lord Home of the Hirsel, who had opened the first IAPB Assembly in 1978, chaired the proceedings. He told participants that, as Commonwealth Secretary in the late 1950s, he had seen at first hand the ravages of tuberculosis and smallpox, blindness, polio and leprosy from which millions in

Africa and Asia suffered and died. He also said that for more than two years of his own life he had been totally immobilized by tuberculosis of the spine. He therefore knew something of disability.

The Leeds Castle Declaration on the Prevention of Disablement was adopted on 12 November 1981. It stated that disablement was a tragedy in terms of human suffering and frustration, and in terms of numbers. Much of the underlying impairment was preventable. Worldwide expansion of a programme of immunization could save 5,000,000 children a year from the disabilities caused by various diseases. This could be done in ten years at a cost of about $3 per immunized child. The use of rubella vaccine should be promoted in all countries because rubella (i.e. German measles) was a prime cause of congenital blindness, deafness and mental impairment. Inexpensive improvements in primary health care could prevent impairment arising from malnutrition, infection and neglect. The world had already seen that trachoma and vitamin A deficiency could be controlled. Similarly, inexpensive and simple treatment could arrest impairment from leprosy, restore sight to 10,000,000 people blinded by cataract and improve the hearing of 10,000,000 deaf people.

Many disabilities of later life could be postponed or averted. Early identification and treatment of raised blood pressure could save millions from premature disability and death due to heart disease and stroke. Avoidable disability was a prime cause of economic waste and human deprivation in all countries, industrialized and developing. This loss could be reduced rapidly. The technology was available to prevent or control most disablement. What was needed was commitment by society to overcome the problems. A programme of action to prevent disablement was a logical and essential part of the follow up to the Year.

The Declaration has Wilson's stamp all over it. The strategic vision matched his earlier vision of action on blindness. Many of the arguments he had used for years to promote the prevention of blindness are here transposed to the more general cause. Just as with blindness, the obstacles were not a lack of knowledge or technology but a lack of commitment from society, in which he would have included government.

The papers submitted to the seminar were brought together in a book entitled *Disability Prevention: The Global Challenge* (OUP, 1983). Formally edited by Wilson, though most of the work was done by the seminar's rapporteur, Kenneth Thompson, the book carries contributions by recognized experts on the principal causes of disability, on research priorities and on the prospects for control. Wilson contributed a short piece on blindness and, I would guess, wrote or at least strongly influenced the concluding chapter on mechanisms for action. Drawing on past experience, he emphasized that the success of a world plan of action must eventually depend not upon the UN but upon the exercise of political will and the allocation of resources by national governments. 'Disablement,' he wrote, 'with all its consequences of wasted resources and frustrated lives need not necessarily be an inescapable part of the human predicament. Prevention on an unprecedented scale and at no great cost is one of the options available to the international community during the next twenty years.'

The Leeds Castle sponsors of the seminar were a little disappointed by the attendance. They had hoped for a larger gathering. They may also have wondered whether it would have any lasting effect. Seminars and declarations are, after all, ten-a-penny and the world tends to pass them by unruffled. But, as we know, Wilson was rather good at ruffling. He above all people would not let the Leeds Castle outcome wither on the vine.

Kenneth Thompson carried the Declaration to a wide range of countries and discussed its proposals with Ministers of Health and non-governmental organizations. He reported back that there was widespread interest in the practicability of systematic action for the prevention of disability, that the Declaration was widely seen as the clearest available presentation of these possibilities and that there was a general welcome for the seminar's concept of a multi-disciplinary approach to the problem and its proposal for the systematic inclusion of measures for prevention within existing global programmes rather than the establishment of a new, vertical programme, which would be prohibitively expensive.

Meanwhile, Wilson concentrated on the United Nations' network of organizations. In December 1981, he attended a special plenary session of the UN General Assembly in New York, convened to mark the International Year. Asked by the then British Minister for the Disabled, Hugh Rossi, to speak on behalf of the United Kingdom, he reviewed the activities organized in the country in the last twelve months. Almost every town and village had marked the Year with some special activity, he said. The media had played an invaluable role in enabling people to break through age-old prototypes and see real individuals behind the disability. Government departments had taken special action and new laws had been passed on facilities for the disabled.

He then briefed the Assembly in detail on the contents of the Leeds Castle Declaration, laying special emphasis on the concept of prevention, and concluded with a personal statement made 'in my more accustomed role as one of the 450 million disabled people'. The Year had given the leaders of the disabled an opportunity for the first time to bring before the world community their aspiration 'to share the right of humanity to grow, to learn, to work, to love and be loved'. 'But the mass of the disabled are not rehabilitated, educated, eloquent. They are destitute street beggars, exposed to the brutalizing triviality of mendicancy. They are outcasts and amongst the loneliest people of the world. Many are victims of diseases which should be an obscene anachronism in our modern world.' There were, he recognized, limitations on the steps that could be taken even by the General Assembly, 'the greatest of human institutions' (a flattering description to which not all who have seen the Assembly in action would subscribe). But this, surely, was a cause which could transcend those limitations. 'It could commend itself to North and South, to East and West.'

Wilson believed that it was the first time anyone had addressed the Assembly from Braille notes. 'It is not an experience I would recommend to others. The reading lamp on that famous podium has some strange thermal quality which heats up your Braille notes to oven temperatures.'

As with most speeches at the United Nations, the effect of this one on the audience or, indeed, on the subsequent course of events is untraceable. But Wilson said afterwards that he was astonished by a yawning gap in the debate. Apart from reports presented by representatives of the United Nations Development Programme (UNDP) and the United Nations Children's Fund (UNICEF), and a few incidental remarks in some statements by country representatives, there had been little reference to prevention in the whole of the proceedings, and certainly none with the precision and detail of the Leeds Declaration.

He took the opportunity of his visit to New York to discuss the way forward with a number of people. The Leeds Castle participants had clearly recognized that it would not be wise to try to create a new, self-standing UN programme to deal with the prevention of disablement. This would be both politically impracticable and prohibitively expensive. Instead, the aim should be to insert preventive measures into existing programmes. Various UN agencies and other organizations were already working on aspects of the problem. Wilson concluded that the main need was for coordination of these activities. He discussed the matter with UNICEF officials but, not surprisingly, was told that since that organization was specifically committed to the prevention of the disablement of children, it could not take on a general coordinating role. On the other hand, Bradley Morse, the senior official of the UNDP, was particularly interested in the theme, partly because his organization had well-established partnership arrangements with the WHO, UNICEF and the Food and Agriculture Organization and had a particular role in promoting cooperation between these largely separate empires.

Morse agreed that what was needed was the simplest possible mechanism to ensure that cooperation. Perhaps, speculated Wilson, it could take the form of a kind of consultative group, small enough to be effective but large enough to represent the various UN agencies and international non-governmental organizations. At the executive level, all that would be needed was, in his view, a full-time senior official with the commitment and inter-agency experience to make a success of this programme, supported by a secretary and with funds for travel. This would need special financing and Wilson undertook to explore the possibilities. In presenting the Leeds Castle Declaration to the Executive Board of UNICEF in January 1982, he put forward a proposal very much on these lines.

Various permutations of these ideas were discussed before there was a clear outcome. Those unaccustomed to the ways of the United Nations may wonder why such matters take so long to resolve. The fact is that proposals for new machinery and new expenditure always encountered sharp questioning at the time (and since). The UN had a reputation for waste and inefficiency. However simple a new mechanism might be thought to be at the outset, experience showed that it grew in size and complexity and over time required a good deal more money than its protagonists had first claimed. Furthermore, the various UN bodies were tightly constrained by their own constitutions and rules as to what they could and could not do.

But Wilson's persistence and commitment eventually produced results. It was agreed that the prevention of disablement should become a major objective of the world programme of action concerning the disabled, drawn up in the months following the International Year. Then, the WHO agreed to establish a multi-disciplinary consultative group to examine the extent to which measures for prevention could be included in global and national programmes of health and development. Finally – but most significantly for Wilson's own activity – the WHO, UNICEF and UNDP agreed to promote 'an international initiative against avoidable disablement'. A small secretariat to administer this new initiative was established in Geneva in January 1983 under the direction of Melissa Wells, an American diplomat who was to become the Ambassador of the United States in Mozambique and then in Estonia. The office was financed by the UNDP for some years. In November 1982 Brad Morse invited Wilson to accept an appointment as Senior Consultant for an indefinite period, unpaid but with reimbursement of necessary travel expenses. Wilson rapidly accepted.

This was a novel arrangement. The new organization, so far as I have been able to discover, was not established by a formal United Nations decision and in any case it was not a formal UN body. The nature of the undertaking of the three agencies to promote the initiative was unclear. No organization of this small size and modest standing could possibly aim to coordinate the activities of the UN agencies, a task which has long consumed the energies of much more powerful bodies. But senior UN personnel were impressed by Wilson's long-standing achievements and by his new commitment to the prevention of disablement. They wanted to find a role for him. With ingenuity and a measure of will-power, it is usually possible to find a way through United Nations rules to launch worthwhile activity.

Wilson now had a new opening. But first, he later recalled, something had to be done about the name: 'an International Initiative Against Avoidable Disablement'. 'The English couldn't pronounce it; the French couldn't translate it; and in Arabic it meant something positively obscene.' Guided perhaps by the initial letters of the French title, the name 'Impact' was adopted (though apparently Brad Morse had always wanted to call *something* Impact and that may have been the determining factor). The establishment of Impact was announced at the World Health Assembly, the Executive Board of UNICEF and the Governing Council of UNDP. The development of this organization from its uncertain beginnings, and the campaign for the prevention of disability in general, were to be Wilson's main preoccupations for the rest of his life.

In 1982 he was sixty-three. At the time the normal retiring age in Britain was sixty-five. He had decided that when he reached that age he would stand down as director of the Royal Commonwealth Society for the Blind, a post he would then have held for thirty-four years. His decision was not principally motivated by a desire to concentrate on running Impact. A person of his ability and energy could probably have combined both jobs. But he felt that the time had come for someone else to take over the Society's reins. Interviewed in late 1983, he said that he 'had no use for the kind of organization that becomes an ego trip for its founder and essentially serves as a monument for him.' He wanted something with the maturity to survive. The Society had reached a fresh take-off point when a new style of leadership was needed.

In an interview for the radio programme 'In Touch', Peter White later asked him why he did not retire altogether when he left the Society. 'I didn't want to stop,' he replied. 'The model we had used for eye problems could so easily be applied to other problems.' People with a genuine vision of an improved world don't stop. You cannot have that vision at one moment and not the next. And when the vision is personally compelling you are driven to continue to reach for it.

Wilson was now re-energized by the wider project of the prevention of disability. With typical farsightedness and commitment, and, yes, with that same touch of naïvety with which we are by now familiar, he was talking of the objective of halving the number of disabled in twenty years. His successor, Alan Johns, was announced in 1983 and Wilson formally retired as director in January 1984, though he was at once made a vice-president of the Society and continued to take an interest in its activities. Jean Wilson retired on the same date.

In the various statements Wilson wrote or recorded about his life, he had nothing to say about his emotions on departure from the active role with the Society which had so occupied his energies for some three and a half decades. The imminent prospect of fresh pastures is often a good antidote to nostalgia. Pride in achievement is often a more than adequate compensation for a sense of loss.

In the case of the Wilsons, those achievements were a matter of record.

In her traditional broadcast to the Commonwealth on Christmas Day, 1981 the Queen had referred to the need for preventing disablement and used as an example of the possibilities the fact that the Society's activities since its foundation had restored sight to over 1,000,000 blind Commonwealth citizens. In 1983, Wilson's last year as Director, a record income of £2,676,000 had been received from 105,000 individuals and organizations. This income had financed projects in thirty-eight Commonwealth countries. Medical teams working in eighteen countries had treated some 1,770,000 people, restored sight to 193,000 and prevented blindness in a further 34,000. Encouragingly, the Indian government was now supporting three times as many cataract operations as the Society. Together with two other charities, the Society was operating thirty-nine mobile units in Africa. An increasing proportion of its budget was being devoted to the training of ophthalmic and paramedical staff, especially at the new training complex in Chittagong (Bangladesh), and in Sri Lanka, Malawi and Tanzania. The training of African administrators in work for the blind was being supported in Kenya, Tanzania, Uganda, Zimbabwe, Sierra Leone and the Gambia. The education of blind children in normal schools in India, Malawi and Jamaica was being fostered. New approaches were being developed to deal with the still major problem of providing genuine employment for blind people. The Society was working with partners in thirteen countries to establish revolving loan funds for self-help projects in small businesses and agriculture. Its 'self-help endowment fund' (SHE) financed the education, training and self-employment of blind women in fourteen countries.

So the Society was flourishing. Sir Edwin Arrowsmith, who had before retirement occupied a series of colonial posts in Southern Africa, the Caribbean and the South Atlantic, had been chairman for fourteen years and was a particularly popular and successful holder of the post. The Council of over fifty members, if a good deal too large for most modern tastes, as I have said, included representatives from fifteen of the countries where the Society worked and also from Australia, Canada and New Zealand.

The scale of the problems faced by the Society was still utterly formidable, but if, as he stepped down, Wilson felt pride and satisfaction in the knowledge that without his efforts, and those of Jean

Wilson, millions who could now see would have still been blind or would have become blind, and that many thousands of irreversibly blind people who now lived fuller lives would have remained hopeless outcasts, he was surely entitled to do so.

Retirement can be more difficult than most people may imagine who have not yet had to think about it. There is plenty of advice available from many sources on how to organize one's finances but very little on the more elusive and difficult question of how to organize one's life. Until they have tried it, most people will probably not know whether they want a full and active retirement or a more leisurely existence, assuming that their financial situation permits such a choice. Mistakes seem to be as common as successes. But John Wilson faced no such dilemma. Those who knew him would have found it impossible to imagine the man embracing with equanimity the prospect of years of inactive contemplation or worse. It was clearly not in his nature. When he was quite seriously ill in hospital in the late 1990s, one of his daughters asked him whether he would now stop work and retire. 'Good God, no,' said her father. 'Far better to die in harness.'

Within a few months of leaving the Society, the Wilsons took up residence at the Fogarty International Centre on the campus of the National Institutes of Health in Bethesda, Maryland, in the United States. This prestigious collection of institutes is devoted to carrying out and supporting basic research on health problems. John Wilson had been appointed a scholar-in-residence for a year though, as Jean accompanied him, the Fogarty Centre in effect acquired two scholars for the price of one. It was an unusual appointment. Most of the scholarship-in-residence awards went to scientists, who worked with the intra-mural staff on the campus. Wilson was appointed in recognition of his work as a health administrator in Africa and India, and at the behest of Dr Carl Kupfer, then director of the American National Eye Institute, who had succeeded Wilson as president of the International Agency for the Prevention of Blindness in 1982. The expectation was that Wilson would use the resources of the National Institutes to further the aims of the Impact programme. That, indeed, was the point. Wilson knew as much as he needed to about blindness. But he had much to learn about other forms of disability and this was the ideal environment. There, within easy reach, were research institutions devoted not only to blindness but also to arthritis, allergy and infectious diseases, child health, ageing, neurological and communicative disorders and other problems (but not deafness. Wilson strongly advocated such an institute at Bethesda and one was eventually established). The National Institutes also had readily usable links to the Centre for Disease Control, Atlanta, the Johns Hopkins School of Hygiene and Public Health and universities in the United States and Europe.

Wilson obtained agreement to spread his twelve-month scholarship over three years from 1984 to 1986. He found it an enjoyable and exhilarating experience. He plunged straight into the study of deafness, a disability of which he now had first-hand and unwelcome experience. With the assistance of resident scientists he sought to develop definitions and standards of hearing impairment that could be used in planning strategies for its prevention. Within two months of his arrival, he presented a paper to the seventeenth International Congress on Audiology in Santa Barbara, California on 'Deafness in Developing Countries; Approaches to a Global Programme of Prevention'. This was subsequently published in the Annals of Otolaryngology, a rare achievement, I gather, for someone outside the profession.

Characteristically, research was not enough for Wilson. Three months later, he was in Islamabad, persuading Pakistan's Minister of Health that his country's delegation should sponsor a resolution at the World Health Assembly in the spring of 1985 commissioning a global review of the prevalence of hearing impairment and deafness, and requesting the WHO's Director General to prepare a programme of action. Government changes in Pakistan got in the way, so it was arranged that Belgium and Kuwait should sponsor the resolution instead. All went well and, says Wilson, an excellent report was prepared by the WHO which estimated that there were 70,000,000 deaf persons in the world (outstripping, it should be noted, the number of blind persons) and that at least eight per cent of every population had some measure of hearing impairment. Unfortunately, as can happen at UN meetings, debate on the report was sidetracked by the Assembly's decision to hold an emergency debate on the health risks of nuclear energy, following the leakage from the Chernobyl Nuclear Reactor in 1986. But, at a subsequent session, the Assembly urged all countries to set up national programmes for the prevention of deafness.

Another international development also interrupted Wilson's

research. The issue of the tension between organizations *of* the blind (i.e. those composed mostly of blind people who advocated the rights of the blind) and organizations *for* the blind (composed mostly of sighted people who provided services for the blind) again raised its head while Wilson was at Bethesda. Back in the 1940s he had convened a study group that had led to the formation in Britain of the National Federation of the Blind – which in time became a member of the International Federation of the Blind. He also played a part in the establishment in 1951 of the World Council for the Welfare of the Blind. So he had a foot in both camps. But as his life progressed, particularly because of his work with the Society, he was thought of as largely a 'for' person, a provider of services.

He often thought about and discussed the 'old, sad issue . . . our inability to reconcile the aspirations of the organized blind with the interest of the executive agencies and to bring both motivations together to power a single national and international effort.' He recognized the strengths of each. 'The organizations of the blind,' he said in 1977, 'however abrasive they may have been, have brought into the cause a freshening vision of the significance of the individual, and understanding and compassion for the human predicament of blindness and a practical awareness that links our cause to some of the strongest convictions of contemporary society: non-discrimination, civil rights and the status of minorities. A single international effort must recognize that and also that, at the executive level, work *for* the blind has become a highly professional business.'

He pointed to the fact that, in an increasing number of countries, national systems of blind welfare were evolving that retained executive efficiency and accountability but with enhanced political awareness and an acceptable and democratic base. He believed that for the majority on both sides of the issue that would be an acceptable and reasonable compromise. In truth, he was impatient with the dispute, which he believed lessened the effectiveness of the campaign to reduce blindness and serve blind people better. So when in 1984 there were moves to bring together the International Federation and the World Council, he worked hard in that direction. He lobbied organizations in various countries to support the merger and could do so the more easily since his credentials both as an advocate for blind persons and as a provider of services were impeccable. The merger took place, and he afterwards flew to Riyadh to take part in the launch of the new World Blind Union. His name was put forward to be its President but he eventually withdrew in favour of the host country's candidate, Sheikh Abdul Ghanim.

Four years later Wilson attended the second General Assembly of the World Blind Union in Madrid. He delivered the keynote speech on the theme 'Progress through Joint Action'. 'Perhaps,' he said, 'the most significant change in the last fifty years has been blind people's perception of themselves not as social victims or as passive recipients of welfare but as convincing advocates and essential partners in the whole development process. With that has come the concept of accountability: any organization concerned with blindness is responsible not only to taxpayers and subscribers but primarily to the blind people it serves. And so two traditions... have come together to form the World Blind Union.' His words were well chosen. Even if the old dispute was not entirely over (nor is it today), the very existence of the new body greatly reduced its ramifications.

Back in Bethesda, the Wilsons planned a book entitled *Avoiding the Avoidable – Strategies for the Prevention of Disability*. Chapters were envisaged on concepts of disability, on data and definitions (based on a workshop at the Fogarty International Centre), on historical interventions against disability (to be compiled by Jean), on the example of blindness prevention as a global model, on deafness and hearing impairment, on the disabilities of movement, on intellectual impairment and developmental disorder, on mechanisms for action and inaction and on other matters. By the time the Wilsons' period at Bethesda was completed, four of the chapters had been drafted. But, sadly, the book was never published because when they returned home they were quickly reabsorbed in practical action on disability prevention and their usual busy agenda.

During his first term, Wilson had also suggested setting up a study group on 'appropriate technology', to include not only the adaptation of clinical procedures to conditions in developing countries but the possibilities of producing low-cost hearing aids and orthopaedic devices. Jean, meanwhile, worked on a paper on 'Immunization as a Means of Control of Disability in Developing Countries' and a second more specific paper on rubella.

By the end of his second term in 1985, Wilson said that, in notes and recorded form, he now had most of the material required for an extensive treatment of the disabilities of movement and of ageing, of the disability factor in programmes of environmental intervention, and of the possibilities of intervention against mental and developmental handicap.

In his time at Bethesda, he gave many lectures and seminars, and attended several conferences. Some were on more or less academic subjects but in most cases he was in advocacy mode. He worked on influential American audiences to drum up support for Impact and his campaign for disability prevention. This, said the Fogarty International Centre's official report on his scholarship, was 'in keeping with his long time role as gadfly and stimulus for action in a field that had been fragmented and lacked form'. The gadfly had a gift for addressing American audiences. His knowledge of, and affection for, the United States usually enabled him to strike the right chords. Thus, in a lecture in Chicago in 1982, he borrowed from an earlier American vision to suggest that the 450,000 disabled people in the world were 'the tired, the poor, the huddled masses yearning to be free, the wretched refuse of those teeming shores'.

Impact had been formally launched before the Wilsons went to Bethesda – not in England nor in the United States but in the country where they had spent so much of their lives working on the problems of visual impairment: India. The then Indian President, Giani Zail Singh, performed the ceremony on 2 October 1983, the anniversary of the death of Mahatma Ghandi. Practical events were organized at the same time. Since at least 1981 Wilson had been thinking about applying the techniques used at eye camps to other disabilities. In November 1983, 32,000 blind, deaf or otherwise impaired people had sight, movement or hearing restored in similar camps at a unit cost ranging from $6 to $25. As part of the campaign, over a thousand middle ear operations were performed by a team from Thailand where techniques had been developed to conduct such operations under local anaesthetics in rural areas.

Wilson referred to these events in a speech in July 1984 to an American audience entitled 'The Global Challenge of Avoidable Disablement', the fullest statement so far of his thinking on the new cause. He set out his credentials: 'I have spent much of the past thirty years among communities of disabled people. There are those appalling villages of the blind in West Africa, where only children have normal sight. There are the islands of Indonesia, where leprosy afflicts most families. There are Caribbean islands with children blind, deaf and imbecile from rubella. Everywhere, in shanty towns and impoverished villages, there are twisted victims of poliomyelitis crawling the alleyways, malnourished children, stunted, dwarfed, disfigured, disabled.

'They are in the poorest communities, the bottom of every social and economic heap. They are beggars, dependants, outcasts, victims often of diseases which should be an obscene anachronism in our modern world. At best they are recipients of aid and charity, at worst exploited in beggars' guilds and brothels by extortionist, mafia-like organisations. In Calcutta, blind beggars fight the cripples for the right to beg in the richer streets.

'Many of you ... will have experienced the mental gear-change which happens when you meet such a community, when our comfortably anaesthetized concept of Third World poverty comes embarrassingly alive with identifiable individuals. For me, there is perhaps the added knowledge that there, but for the luck of geography, might I be, holding my beggar's bowl outside some Asian railway station, listening for the rich tap of a tourist footstep.'

His main plea was for the development of a multi-disciplinary strategy for dealing with disablement. The principal thrust must, he argued, be at the level of primary health. 'The statistics of deprivation assail us in every television documentary. 5,000,000 children disabled each year by diseases against which we have inexpensive vaccine. Foetal and post-natal malnutrition; the whole medical zoo of viruses and bacteria; grotesque birth practices; too few health workers and too many quacks and dirty grandmothers. Bad housing, unclean water, primeval pests, from the blinding flies of West Africa to the Chagga disease ticks of Latin America. These conditions disable even more people than they kill.'

To attack avoidable disablement, it was necessary to explore in detail the potential for control, to formulate real priorities, to identify linkages between different disciplines and the needs of motivation and delivery. Immunization was clearly the most powerful weapon. As to those who talked of the difficulty of distributing cold vaccines in hot climates, he asked why that should be such a problem 'when in practically every African and Asian village you can buy ice cream.' Xerophthalmia, endemic goitre, lassa fever (an infection that attacks the visceral organs) – given the minimum of community involvement, these and many other problems might be remedied quickly and inexpensively. 'In areas where a primary health system really works, disabilities which have seemed an immemorial part of traditional life can be controlled by a simple intervention.'

He expressed his total conviction that the sort of action taken to restore sight could be applied to deafness and orthopaedic handicap. 'We have established that some ear operations and many orthopaedic interventions can be performed in camp conditions. Is there an advantage in moving forward from eye camps to disability camps, and expanding our objectives from clearing the backlog of cataract to clearing the backlog of curable disablement?'

So often when, in the industrialized world, one hears accounts of disease and suffering in developing countries, one has the false comfort of the illusion that these things cannot happen in the industrialized West. But of course they can and do. Such diseases, he told his American audience, were 'only a grandfather away here. Helen Keller went deaf and blind from an infection which today could be cured by a short course of antibiotics. Roosevelt was crippled by poliomyelitis. Edison was deafened by a condition which, today, could be cured.'

Wilson was now moving towards the concept of a network of Impact Foundations in a number of countries, linked in a very loose federal arrangement, but otherwise independent in their decision-making and working for the establishment in each country of a national programme of disability prevention. The United Kingdom Impact Foundation, with himself as Chairman, was established in 1984. Naturally enough, it was seen as the prototype organization and the one most likely to mobilize appreciable resources for action at home and abroad. In the same year Impact was launched in Africa at a conference in Nairobi. A 'Nairobi Declaration' outlined strategies for the prevention of some of the major causes of disability in Africa and a series of treatment projects were inaugurated in Kenya. In November 1985, the Wilsons visited Thailand for the inauguration of the Impact programme in the Western Pacific. A 'Bangkok Statement on the Prevention of Disability' was issued, and a ten-year programme of action against the principal problems of disability in Thailand formulated.

While still at Bethesda, John and Jean took the initiative to establish the American Impact Foundation, to be concerned not only with international action but also with promotional activities for the prevention of disability in the United States. The founding directors included David Morse, for many years Director-General of the

International Labour Organization, and Norman Acton, Secretary General of an organization called Rehabilitation International. It was envisaged that the American Foundation would concentrate initially on disability in Latin America.

All these foundations were small, with limited resources both of people and money. The spectrum of disabilities was wide and the scale vast. The hope was that Impact's projects, where successful, would be replicated through the national health and development programmes of governments, and that the United Nations Organization which had promoted the initiative would spread the message.

By the end of 1985 Impact claimed a number of achievements. In India, it organized a 'polio-free Madras' campaign, to demonstrate that with community involvement and effective management it was unnecessary that 400,000 children across the world should be paralysed by poliomyelitis each year when an effective vaccine existed. A large Asian refrigeration company voluntarily guaranteed a system for refrigerating the vaccine. Many sizeable companies in Madras (now Chennai) provided other facilities; 5,000 volunteers were recruited; vaccination points were established across the city; and 240,000 infants were registered for treatment. The mobilization of private resources was so effective that the cost to Impact's central funds was less than $6,000.

In the sub-Himalayan region of India, 20,000 babies were born each year with severe mental and hearing impairment because their mothers had goitre during pregnancy. The remedy was to add a small quantity of iodine to domestic salt. Impact persuaded the Tata Company – then and now one of India's biggest enterprises – which provided eighty per cent of the salt in the area, to iodize its produce by a process that added so little to the cost that it was not reflected in the selling price.

Similar imaginative and low-cost ideas were advanced for dealing with hearing impairment in Kenya and for providing callipers (metal splints) and artificial limbs for disabled people in both Africa and Asia. Impact was also pressing for new international action on mental handicap and guinea-worm disease. In a survey it conducted in Northern Mali in 1987, Impact found villages where nearly a third of the people were incapacitated, at least temporarily, by this latter disease which comes from polluted water. The survey was followed by a control project which treated disabled people, disinfected water sources and taught the population about risk factors.

The new organization had made a creditable start, but the wider scene was discouraging. Wilson told an All Party Joint Disabled Group in the House of Commons in July 1986 that the International Decade of Disabled Persons, launched following the International Year, was, in his view, failing. 'There is a lack of commitment by most governments, funding difficulties within the United Nations and other priorities for international attention.' It was ever thus. But while many might have accepted such a situation as a harsh reality, Wilson, with a stamina which compels admiration, launched a proposal for a global publicity and fundraising event in support of the objectives of the Decade. 'The aim, using the fundraising techniques so brilliantly developed in Band Aid and Sports Aid, is to raise a large sum of money and also, in every participating country, to revive interest in the needs and aspirations of the disabled.' Working with the United Nations and international non-governmental organizations, he developed the project, whose aims were to strengthen global awareness of disability issues and raise funds to finance schemes for prevention and rehabilitation and the equalization of opportunities. But, despite his efforts, it became clear that the idea of a global fund would not run and the emphasis switched to an effort to provide information and guidance to disabled people and their organizations so that they could campaign for themselves.

In 1987 Wilson attended a meeting in Sweden whose task was to evaluate the progress of the Decade of Disabled Persons at midterm. The gathering was not able to note much progress of significance beyond the increased salience of groups working for the rights of the disabled, and a degree of advance in raising global awareness of the problems of disability. On the negative side, to quote a UN document of January 1989, 'It was clear that discrimination and segregation widely persisted, that national planning had not yet integrated the needs and concerns of the disabled population into most programmes and projects, and that human and financial resources were sorely lacking in the disability field.' A modest voluntary fund established by the UN for the Decade had produced only $2,000,000 for projects related to disability.

If international interest was flagging, his own was not. In the first four months of 1988, he pursued the cause in India, France and the United States. In January he spent some time in Mumbai where Impact was organizing a three-year programme to immunize 600,000 children and to restore sight, movement or hearing to 70,000 people in a project that, it was hoped, would be a model for the city complexes of Asia. In March, he attended a meeting in France as a member of the International Task Force on Child Survival which was promoting an acceleration of immunization coverage in an attempt to ensure that by 1990 seventy per cent of the world's children would have access to protection against the six major disabling diseases, perhaps saving a million children a year from disability.

In April, he addressed the American Impact Foundation in New York, appealing for the technological resources and the vision of North America to be brought to bear 'to attack in every country the excessive prevalence of avoidable disability.' His audience may have been surprised to learn that, adapting the mass-treatment techniques learned in Asia, Impact had promoted a cataract project in an area of southern England where there was a distressing backlog of people waiting for eye surgery. Using a local hotel for after care, a hundred cataract operations were performed in ten days, at a unit cost of $760 compared with the $1,300 which the National Health Service normally charged. The backlog of cataracts in a country with the resources and expertise of Britain was particularly striking, indeed rather shameful. (Not until 2003 did the British government announce a new programme to clear in five years the very sizeable queue of cataract patients.) Impact conducted many 'Operation Cataract' projects in the United Kingdom. They helped to change clinical practice and were cited as a model of good practice by the Department of Health.

Wilson continued his efforts to revive the international campaign, reminding the governing council of the UNDP in 1989 that they had helped to launch Impact, that the prevention of disability was a declared priority of the United Nations and that decisive advances were possible. Impact wanted to collaborate with governments in developing integrated national programmes. It was well placed to do so, he argued, through its alliances with non-governmental organizations and its ability to recruit expert and often free services from specialists in many disciplines. Mobilization of the talents and resources of the private sector remained essential. So, over the next five years he wished to establish new Impact Foundations in twenty countries as a channel for project funding and a focus of community action. But some of these foundations in the poorer countries would, he said, need support.

Engrossed as he was in his global campaign against disability, Wilson's ear was attuned, as it always had been since his school-days, to broader world developments. His diary entries are few and far between by this time, but they show that he was acutely aware that 1989 was a year of extraordinary political change. He followed events in China leading to the Tianamen Square massacre and recorded the fall of the Berlin Wall and the collapse of communist regimes in Europe. 'Dare we believe,' he wrote, 'that this is the beginning of a new age in Europe? A new re-orientation with the East? Will Germany, if reunited, not only dominate Europe commercially but again perhaps become the aggressor? Can Communism mutate into some form of democratic socialism without losing whatever remains of its saving originality of idealism? Will the United States, freed of the balancing menace of the Soviet Union, itself become an aggressor under the guise of a compassionate market economy?' Two years later he was dismayed at the allied invasion of Iraq. 'What an appalling sequel to last year with the tentative feeling of an awakening renaissance in Europe.'

By the end of the 1980s, Wilson felt the need to take stock, to assess where all his efforts were leading, where the campaign for preventing disability was succeeding and where not, and what the future of Impact should be. He decided to convene another gathering at Leeds Castle and draw on the brains of acknowledged experts in the field. In preparation for the event, he asked an old colleague, Dr Ramachanda Pararjasegaram, to review Impact's programme to date. Dr Pararjasegaram, a Sri Lankan by birth, is today a WHO consultant on the prevention of blindness and deafness. He had set up the Ceylon Society for the Prevention of Blindness as long ago as 1957. He first met Wilson in the mid 1960s, and subsequently took on assignments both for the Society and the WHO. In 1976, he ran a mobile unit in Northern Ghana for the Society. 'The whole of ocular pathology was there,' he told me with professional relish. The two men were to take part in the WHO advisory group on the prevention of blindness, and in 1982 Wilson prevailed on Dr Para, as he is familiarly known, whose preference was to continue with his ophthalmic work, to become the WHO's regional adviser on the prevention of blindness in Delhi. Dr Para is one of the many distinguished experts who freely acknowledge Wilson as their 'mentor'.

He began his substantial report by summarizing a policy review of Impact conducted at UNDP headquarters in April 1989, which described the organization's role as 'supportive and contributing a factor of additionality to the activities of its sponsoring organizations,' i.e. UNDP, WHO and UNICEF. In the report's view it could be a 'pathfinder' on global issues that could benefit from an innovative and flexible approach, and it was encouraged to concentrate on small-scale, innovative programmes providing modern technologies to needy countries. The review also called for a vigorous expansion of Impact's activities worldwide, which would require a new five-year strategy and programme, more funding and the establishment of more Impact Foundations in individual countries.

The international office of Impact was now accommodated by the WHO at its Geneva Headquarters and the organization was drawing on WHO's network of overseas offices for technical support. The UNDP had made seed funds available to support national Impact Foundations in India, Thailand, the Philippines and Kenya, and was helping to finance specific pilot projects in Africa and Asia. Now, Dr Para proposed a five-year plan for 1991 to 1995 containing various suggestions for clarifying Impact's relationship with its sponsoring organizations, strengthening the technical and managerial support it received from the UN system, expanding the network of national committees and foundations, and establishing models of 'integrated intervention against avoidable disability' on lines already being tackled in the field in Asia.

The Leeds Castle International Conference on the Prevention of Disability met in September 1991. The United Nations itself, as well as the UNDP, WHO, UNICEF and the International Labour Organization (ILO), was represented, and around thirty experts on blindness and visual impairment, deafness and hearing impairment, orthopaedic and mental impairment attended. As at the 1981 Leeds Castle gathering, a former British Prime Minister, this time Edward Heath, took the chair for most of the conference and observed that while the 1981 event had drawn international attention to the nature of the problem of prevention and what might be done, 'We have the infinitely more difficult task of getting something done.' The President of the United States, the Prince of Wales and the UN Secretary General sent messages of support and encouragement – not too difficult to organize for a good cause but an indication that Impact had grown in stature.

John Wilson, of course, made a major contribution to the

proceedings. First, he produced a remarkable background paper, written in consultation with specialists at Bethesda and elsewhere. This distilled the knowledge he had acquired since he had begun to address the general problem of disability eight years earlier. Aware of the detailed definitions and measurements of disabilities produced by the WHO he nevertheless introduced, with the gift he always had for the lucid, simple sentence, his own concept: 'A disabled person is...someone who, from whatever cause, has a severe and enduring limitation in sight, hearing, movement, intellect or behaviour.' He surveyed the statistics for the various categories of disabled persons in the world and estimated that there were at least 70,000,000 people in developing countries whose sight, movement or hearing could be restored for $15 to $40. He considered in turn the efforts being made to immunize children against six basic diseases; to reduce the incidence of maternal death and maternal disability; to attack problems of visual and hearing impairment; to help those disabled by poliomyelitis; to control guinea-worm disease which was affecting millions of people in Africa and Asia and permanently disabling many; to reduce the prevalence of leprosy; to tackle the huge problem of disablement brought about by traffic, domestic and occupational injuries (perhaps then responsible for 100,000,000 of the world's disabled); and to begin to deal with the widespread incidence of mental and neurological impairment. He thought more attention should be given to the use of tobacco, the 'brown plague', as a cause of disability. If he did not deal in detail with tuberculosis and various parasitic, diarrhoeal and water-borne diseases, this was because he thought more work was needed on the degree of disability they caused, and the means of control which could be devised.

In both the industrialized and the developing worlds, the link between disability and ageing was growing into a major cause of concern. He saw 'a race between the science which increases the span of life and the science which can influence the quality of that life. The winning of that race must be a major priority during the coming decades.' The technology to deal with most of these problems existed, he wrote, but most of it was not being used. The necessary global mechanisms for action existed (and Impact was part of this), but the essential action must be at the national level, acting through integrated national programmes for the prevention of disability. The cost of such programmes was modest and they were demonstrably cost effective. But, as always – and how many times had he said this in the last forty years? – what was needed was 'political commitment, encouraged by public demand and nourished by a climate of awareness and cooperation within the international community'.

This summary cannot do justice to his lengthy, thoughtful and practical paper. It tackles a vast canvas. Disability is on the face of it a simple enough concept. But the term embraces a considerable number of effects of a large number of diseases and other causes of disability and the interaction of people with impairments with social environments and attitudes. The intellectual effort involved in achieving even a basic grasp of the many complex issues at stake, and then in trying to chart a course of action to deal with them, would be impressive enough in someone at their prime. For a person of seventy-one, and blind and progressively more deaf, it is a particularly striking accomplishment.

At the conference itself, Wilson's speech emphasized the notable advances that had been made: the phenomenal success of immunization linked to expanding primary-health-care systems; the remarkable progress in preventing blindness and the beginning of similar progress in dealing with hearing and orthopaedic impairment; the simplification of surgical techniques; and intervention against some major causes of mental impairment. Yet, he added soberly, 'In our three days here it is likely that some 80,000 people, somewhere in the world, will become blind, deaf, physically or mentally impaired.'

Margaret Anstee, Deputy Secretary General of the United Nations, produced a striking statistic: the number of disabled in the world exceeded the combined population of the United States and Soviet Union. Yet, she said, every second cause of disability could be prevented by effective primary health. The underlying cause, particularly in developing countries, was poverty.

The UNDP and WHO reiterated their commitment to collaboration with Impact. Another WHO spokesman brought to the conference's attention the contents of Dr Para's report, singling out his proposal that an integrated disability project should be developed in each WHO region and that governments should be encouraged to develop comprehensive national plans with the active support of Impact Foundations which, he continued, should be developed over the next four years in at least twenty countries with the roles of advocacy, community motivation, and the mobilization of both funds and the managerial talent of the private sector. The WHO, the conference was told, now had four taskforces concerned with the prevention of disability amongst children, adolescents, workers and the elderly.

The conference ended with a Declaration. It emphasized that, in the next decade, at least 30,000,000 people could be saved from disability through preventive action. Also, if basic surgery were available, over 40,000,000 disabled people in developing countries could have their sight, movement or hearing restored at a unit cost of between $15 and $40 (these figures represent a considerable scaling down of Wilson's earlier goal of halving the number of disabled in twenty years). In the decade since the last Leeds Castle gathering revolutionary change had begun. Advances were possible in many fields: universal immunization, the provision of essential nutrients such as iodine, vitamin A and iron, safe motherhood, the alleviation of birth asphyxia, community-wide programmes for parasitic control, the prevention and early treatment of middle-ear disease, the improved treatment and prevention of leprosy, the prevention of injury, reduction in the use of tobacco and the provision of basic surgery to restore sight, hearing and mobility. The continuation and development of the role of Impact as a link between the UN system and the resources and managerial talent of the private sector was re-affirmed.

The conference proposed, among other things, that the government of each country should develop a ten-year national programme to prevent, and where possible, reverse avoidable disability; that aid agencies and the UN should recognize that the prevention of avoidable disability should be a prime objective of development policy; that on the model of the prevention of blindness programme, other global programmes should be rapidly developed for the prevention of hearing loss, orthopaedic and neurological impairment and mental disability; and that disabled people and their organizations throughout the world should be fully consulted and encouraged to participate as essential parties in all action to prevent avoidable disability.

The overlap between Wilson's background paper and the Declaration is too obvious to need further description. The Declaration itself now became a launch pad for another round of Wilsonian advocacy. In September 1992, he presented a paper on disability prevention to a world congress of Rehabilitation International in

Nairobi. In October he distributed a statement on the theme at the UN General Assembly. In that month, also, he took part in the inauguration of Hearing International, an organization set up to promote and develop global programmes for the prevention and management of deafness and hearing impairment. Wilson became a consultant to it, helped to draft its constitution and guided it during its formative years. Yash Kapur, a previous president, told me that he owed Wilson a great personal debt for changing his focus from the treatment of hearing disorders to their prevention.

For the rest of his life Wilson would promote the cause ceaselessly. He would continue to argue that action for the prevention of disability should be integrated into national and international programmes of health and development. But he came to realize that this must be a long-term aim rather than tomorrow's achievement. For Impact itself, he refined over time his agenda of action, settling on six points: immunization; safe motherhood and child survival; early identification and treatment of disease; accessible surgery; control of the disabling consequences of micronutrient deficiency; and research into the links between disability and ageing.

The international debate was crucial. In the end, only the UN system and national governments could make a real impact on the towering problem of disability. The Decade of Disabled Persons had been disappointing in its results. But Wilson also had great faith in the power of demonstration on the ground, as we have seen. Indeed, he believed that was Impact's essential function – 'to demonstrate, not to do. It is the job of governments to do. We establish a possibility with their help. But then we get out of it and let them get on with it.'

Perhaps the most striking example of this approach was the 'Lifeline Express'. According to Wilson, he had once met Pandit Nehru, the first Prime Minister of India, who had told him that he should think of using the railway system to deliver health services in that country. In the late 1980s, Wilson prompted the Indian Impact Foundation's representative to call on the Indian Minister of Railways and request the donation of a train to serve as a travelling hospital. The Minister promised to make one available provided it visited his constituency in Bihar (*plus ça change*). The train was received in 1991 and was fully equipped for the task. It began to visit remote areas all over India. Impact India would spend a month in each area before the train's arrival to identify disabled patients.

The train would then be stationed in that area for a few weeks. Impact provided the equipment and staff. Doctors provided their services free. Local sponsors put up money to cover the cost of accommodation, food and medicine. Treatment was free for patients. In 1992 alone, some 200,000 people with different ailments came to the train and some 20,000 operations were performed to restore sight, movement or hearing.

In 1993, the Wilsons visited this, 'the world's first hospital train'. 'We stood on the station platform as the train, vividly painted with carriages equipped like a modern hospital, clanked in to the cheers of a crowd of school children who had been given a holiday to greet what has become known as "the magic train".' They watched the operation: 'There was a seven-year-old girl, Bismilla, her limbs twisted and contorted from polio, crawling painfully on all fours, like an animal. After surgery on the train, she walked upright, excitedly, into her new life. She was one of 1,200 people who had life-transforming operations and treatment on the train. It was like a biblical scene: blind people regained their sight, deaf people heard, crippled children walked again.'

But there was more. While the train was being packed up for the next task an emergency telephone call came from New Delhi. There had been a devastating earthquake in Western India. The district hospital had been destroyed and there were thousands of casualties. Could 'Lifeline Express' help? The authorities cleared the track and the train rushed through the night. 'A wonderful thing happened: in response to the radio news bulletin, at different stations along the route volunteer doctors, many of them Rotarians, were waiting to board the train with drugs and equipment donated by Indian companies. At the epicentre of the earthquake, a scene of utter devastation, over 700 operations and treatments were performed on the train, mending fractured limbs and fractured nerves. People often think of Rotary as a cosy luncheon club; it is at its best in an emergency like that, when the earth cracks, coping quietly and professionally at the centre of disaster.'

By the end of Wilson's life the Lifeline Express had performed 150,000 operations in seven years. It was known all over India and was the subject of several television documentaries. On the BBC radio programme 'Desert Island Discs' in 1994, Sue Lawley observed to Wilson that he had only one train. She had missed the point. He replied that he had been offered sixteen different ones.

But it was not Impact's job to run a health system. Their task was to show what could be done. He could have told her, but did not, that a group of Hong Kong businessmen had visited India to see the train and later presented a similar one to the government of China where there are now three such trains operating.

In 1993, Impact United Kingdom gave £5,000 to two Bangladeshis, Monsur Choudhuri and Rezaul Haque, to help start an Impact Foundation in Bangladesh. In the same year the director of Impact India visited Bangladesh and discussed the possibility of launching a train in that country on the lines of the Lifeline Express. But the Bangladeshis argued that their country was riverain. A third of it was under water. Many villages were accessible only by river. Flooding was a permanent hazard. If you wanted to reach the remote areas it made more sense to use the waterways. This view eventually prevailed. It was decided that a flat-bottomed engineless pontoon should be built, rather than a more expensive vessel. When it needed to move to a new area, it could be towed.

The local view was that the boat should be built abroad, but Wilson insisted that local builders and, so far as possible, local materials should be used. A design was provided by Geoffrey Martin, a civil engineer and father-in-law of Wilson's younger daughter. Steel was imported from Singapore and construction began. It was a daunting business. On one occasion the half-constructed boat was entirely submerged by floods. Finally, it was completed on time and within budget and in February 1999, after twelve days of hauling by hand, the 290-tonne, three-decked craft entered the water ready for business. At the launching ceremony it was given the name Jibon Tari – the Boat of Life.

It was quickly in use, complete with operating theatre and recovery ward. The Boat of Life spent about two months in each mooring. At one such in 1999, more than 3,000 patients were treated and 500 surgical operations were performed, including 272 for the restoration of sight. Orthopaedic and ear, nose and throat problems were treated as well as eye conditions. Payment was waived for destitute patients. Surgeons were paid only a small honorarium. Again, the main value of the boat was its power of demonstration. It showed what could be done. But in the showing it also brought relief to suffering in far-flung corners of Bangladesh where access to orthodox medical services was extremely difficult.

Bangladesh and India were of course familiar environments

for John Wilson. But in the 1990s his work also took him to less familiar places and topics. In November, for example, he attended a conference at the Vatican on the Church's attitude to disability or, 'as they put it, the inclusion of disabled people in the body of Christ'. Pope John Paul addressed the first meeting. Wilson says that he had arrived with his Protestant prejudices fully alert but when the Pope, only two weeks out of hospital after an abdominal operation, passed before them it was a moment of blessing. 'He touched my hair and then, after moving further away, came back and joined my hands in Jean's and said softly "In nomine Patris et Spiritus Sanctus".'

Wilson then visited Saudi Arabia as the guest of Prince Abdul Aziz Bin Ahmed Bin Abdul Aziz Al Saud. He recorded 'a spectacular evening at the Prince's palace in Jedda. Camels in the gardens, disgusted to give rides to the American ladies. Dangerous falcons tethered to their poles.' He spent a day in the desert with Prince Abdul Aziz, visiting a camel market, during which the Prince's Nubian secretary described to him 'the Muslim belief that there will be a final coming of a great prophet. He will try to turn mankind from its destruction of the planet. He will fail and the world will be destroyed.' Wilson commented in his diary that the fundamentalists were doing their best to prepare the world for the prophet and that they had become much more insistent since the American troops came to Saudi Arabia, and were harassing in particular the short-skirted American women.

During this visit to Jedda he discussed with his Saudi hosts the possibility of an Islamic conference to draw up a plan for the prevention of disability in Islamic countries. Two years after that the Wilsons toured the Gulf States with the Prince. John produced a paper on disability prevention in the Gulf. They travelled in the unaccustomed luxury of an aircraft of the Saudi Royal Flight. Back in England in midwinter they came down to earth: 'After the luxury and princely pomp we queued at the Town Hall for our old age pension bus passes.'

In the autumn of 1995, the UN Secretary General asked Wilson to represent him at an Arms Control Review Conference about to be held in Vienna. Among other things, the meeting was to discuss a new laser gun, which projected a laser beam in order to blind opposing troops, and also the issue of landmines. Wilson told the conference that the laser gun was abhorrent to the conscience of

humanity. There was a practical opportunity to ban it before it became part of the international arsenal and available to terrorist
groups. 'There are 40,000,000 of us blind in the world. Surely,
Mr President, that is enough.' The conference recommended that
the use of the weapon should be prohibited.

He was appalled by the statistics relating to landmines. There
were, he learned, over 100,000,000 of them planted in various
countries and the number was increasing. Three years later he was
delighted to learn that the British government had joined the campaign for their global eradication.

Towards the end of November 1997, he and Jean were in Denmark for a conference of Hearing International. A rare diary entry,
showing that his sense of humour was still intact at the age of
seventy-eight, runs: 'They lent me some thin rubber gloves in the
Carlsberg Museum so that I could feel the statuary. The Degas
bronzes of the ballet dancers – those athletic nude girls were a joy
to touch. But not the three Graces which Jean says are wonderful to
see but to touch impossibly obscene, with the Grace in the front
mostly notable for her very large bottom.'

The next year was similarly charged. September of 1998 provides
an example of Wilson, at the age of seventy-nine, acting with undiminished energy and focus. Bangladesh had been assaulted by
particularly devastating floods. He received a distressing message
from Impact Bangladesh about two districts in the north where
1,600 people were said to be victims of the floods, marooned on
rooftops of damaged houses and wandering about flooded fields in
search of sanctuary. 'I got in touch with the President of the Rotary
Clubs in the United Kingdom. With his agreement, and that of the
district governors, I wrote a letter to 1,800 Rotary clubs inviting
each of them to contribute £41, the estimated cost of assisting one
of these families. Within three weeks £60,000 had been contributed
and the teams went into action in Bangladesh, eventually providing
assistance to over 2,000 disabled people who, with their families,
totalled over 8,000 people. Towards the end of that year they were
able to rebuild 240 village huts and restore safe drinking water and
sanitation.'

The winter of 1998 took him to India, Bangladesh, Malaysia,
Singapore, Thailand and Hong Kong. 1999 began actively. In
January, the month of his eightieth birthday, he went to India to re-
ceive a special award from the Mohanlal Mehta Charitable Trust

and then on to Chittagong in Bangladesh for another ceremony. In March, he visited Egypt for meetings of the International Council of Ophthalmology which commemorated one thousand years of ophthalmology in the Middle East. In November, he attended a symposium of Hearing International in Kyoto, Japan. He was occupying himself at this time with two new projects, the establishment of a Hearing Conservation Council in Britain and a scheme for contingency plans to assist disabled people in areas subject to frequent natural disasters. But the travelling and the project making were about to end.

Some years earlier, Wilson had been asked on the BBC radio programme 'In Touch' that stock but not uninteresting question: 'If you started again, would it be different?' He replied in the affirmative: 'Yes, I think I would probably have been involved in the whole business of disability rather than the specific disability of blindness. I would also have been more involved in the *prevention* of disability. In the last forty years there has been a revolutionary change in the world's ability to prevent and reverse disability. I could have got involved a bit earlier.'

The statement is a little confusing. The notion that he might have been involved rather earlier in disability prevention is uncontentious. But the thought that, from the beginning of his working life, he might have campaigned on the general rather than the specific issue is hard to credit. In the 1950s, it was difficult enough to get attention for the narrower issue of blindness. It is not easy to imagine that he could have successfully advocated the general disability cause at that time. The wider issue was so diffuse and so complex that, in my view, he would have achieved much less than he did by his concentration on visual impairment.

When in the early 1980s Wilson took up the broad cause of disability prevention, he lost the sympathy of a few of his earlier supporters. They thought the target too wide. They feared a loss of focus and effectiveness. They thought, too, that the problems of visual impairment still needed his attention. It was an understandable reaction. But I find it hard to see how he could have continued to add value to work on the problems of blindness. The Society to which he had devoted so much of his life was flourishing. After more than three decades, it surely needed new leadership. He had been president of the International Agency for the Prevention of Blindness for two terms and could not, constitutionally, serve another. In my view he judged rightly that he should develop a new field of activity.

The one he chose was vast in its scope. His optimism as to what could be achieved was often unrealistic. Nor was it clear that he could add a great deal to the work on the prevention of disability in which the international community was already engaged. That said, his advocacy certainly had its effect on the main United Nations organisations involved. Impact demonstrated on a limited canvas what might be achieved in some areas. And in certain respects he was, as so often before, ahead of the game. In perhaps the last article he wrote, published posthumously, he said, 'The time may come when to mobilize the resources and political will necessary for continuing progress, we shall need to join with other specialists in advocating that action for the prevention of disability should be a basic component of all national and international programmes of health and development.' But that of course had, broadly speaking, been one of the main conclusions of the Leeds Castle seminar nearly twenty years previously. It had been an uphill struggle.

Nevertheless, some progress had been made. The Decade of Disabled Persons had had at least one practical result of enduring value, the adoption by the UN in 1992 of the Standard Rules on the Equalization of Opportunities for Persons with Disabilities which, though they had no compulsory legal force, imposed a moral obligation on the governments of the world to promote equal opportunities for people with disabilities. Wilson had – as earlier in the field of blindness – helped to entrench the notion that the prevention of disability in general should be a priority concern. Some time after he started to argue the disability cause, national governments and aid agencies began to formulate policies on general disability and development. Away from the policy debates, very large numbers of people benefited from his efforts because their disablement was either prevented or cured. The last twenty years of his working life, like the first forty, had reduced much actual and potential human suffering.

Chapter 7

The Man

It would be hard not to be impressed by the qualities John Wilson brought to his work – the energy, the will-power, the courage, the conviction, the remorseless pursuit of objectives. But those who knew him best saw other qualities, too. He relished life. His enjoyment of the people and things around him was full-blooded, his enthusiasm infectious. It would be easy, in concentrating on his work and achievement, to miss the whole person – his attitude to life, his beliefs, his interest and occupations other than work, his relationships with family and friends and pre-eminently with his wife, Jean. His rounded personality is full of interest.

We have seen that at school in Worcester and at Oxford University Wilson, despite his blindness, had acquired great confidence in his physical ability. He was remarkably mobile. Throughout his life, those who met him found him physically courageous. Some sighted people even found him foolhardy in the physical risks he ran, as I have said, though in reality he assessed the risks more carefully than they appreciated. His blindness did, of course, impose limitations, but he was more inclined to push at the constraints than to resign himself to them. One person, not a close contact, met him at a dinner party in Kuala Lumpur in the 1960s: 'He had a great air of confidence. He held himself very upright and walked ahead as though sighted. He carried everything off with a great air of being normal.' After dinner, there was dancing. Wilson invited her to take the floor. 'He steered me with great skill. He was a very good dancer.'

The dancing classes and balls at Worcester had paid dividends. In the early 1980s Wilson attended an event in California arranged by an American non-governmental organization. A Muslim guest had been invited to explain and demonstrate the art of Sufi dancing. When he finished, those present were encouraged to try it for themselves. Typically, Wilson was quickly on his feet. I am told that he intuitively grasped that the dance was part worship, part ceremony and made a strong impression. 'He was the best dancer on the floor.'

Some found him physically attractive. He was slender and not particularly tall (about five foot ten inches). His face was usually tanned and very expressive. But the feature that most impressed many who met him was an unexpected one. 'He had deep blue eyes,' said a close Indian friend. 'He did not look as though he was blind.' That was partly because, when talking or listening, he looked at people as though he could see them. Many, at least on first acquaintance, were transfixed by those eyes.

Wilson used to say that it was up to blind people to make sighted people feel normal. He understood the importance of body language. When he met people, especially when travelling abroad, he knew he had to take the initiative in this area, using the correct hand gestures according to the custom of the country. He was always careful to face a person openly and to develop facial expressions which showed interest, aiming to put individuals and audiences at their ease.

Then there was the voice, once described by a *Yorkshire Post* journalist as 'cultured, with precise delivery and a hint of the military'. I can testify, from many hours of listening to Wilson's voice on tape, that that is an accurate description. I was initially intrigued as to why this man, brought up in northern England, showed no trace of a north-country accent, although his brothers and sisters had quite a strong one. I suspect that the answer lies in his years at Worcester. In his autobiography *See It My Way*, from which I have already quoted, Peter White, another Worcester alumnus, states that, 'Despite our polyglot class origin Worcester boys developed a corporate and wholly recognizable voice, distinctive not so much for any tell-tale accent... but because of the clipped certainty of its delivery. Almost all of us acquired "the voice", whether the confidence it suggested was real or imagined.'

That Wilson had formidable energy will have been plain from the story of his life so far. Without it, he could not have carried through his relentless travelling in rural Africa and Asia. But, physically, he was not super-human. He was never inclined to pay undue attention to his own health, but he did have his problems. His sightless eyes gave him considerable pain from time to time. As mentioned earlier, in 1941 he had an operation to relieve what was then called 'traumatic glaucoma'. 'I have often since wondered what that was supposed to be,' he dryly commented in his diary. He continued to have trouble with his eyes until the 1970s when he had two successive operations to replace his natural eyes with artificial ones, skilfully hand-painted and designed to catch the light.

But physically, his biggest setback occurred later when he fell ill in Africa and was treated locally for amoebic dysentery. The antibiotics used were toxic to the ear and started him on a gradual process of hearing loss. He always said that this was worse than losing his sight because his ability to orientate himself through his hearing progressively deteriorated. He experimented a great deal with hearing aids but found them generally unsatisfactory. In 1994 and 1999, he had operations to replace both hips. He also developed cardiac problems in the latter part of his life.

Those who knew him well, both family and friends, insist that, although he found his physical disabilities frustrating, he did not complain about them. Indeed, he steadfastly ignored them. In particular, he did not complain about his blindness. His stock statement was that it was a confounded nuisance, nothing more. This was partly a matter of education. Peter White again, recalling his days at Worcester, says, 'I can't stress enough how unconcerned we were about our lack of sight...My stance – the stance of many young blind people – was that blindness is a nuisance which should not be dwelt upon.' In Wilson's case, it was partly a matter of vocation too. His message to the blind people of the world was that disability should be kept in perspective. He once wrote that he wanted Africans to realize that blindness was a 'confounded nuisance, not a crippling affliction'. He believed that whether a particular disability amounts to incapacity depends less on its apparent severity than on the character of the individual who has to cope with it and the attitude of the community to which that individual belongs.

His own life and achievements were a triumph over disability. But naturally he often thought about the problems of blindness. In a revealing passage in *Travelling Blind* he wrote that, 'the disabled are accustomed to being treated either as total wrecks or heroes. The blind are particularly subject to this and are frequently credited with extraordinary moral and spiritual virtues. This would be flattering if it were not accompanied by an equally strong conviction that they are incapable of normal everyday activities. People are prepared to believe that we can be prophets, seers or sages (which is unlikely) but they do not believe we can be competent farmers or engineers which is, in fact, well within the capacity of most of us.'

Throughout his working life, Wilson made many speeches and wrote many documents about eye diseases and techniques for controlling or preventing them. Rarely did he reflect publicly on the personal problems that blindness may cause. A notable exception is a paper on 'Adjustments to Blindness' which he read in 1946, at the age of twenty-seven, to the British Psychological Society. Delivered shortly before he left on his first visit to Africa, he observed that a blind person is a curiosity to all but his intimates and that, wherever he goes, he is on show. Travelling alone, he must develop a macabre humour to survive situations in which he is treated as a hero, an invalid or a beggar. One of the main problems for a blind person is, he continues, to achieve a right assessment of his abilities. It is easy to conform to the traditional pattern, to become a hero or a dependent, but that way lies moral and often physical disaster. Instead, one must find, and where possible express, one's own standards as a developing individual. That demands considerable integrity and an intellectual discipline beyond the average. Moreover, it involves a mental and physical strain which is too often disregarded.

The most far-reaching handicap imposed by blindness was, he thought, the limitations on physical freedom and its mental consequences. 'All our movements are controlled by pre-determined techniques...even on known ground we must proceed warily, calculating every angle, attentive to catch the shade of meaning in an echo. I often return from a country walk alone with a positive headache from the effort of concentration it demands.'

His paper was in substance a discussion of how the various categories of blind people adjust to their visual impairment. His own experience suggested to him that the more a person who has been blinded achieves such an adjustment, the closer will his imagery approximate to that of a person who has always been blind. 'Memories of colour and perspective soon become uncertain, requiring an increasing effort of will to recapture. Words and phrases based on visual concepts lose their power to evoke a clear response in visual memory. My own experience is, I think, typical of many who, like myself, retain visual memories from childhood but have lived half a life without sight. With few exceptions, mainly in respect of things I knew intimately as a child, my conception of objects of feelable size is tactile and three-dimensional. To imagine a scene two-dimensionally, I have to exert as great an effort as would be required for a sighted person to imagine it three-dimensionally.'

Lastly, the limitations placed by blindness on cultural and aesthetic life formed, in his view, a constant barrier to intercourse with the minds of his fellow men and to the appreciation of universal forms of expression. The problem was most marked in the appreciation of literature. 'Almost every page of every book is studded with words and metaphors which can evoke no response in the experience of the always-blind, and which recall but a fading, phantom image to the blinded.'

I have quoted from this paper at some length because it is the best example I have discovered of John Wilson's considered views on the personal problems resulting from his blindness. But it should not mislead. As I have said, he dwelt only very rarely on this issue. The tape recordings of his personal diary contain few such reflections, and there is not an iota of self-pity in them. The fact is that his visual impairment played a much smaller part in his life than sighted people may imagine.

Nor, when those who knew the man best describe him, do they give any prominence to these things. In their accounts of his personality, the quality first selected, time and time again, is 'vision'. Helen Keller, the other great (and doubly disabled) pioneer in work for the blind, once said, 'A tragedy is a man with sight and no vision.' John Wilson was regarded by many as the reverse. 'A man without sight, with a worldwide vision,' wrote Sir Patrick Nairne, the former head of his Oxford college.

Almost from the beginning of his working life this visionary quality led him to address the global implications of specific actions on the problems of blindness, whether in the villages of Africa or Asia, the sprawling cities of the Indian sub-continent or the scattered islands of the Caribbean. He was perhaps the first person to advocate the cause of blind people in global terms, to focus public attention on the types of blindness and their causes, and to address the means by which the issues could be tackled internationally. He inspired practitioners to look at the broader picture of eye care when their focus hitherto had been on the clinical aspect. He once said to a congress of American ophthalmologists: 'As ophthalmic surgeons, you were disciplined to see the problem in clinical terms

… it may require a special effort of imagination for you to see the millions of other eyes in the deserts, the jungles and the mass, disorganized populations of the world.'

Increasingly, as we have seen, his vision was of a world movement to eradicate or prevent the vast bulk of blindness which he knew to be unnecessary. From the mid-1960s, he had been all too well aware that the problem was getting bigger, not smaller. 'As to the future, it is a race between the mothers and the doctors and, for the present, the mothers are winning.' The growth in world population and the ageing of that population meant that the number of blind would inevitably increase unless an extraordinary international effort was mounted. He wanted 'to lift the subject from the textbook and give it the impulse and purpose of a world movement.'

One famous orthopaedic surgeon likened Wilson to Winston Churchill in the way he could turn vision into action. It would not be sensible to pursue the comparison too far, but for Wilson it was certainly deeds that counted. 'Action this day' is a slogan to which he would have wholeheartedly subscribed. He frequently quoted a passage from Goethe: 'Until there is a commitment, there is avoidancy, confusion, a chance to draw back. But at the moment of commitment, Providence moves too. Commitment has its genius, its power, its magic. Whatever you can do, whatever you can dream, begins to be possible.' Wilson's commitment to action was pursued with a single-mindedness, a tunnel vision, which inspired some but deterred and perhaps disturbed others.

In January 2003, I discussed his personality over dinner in Mumbai with two Indians who had known him well and had worked with him in establishing the Indian Impact Foundation. They were both strong admirers. I asked them, as I have asked many others, 'What, if any, were his faults?' After a longish pause, one said, with an air of resignation, 'If John was determined to do something, or get *you* to do something, there was no stopping him. You had better do it.' The other said, 'That is not necessarily a bad thing.'

Peter White asked Wilson in a radio interview: 'Don't you ever get depressed, feel you are banging your head against a brick wall? As you solve one problem another occurs. How do you motivate yourself?' Wilson replied that he did not have the slightest trouble. It was all 'self-motivating'. It is true that he rarely, if ever, allowed himself to be daunted by problems. The combination of clear objectives, a conviction based on long experience that they were realizable and a passion for the cause provided powerful motivation throughout his working life.

Testimony to Wilson's tenacity of purpose is abundant. It often achieved highly significant results where a less determined person would have given up the struggle. That is true of his general lifelong campaign against unnecessary blindness. But there are specific illustrations too. For example, he fought long and hard to persuade the World Health Organization to organize the systematic collection and analysis of data on world blindness. His own efforts and those of others had been dogged by a lack of adequate statistics for many years. Anyone who has dealt with international organizations knows how much energy may be needed to get them committed to a new objective or task. But in the end the WHO was goaded into the proper collection of data. Later in his life, Wilson campaigned on the problem of hearing disability. Once his mind had become focused on that issue, he single-mindedly sought to involve others in the new cause. He had less success. They had their own priorities and were unwilling to be diverted.

People who determinedly pursue a particular objective run risks. They may get their way but in doing so may distract attention from other causes and distort priorities. We have already seen how in the 1950s Wilson was so preoccupied with river blindness in Africa that he was initially slow to appreciate the growing significance of blinding malnutrition, although he made up for this afterwards. It can be argued, too, that, partly as a result of his own advocacy, river blindness itself received too much attention, since it was geographically limited and, in global statistical terms, was not one of the major causes of blindness. Yet my own sympathies are with Wilson. It is always easy to find objections to a course of action, especially an innovative one, to argue for more time, more research, for better refinement of priorities. All too often the result is that nothing gets done. Better action now than no action, in most cases at any rate.

Some who worked with him felt that he tended to impose ideas and methods, sometimes without adequate thought, occasionally with an inadequate appreciation of local circumstances. Some, too, thought that he could be simplistic, somewhat detached from reality, a little naïve about what could be accomplished, rather too trusting of strangers making a case for the first time and rather too ready to take on commitments and then discover that it was difficult to keep to them. He could also be very stubborn, when his desire to achieve something was in danger of being frustrated. All these criticisms, in my view, have some force. But they are relatively common where a person is passionately committed to a cause and has not yet convinced others of its merits. There is sometimes a price to be paid for positive action. I believe that in the case of Wilson's work it was a price usually worth paying. It cannot be emphasized enough that throughout his working life he was seeking to do new things. He had a great capacity for innovation – the introduction of 'open' or 'integrated' education to Africa, the use of mobile outreach clinics, the training of ophthalmic paramedics, the introduction of new disciplines for eye camps, the education of mothers about the causes of blinding malnutrition, and the creation of an international structure to deal with the world's eye problems. Innovators typically meet resistance. The resistance is not always wrong, but if it succeeds too often a great deal of good is lost.

Wilson had no medical training. He was avid for knowledge of all kinds and worked hard to understand the medicine of eye problems and other forms of impairment. A prominent ophthalmologist tells me that Wilson was good at listening to others who did understand this medicine, and that he had the ability to grasp what he was told and to convey it publicly. But, because he lacked the background, he could not always judge whether the medical information he was being offered was sound and he would occasionally advance dubious medical arguments and propositions.

Few of the staff who worked with Wilson at the Society still survive, so it is not possible to give a rounded account of how they regarded him as a leader and manager. Not all found him easy to work with. He was intuitive, an improviser. Like many such, he knew what he wanted himself, but his aims could be less clear to some of his staff. They were sometimes not sure that they were delivering the right thing. As a result some felt, in modern parlance, that they were 'under-achieving'. He could be very hard to shift once he had made up his mind. One or two people who worked with him said that he was inclined to be 'tetchy' when challenged. His passionate feelings about issues could erupt without warning, often because of his 'bubbling rage' about disability, which he refused to accept might be an unchangeable part of the human condition.

I am struck by the fact that those who made these criticisms invariably put them in a broader context of admiration, respect and, often, affection. While some consider that there were flaws in the man all, without exception, felt that those flaws were far outweighed by the virtues, the strengths and the achievements.

Few people could help being affected by the Wilson charisma. He had a very strong capacity to inspire. His deep personal conviction about the cause in which he was engaged, his infectious enthusiasm, his confidence that practical action could be taken, his wit, his eloquence and his presentational skills, all combined to inspire others to action. This inspirational quality readily crossed the barriers of nation, race, religion, class and sex.

Dr Venkataswamy told me that Wilson had a wonderful capacity to 'go down to the poorest, to sit with them with the same composure as with a head of state.' Dr V had seen him in action in both capacities. In his work Wilson dealt with people of many races and he encountered many situations of racial conflict. But he observed that the Society's work bypassed barriers of race and politics. 'In Cyprus, Greek and Turkish children lived happily at the blind schools throughout the communal tension on the island. In Kenya, a mobile eye clinic worked in the Kikiyu villages despite the Mau Mau trouble. And in Malaya, even the bandits are said to have subscribed to the fundraising appeal.' That the organization did not become enmeshed in racial and tribal problems owes much to his own outlook. He once said that to someone who cannot see there is a lunatic quality in racial controversy.

Distinguished figures of both sexes, working today on eye problems – in Africa, Asia, the United States and Britain – freely talk of his crucial influence on their lives. When they reach for a single word to describe the role he played in their lives they select either 'mentor' or 'guide'. They felt his interest across the continents. He frequently telephoned with words of encouragement, or seeking advice, or proposing a new project. Colleagues from Asia, Africa, the Caribbean and beyond were made welcome in Britain and several were regular guests at the Wilsons' home.

There is plenty of evidence, not just that John Wilson was an exceptionally effective orator, but, which is more rare, that his speeches really did inspire people to take action. Larry Brilliant is an American who led the successful campaign by the World Health Organization to eradicate smallpox in India. At a WHO meeting in

1975 in New Delhi to mark the successful end of the campaign, Wilson was invited to speak. He chose the theme 'If smallpox, why not blindness?' Brilliant says that Wilson had been visibly, palpably moved by the story of the eradication of smallpox which had earlier been regarded as ineradicable. Why could not the world do the same for avoidable blindness? He delivered what Brilliant calls the 'best sales pitch I ever heard in my life'. It had an inspirational effect. Brilliant had earlier decided that on retirement from the WHO he would set up a charity to work in the Third World. His intention was that it should focus on the problems of diarrhoea. Wilson's speech persuaded him and others that it should instead concentrate on blindness. The Seva (meaning 'service' in Sanskrit) organization was duly founded in 1978, is based in California and states that in the past twenty-five years it has assisted in restoring sight to 2,000,000 people in India, Nepal, Tibet, Cambodia and Tanzania.

Mike Hicks, Wilson's son-in-law, who often went to gatherings Wilson was to address, and who is perfectly capable of being objective about his father-in-law, told me that people were frequently visibly moved by what he had to say, which was usually simple and easily comprehensible. 'The effect was quasi-religious; people would gather round.' A grandson, Damian Hicks, who had some experience of travelling abroad with his grandfather, wrote that 'he could move conference members to tears with a speech, construed from one long stream of dictation.'

He addressed numerous audiences on the misery and waste caused by unnecessary blindness and other preventable disabilities. But he was always delighted when humour intruded into the necessarily grim story, as we have seen. In 1978, he went with his daughter, Claire (Hicks), to a Lions International Convention which he had been invited to address in a stadium built for the Tokyo Olympics. He was told that there were twenty-eight thousand people in the audience. After his speech the Brazilian president of the Convention clapped him on the back 'and,' says Wilson, 'reduced Claire and me to hysteria by saying "you are now receiving a standing ovulation".'

His effectiveness in presentation owed a good deal to sheer hard work. He prepared all his public appearances carefully; his speeches often went through several drafts; and he usually kept Braille notes in his pocket to assist delivery. He was skilful at judging his audience, which must have involved a good deal of prior thought since he could not see them, and adjusting his style correspondingly. He would often insert a joke early in a speech so that he could judge from the laughter how many people were in the audience and how they were distributed in the building. Whether he was appealing for funds to a gathering of potential donors or trying to persuade a United Nations body to take a new decision or attempting to shift the traditional attitudes of the ophthalmic profession, he fitted his themes and words to his listeners with considerable subtlety. It is true that the same images, phrases and jokes recur fairly often, but that is only a mistake when an audience feels it has heard the speech before and I do not think that happened in the case of Wilson. It is pretty rare in public life for a speaker to attract no criticism of the quality of his or her speechmaking. I have heard none of Wilson's.

He was also an effective and regular broadcaster. From the early days of the Society he would make radio appeals for funds. Later, he would take part in more extensive programmes, usually about his travels. In 1967, the producer of the BBC African service wrote to him to thank him for 'one of the most impressive pieces of radio description I've ever heard'. Another BBC presenter comments on his 'capacity for painting word pictures; I never managed to find another traveller with his gift for evocative description of his experience.'

At Worcester, Wilson had believed he might devote himself to writing. It was largely because of a fascination with words that he had begun keeping a diary. He had also begun to write poetry, as I have mentioned. At Oxford, and subsequently, his ambition to write remained quite strong and his passion for poetry, and literature more generally, continued. But his poetry remained largely private. He would occasionally read to his family a poem with which he was especially pleased but in general, Jean apart, they had little access to his verse. Apart from official publications, he wrote only one book. His talent for using words was diverted, and very productively too, into his speechmaking and the abundant high-quality reports and analyses which he produced in the course of his work. He also wrote a large number of articles about his professional activities. The library of the Royal National Institute of the Blind contains more than seventy.

Clearly, he was a consummate publicist. Some go so far as to say that he was, first and foremost, a 'PR man', a salesman. Others say that he was not above shading the facts to support his case. The latter point has substance. But which advocate of a good cause has not been a little guilty of doing so? His embellishments of the facts were a very pale reflection of the modern scourge of 'spin-doctoring'. His ends were always admirable. I do not doubt that he was a brilliant presenter but I would defend him against the charge of being only, or even primarily, a showman. What fired him was primarily a cause, not the pleasure of self-display on the big occasion. Nor can he ever be accused of the shallowness that often characterizes the contemporary 'skill' of presentation. He thought deeply, not only about his work but about his relationships, about life and about the world.

When she interviewed him for 'Desert Island Discs', Sue Lawley suggested that he was 'one of life's doers'. She was right but Wilson modestly disclaimed the description. He went on to add, 'I don't do things because of a philosophy. I've never been able to develop a philosophy. You build one thing on top of another and see if it works. If it does, you try to repeat it.' He may have liked to see him-self as a pure pragmatist, but I believe that was only part of his approach to life. He had a core of beliefs that informed much of his behaviour and action and probably *did* amount to a philosophy.

He had been brought up in a rigidly Methodist family. But it is evident from his diary that by the time he was a teenager he found that inheritance too constraining. When at Oxford he usually attended Anglican services. Shortly after his marriage to Jean he joined the Anglican Church. I suggested earlier that there was always a degree of tension between his Methodist roots and the attractions of Anglicanism. A puritan streak was detectable in him, despite his relish for some of the good things of life. In 1955, back home from Central Africa, he meditated on the welcome sense of permanence produced by his home and family and wrote: 'Avoiding the scourge of asceticism, it is our task to develop our individuality and cultivate its awareness and integrity.' He could joke about this inner tension too. Commenting on the 'black art of fundraising', he once said that, having been brought up as a Methodist, he regarded lotteries as a manifestation of the devil, but that if one produced half a million pounds for his cause, that was beyond his resistance point.

His travels brought him into contact with other religions and creeds – Buddhist, Hindu, Islamic and others. He studiously sought to understand their beliefs and developed the view that there was good in every religion which should be respected and celebrated. But his own choice was clear. In a sermon delivered at his home church of Rottingdean in 1976, he said, 'Amongst all religions it is surely the Christian religion that most recognizes the status and the integrity and the worth of each separate human being.' He had, he continued, tried to understand something of the wonder of other cultures. But, 'how fortunate we are to have inherited a faith which does not impose on its believers an intolerable weight of ritual or a pantheon of improbable Gods.' Our reverence is for life, he once said, adding, 'but reverence also, surely, for the achievements of human life: art, philosophy, science and the wild, true leap of religious insight. That these achievements also evolved from our biological make-up is a matter not only for wonder but also for faith and a cause for optimism.'

Christianity's emphasis on individual worth linked with and informed his work on blindness. Throughout his life, as the statistics of world blindness became clearer and more overwhelming, he insisted – much as he loved statistics – that it was the individuals behind the statistics who mattered. Time and again in his speeches, having sketched the numerical scale of a problem, he would bring his audience back to the human reality: 'People don't go blind in millions. They go blind individually...It will soon be morning in Northern Ghana. From those river blindness villages, the blind farmers, with their bamboo canes, will be walking to their fields. Blind women will carry the water buckets, feeling along a hemp rope which leads them to the well...' (Yes, these images have appeared before in this account. But Wilson returned to them often both because they had made a deep impression on him when he first went to the 'country of the blind' and because they illustrated so well the effects of unnecessary blindness.)

The treatment and care of such individuals was more than a moral obligation, in his view. It was their right. Where the opportunity existed to restore to a human being a lost function, perhaps of the eye, that person had a right to its restoration. And if that was not possible, he or she had a right to, not just a need for, the maximum degree of integration with his or her family and community that was possible for an individual. As described earlier, Wilson's lifetime saw a shift in world attitudes from treating disabled persons as objects of charity to emphasizing the rights of the disabled. The process is not complete but it should be noted again that Wilson was an early advocate of a rights-based approach.

Dr Venkataswamy, the Indian eye surgeon, used to discuss religion with him. He told me that he felt Wilson was more spiritual than religious. 'He was so wide you could not confine him to national or religious boundaries. He was more interested in the spiritual core of religion than its external manifestation, whether a man is sensitive to his soul'. I think there is something in this. I do not doubt Wilson's devotion to the Church of England, whose services he attended regularly and in whose churches he often preached. But a good deal of his spiritual inspiration seems to have come from above and beyond orthodox Anglicanism.

In 1973 he wrote: 'I have an awareness, amounting almost to a conviction, that there is in our life an intermingling spiritual significance, an outreach, a faintly-glimpsed totality. I accept this as I recognize consciousness and existence, something understood, beyond the possibility of proof or the need of validation. This awareness is dimmed by the detailed business of life but never totally exhausted. We live on two planes and our consciousness is for the most part adjusted to the physical. We see through a glass darkly because, perhaps, otherwise the dazzle of absolute awareness would make daily life impossible. We glimpse the other existence briefly, disturbingly, experiencing it only in part, in the mysteries of contemplation, the best appreciation of art, in the experience of love.'

He came to share with Dr V a conviction that, in his work and life, he was not a free agent. In 1985, he delivered a sermon on the same text as his father had used in 1931, following the accident that blinded him: 'All things work together for good to them that love God'. He gave an account of his efforts to deal with the problem of blindness and told the congregation that, throughout, he had been conscious of a sense of guidance. In 1999, a few months before he died, he stated, in the same church using the same text: 'I can truly say that, throughout these years, we have been aware, often against all rationality, of what I can only describe as a sense of guidance and, so often, in advance of focused judgement, an awareness of moving towards an objective.'

Wilson could not have continued for many years to devote his tireless energy to his daunting tasks without the optimism that was part of his personality. The text chosen for his Scarborough sermons quoted above is one way of expressing it. He was also fond of quoting Julian of Norwich: 'All things will be well and all manner of things shall be well.' And he found a passage in the works of the French Jesuit philosopher, Teilhard de Chardin, which must have struck a strong chord with him because he would cite it often: 'Men will one day harness the energies of gravity, of ether, of the winds and tides, and then the day will come when they will harness the energies of love – and on that day, for the second time in the history of mankind, man will have discovered fire.' There is, Wilson told the BBC World Service in 1983, 'no alternative to optimism in this tinder-box world'.

That positive approach to life carried him through many difficulties and the practical problems of dealing with governments, bureaucracies and vested interests, and with resistance from the unimaginative and the uncommitted. It sustained him, too, during his incessant world travels. Damian Hicks, his grandson, accompanied him on a journey through South-East Asia in 1992. 'I saw a man reacting with equanimity to the inconvenience of unknown terrain, difficult climates, jet-lag, stomach upsets, hellish transport and sandwiches unexpectedly containing cucumber.'

While Wilson's diary is often, inevitably, introspective, and while his days tended to be dominated by his work, Wilson had a zest for life that many found infectious and an important part of his personality. He once wrote a poem based on the Greek legend of the boatman who ferries souls across the river between life and death:

> 'Mix not that Lethe drug of yours so strong
> That we forget the wonder of the world,
> Its beauty, and its laughter and its song
> And the togetherness of love.'

His many accounts of his travels show a thirst for knowledge, an enthusiasm for people and places, a restless search for new experiences, sensations and ideas and, never far away, a sense of the humorous. 'He was fun,' says Miriam Benn, his Oxford girlfriend. 'He was funny,' says one member of the Society's staff. 'He had an innate sense of fun,' says another. Geoffrey Salisbury, who worked with him for so long in Africa, found that in many uncomfortable situations they faced together, for example when their jeep was bogged down late at night in a malarial swamp, it was Wilson's sense of humour that saw them safely through until the dawn.

Blindness was not an obstacle to his humour. It often fuelled it. Once, when he was staying in a hotel in Ghana, he noticed 'two old coasters...who used to take bets on whether I would make it without knocking over the plant-pots. They were good enough at the end of my stay to pay the winnings into the local fund for the blind.' In Bangladesh, he went to a Chinese restaurant with a group of Bangladeshi friends, including Monsur Choudhuri who had also been blinded as a child and was associated with John Wilson in many endeavours. As they were about to start their meal there was a power failure and the lights went out. Wilson spoke, 'The rest of you will have to wait until the light comes on. Monsur and I will begin our soup straightaway.' He used to tell a charming story of rehearsing for a radio fundraising appeal so often that when he sleepily told a fairy story to his small daughter early one morning, she asked 'But Daddy, why did you end by saying "please send as much money as you can spare"?'

Music mattered to him. Since school days he had played the tenor saxophone and piano accordion, and later he played the piano. He collected recordings and listened to music a good deal, especially at weekends. His taste was catholic, ranging from the classics to the Beatles and Bob Dylan. His choice of music for his 'Desert Island Discs' programme is not as revealing as it might have been since the pieces were obviously chosen mainly to reflect the various stages of his life: Duke Ellington's 'Basin Street Blues', which he had played on the tenor saxophone at Worcester; 'Jesu, Joy of Man's Desiring', which reminded him of Oxford; Schubert's C Major Symphony, which he had listened to in the Albert Hall in London during a bombing raid; the drums of Burundi, reminiscent of Africa; the water music of India; a John Ireland song, selected because the words attracted him; and a calypso called 'Last Train to San Fernando', which evoked the Caribbean and blind calypso players. The last piece he chose was Bach's B Minor Mass, the musical composition he favoured above all. He spoke of 'the soaring, swaying magnificence of the Credo' and 'the great, swaying, surging, wonderful acclaim of life in the Sanctus'.

He listened to the radio all his life. He had, says the family, a radio in every room and another in his dressing-gown pocket. He almost never missed the news. He listened to plays and poetry and loved 'The Archers', the BBC's long-running radio serial about country life.

Telephoning was almost a hobby. Of course, he used the telephone a great deal for his work. He was in constant contact with fellow workers in his field, whether in India, Africa, the United States or anywhere else, enquiring, encouraging, pressurizing. He greatly preferred this form of communication to letter writing and, when he was at home, the telephone would ring at all hours. Overseas contacts got used to the fact that he did not mind being rung up, regardless of the time difference, partly perhaps because in later life he did not sleep all that well. When he retired from the Society in 1984, his successor, the late Alan Johns, and his wife, Joan, found that their nights were frequently interrupted by calls from across the world until they managed to educate callers to the fact that their own preference was to sleep at night.

His daughters used to read to him a good deal, up to the end of his life. They had to read at a speed of knots because he absorbed words so quickly. He found the commercial talking-books service unsatisfactory since acting tended to replace pure reading. He preferred a plain text to be read to him straight and fast while he concentrated intensively and took it all in. He liked *Private Eye*, the *Times Literary Supplement*, the *New Scientist*, the *Economist* and the *Investors' Chronicle*. He enjoyed detective stories for light relief, and he sometimes chose novels from the talking-books service despite its frustrations. The diary shows him reading philosophy, religious thought and a good deal of poetry.

His skill in story telling, which his contemporaries at Worcester remember so well, never diminished and was put to good use as his grandchildren began to appear on the scene. He was also very imaginative in the games he invented for children's parties. Indeed, he was fond of games generally. The family played cards, using the Braille design, and a version of the game of charades that does not depend on the ability to see (The action is spoken, not mimed, and the key words of the phrase being presented are buried in the speech.) He was fond of chess and chose a chess strategy book to take to his 'desert island' along with the supplied texts of the Bible and Shakespeare (which, he told Sue Lawley, 'would have to be in Braille and would run to 127 volumes').

He was always game to do a little work in the garden but he was not perhaps an entirely dedicated gardener. He was fond of drinking wine and usually selected personally the wine for the evening meal. He also made his own wine enthusiastically though it is doubtful whether his family's enjoyment of it quite matched his own confidence in its quality. He enjoyed whisky, especially Chivas Regal, but controlled his intake carefully. His grandson, Damian, writes: 'Conspiratorially and ceremoniously handed another thimble of Cointreau at approximately half the legal age for alcoholic consumption, I was righteously instructed that he had never been drunk and never wanted to be.'

He was rather squeamish about the food he ate. Despite all his exposure to other cultures he had a strong preference for plain English food. He did not like spices. Garlic was excluded from the table because he did not like its smell. Perhaps it was his very experience of foreign travel that limited his tastes. Most of us have to be careful what we eat when we travel if we are not to have those tedious stomach upsets that so disrupt activity. If you cannot see what you are eating you have to be doubly careful. John Wilson's caution did not extend to chocolates and biscuits which he would squirrel away in notable quantities, always keeping a never-empty biscuit tin under his side of the bed.

He loved to walk. He and Jean walked together a great deal, in Devon, Ireland and elsewhere. The South Downs were favourite terrain and his best-loved route of all was the Seven Sisters Walk on the Sussex coast near Brighton. He was a keen swimmer. When he returned home in the summer from work by train and bus the family would often meet him and proceed to the beach to bathe. His swimming was of the vigorous variety. If you were wise, you kept out of the way.

Most of all, he loved his home and family, far beyond the conventional affection that many profess. In 1955 the Wilsons had searched for a home outside London because Claire suffered severely from asthma. The ideal requirements were chalk, sand and no morning mists. Jean eventually found a house on the south coast just outside Brighton, a long, low and attractive building with a garden that sloped down towards the sea, with sea views not then, as now, partly obstructed by buildings. When they moved in, Wilson was lyrical: 'Such a sense of freedom here, freedom and air. The wind carries a sense of salt from the sea and the springy downs grass smells of thyme. At night the swish and wash of the sea. The wind blows organ-notes from the verandah'. 'I love the cold, pure air of the Sussex coast,' he wrote, contrasting this with the 'New Forest with its convoluted, coiling, breeding trees' (where, I might mention, I am at home, happily writing this book).

He lived in this house for the rest of his life and it was a constant source of peace and refreshment. He knew every inch of it and felt comfortable there as nowhere else. A life of physically and mentally demanding work and travel is much more supportable if there is a loved home to return to. *Travelling Blind* ends with the words: 'Whenever I return home after a long journey there is an instant re-discovery. In that instant, between two ticks of the grandfather clock, the house is as unfamiliar as the day Jean and I first found it; each piece of furniture has a sharp new existence, my children are exciting strangers. This is the circle as the outsider would see it. The clock ticks again, the circle has opened and closed – and in the whole turning world there is nowhere I would rather be. For a while I feel exempt from that Commandment, which I have such difficulty in obeying, that I should love the world as I love this place.'

Throughout his life he had a strong sense of family. He delighted in his relationship with his father, George, and his mother, Norrie. They died in 1962 and 1967 respectively, and his brother, Ernest, died in 1975. John then became the focal point of the family. He put much effort into maintaining regular contact with its numerous members. He was fascinated by the family tree and helped Claire to update it in the 1970s. Large family gatherings were invited to Brighton from time to time. They sometimes had an organized quality. On his eightieth birthday in 1999, twenty-six members of the family came, each commissioned to remember some incident of their childhood and to exchange memories. Not, you may think, altogether relaxing. But then there is a sense in which Wilson never relaxed. It was not something he was good at. He liked constant activity. 'Restless throughout his life,' is the comment of one who knew him well in the international arena. If he did manage some re-laxation on family holidays abroad, even then it was common for large quantities of Braille to be sent ahead for him to read and he would take a tape recorder to record his thoughts, though not at the expense of joining in family games and swimming expeditions.

If he set very high standards for himself, he did so for others too, not excluding his family. He always wanted to understand what his daughters and their husbands and children were thinking and doing. Both with them and with people outside the family his method of achieving this was to question, to challenge, to provoke, with an intensity of thought and concentration that was one of his most striking characteristics. He would play devil's advocate to deepen the argument. He wanted the young members of the family to form opinions on issues and be heard. Damian Hicks told me that he was about five years old when Wilson asked him whether *homo sapiens* was still evolving and about seven when asked for his views on euthanasia.

But that was only part of Wilson's personality. His affection for his children and his genuine interest in them were doubted by no one. He always made time to talk things through with them and help them through the inevitable bad patches. Claire and Jane recall a very happy childhood, enriched by family outings and holidays, by imaginative bedtime stories, by shared reading and by their father's warm embrace and his special habit of kissing the palm of their hands and enfolding their fingers on that kiss, telling them to keep it safe until they were together again. From an early age, when they were apart, the girls wrote to him in Braille and received type-written letters back. He was always in touch by phone, too.

Children and grandchildren alike recall his skill in imitating the sounds of birds, good enough to produce responses from the genuine article from time to time. When he wished to draw the family's attention from a distance, his signature tune was an imitation of a bird song heard on his African travels.

The many attractive features of his personality were mixed with a certain inherent tension, a degree of stubbornness and occasional testiness. Was he lovable then? The evidence is positive. Some foreign friends and close members of his staff, have, unprompted, used precisely that word in describing him to me. So, not surprisingly, have his family.

I marvel at the confidence with which many writers describe relationships between people they have never known. All experience suggests that, even when you are personally acquainted with two people, much of how they feel and think about each other is hidden, and not readily open to outside inspection. In the case of John and Jean Wilson three sources are available – John's own views as recorded in his diary and other writings, Jean's comments and the observations of those who knew them.

When he was recording part of his diary in 1991, Wilson played the tape to his wife. She told him that it was much too intimate for anyone else to read. Wilson decided that he must respect her privacy and edit the entries. He thought it was a pity to do so because they were 'full of joy and grace and awakening'. In the material that survived his editing he always speaks with special tenderness of this relationship. Thus, in the early 1940s, he writes of 'the wonderful and holy advent of Jean in my life and the exciting and happy days leading up to our marriage'. He found their marriage 'an incredible and preposterously undeserved discovery,' enhanced by the adventure of parenthood and the birth of their children. Love illuminated things and events for him. When the Second World War ended in 1945, he recorded 'an extraordinary feeling of liberation and freedom of spirit again, augmented for Jean and me by the beauty, peace and incredible happiness of our marriage'. He found it almost unthinkable that in 1946 he should be proposing to leave for Africa without her. But they discussed the plan and decided he should do it. As soon as the children could be left behind, they almost invariably travelled together.

There are attractive glimpses of the couple in later diary entries. Returning home from a journey in 1955, Wilson found it 'wonderful to be back in this lovely house which seems hallowed by the happy presence of Jean and our two wonderful children.' At another point, he describes how Jean and he ran through the sea below their house with Jean singing 'A Road to the Isles', 'as she so often does when she is happy.' Then, on a visit to Glyndebourne to hear *Così Fan Tutte*, he describes 'a still summer evening with all the flowers in perfume. Roses, tobacco plants, orange blossom and a remarkable waxy tropical lily with a great heavy scent which Jean helped me to feel. And, finally, round a corner a perfume I thought must be another of those tropical lilies. I wanted to feel that too but Jean said, "You had better not. It's a perfumed lady, a member of the audience".' These are but a small selection of the happy shared memories that emerge from Wilson's diary.

Of course, it is unlikely that their marriage, any more than others, was one of total and unsullied harmony. There must have been awkwardnesses, problems, anxieties, but Wilson does not record them. Even members of the family found it hard to penetrate this relationship. The two were so close that they seemed at times to shut the rest of the world out. John was very protective of Jean and would not allow their children to confront her in argument.

What began as an intimate personal relationship became, and endured as, a close working relationship as well, as we have seen. Dictating from his diaries in 1993, Wilson put on record a statement of Jean's contribution: 'Throughout the whole work and growth of the Society, Jean was the indispensable partner. We travelled a million miles together, discussed together every decision and every new plan, far, far beyond just encouragement but in the fullest sense of participation . . . From 1967 onwards, when Jean joined the Society's staff, first in charge of funding and public relations, and then later on as Deputy Director, she played an altogether indispensable part in developing so rapidly the resources of the Society, and, through her talent for human relations, adding an indispensable human face to the whole work and effort of the organization.'

Their friends and acquaintances are in no doubt about the solidity of either the personal or working relationship. But it is harder to decide precisely what each brought to it. Certainly, Jean compensated for many of the shortcomings John's blindness might have caused. She described to him the visual world around him, and the people in it, in astonishing detail. Many of his brilliant descriptions of people and places could not have been written without her. Then, over the years, they discovered methods of reading and research that enabled them to cover together a range of subjects which would probably not have been possible for each of them separately. It is clear from the observations of their circle of acquaintances that it was John who produced the main ideas for the Society's work and decided the nature of its programme. He wrote the speeches and became the public face of the Society. But they always discussed everything together and Jean would question and challenge.

She was no mere follower. She had a mind of her own and made distinct contributions to their joint work. Her successful development of the Society's fundraising and her publicity work, including her photography, were mentioned earlier. She used these public relations skills in 1975 to help the World Health Organization produce an international publicity campaign in more than eighty countries on the theme 'Foresight Prevents Blindness'. In the early 1980s she played a major role in the formation of a consortium of non-governmental organizations concerned to prevent rubella by raising the level of immunization. She became chair of the National Rubella

Council in Britain, was for a time vice-president of Hearing International and a Council member and subsequently became president of the United Kingdom Impact Foundation.

Her intellectual ability, personal skills, shrewdness and practical common sense were rich elements in the working partnership with John. Some feel that her own achievements have been overshadowed by his. While her loyalty to his memory is such that she would reject the suggestion, I think it is right to underline her own part in the scheme of things. Given that John was the orator, the negotiator, the presenter and the advocate, and given that it was his charismatic personality that drew people to the Society, it was inevitable that Jean would at times appear to be in his shadow but I suspect it was a place where she was perfectly content to be.

It was a strong combination. Wilson well knew that a blind man alone has many limitations, but he also believed that, with an intellectual seeing partner, he could in many respects cease to be disabled. Jean was that partner. Asked on a television programme what he would like to be in his next incarnation, he did not give the expected answer, 'A man with his sight restored', but 'I would like to be my wife's next husband.'

In 1984 this man, who claimed to have no philosophy, penned for himself a document that is both a creed and a statement of experience. He entitled it 'Maturity' and describes it as a 'rather solemn poem'. But it is best read as prose:

'To have tried on every mask and eventually to have confidence to walk unmasked.

Having experienced many places, to appreciate, in its infinite variety, one's own place.

To achieve, for one's dependants and oneself, an adequacy but to recognize its transitoriness and to hold possession lightly.

Having explored the potential of temperament and mind, to be able to maximize that potential and to harmonize its power into a way of equanimity.

From various experiences and study, to crystallize principles of conduct and judgement without losing the curiosity of the seeker nor the zest for enlightenment.

Despite failure, to retain hope and the capacity for new enchantment.

To fear neither life nor death and, whilst seeking mitigation of suffering, to accept the inevitability of loss.

To revere beauty and art without being obsessed by them and to recognize a supremacy of the art of human understanding.

Having explored love to have found with one person, in humour and grace, the limit of understanding and fidelity; yet to recognize without fear the aloneness of one's individual being and to respect that aloneness in others.

To despise no manifestation of love.

To see the compassionate face and active force of God in every religion and, having chosen one way, to approach holy ground there – in the uncertain light of inadequate understanding – to see the majesty of God.

To feel the inter-relationship of all things with compassion for all humanity.'

This is not one of his clearest statements. Admittedly, he is attempting to express complex ideas. But the sometimes obscure phrasing and choice of words suggest that he found considerable difficulty in conveying his innermost thoughts. That said, the passage does illuminate many of the most important features of the man: his drive to maximize personal potential, his optimism in the face of failure, his gratitude for the love found in his marriage coupled with a respect for individuality, his belief in the value of all religions but confidence about his own choice, and his compassion for humanity.

Introspective reflection always played a part in his life. But in truth it was action more than meditation that defined the man. He is unlikely to be remembered for his philosophy or his poetry. But he will be remembered by countless people in many places across the world for a life of action and its results.

Chapter 8

The Legacy

The eightieth year of John Wilson's life, 1999, was, as usual, packed with work and activity. His visits to Bangladesh, Egypt and Japan were mentioned earlier. In September, he was unable to attend the Sixth General Assembly of the IAPB in Beijing, which was attended by 600 participants from fifty-seven countries, because he had just had an operation to replace a hip. Later in the year he was planning a trip to Prague.

24 November began as a normal day. His secretary came to his home as usual. He had a long talk on the telephone about his Japanese trip with David Williams, a former trustee and vice-president of the Society. In the afternoon, he went to see his heart specialist, from whom he had been receiving treatment for about ten years for an angina condition. In the evening, Claire joined John and Jean for the evening meal. John decided to cook a special supper in the microwave. Among other things, he and Claire talked about a project Impact was organizing to develop a new low-cost, digitally-programmable hearing aid, using solar-powered batteries, which was to be assembled at Aravind in South India.

When Claire left at about 11 pm, John loaded the dishwasher and he and Jean went to bed. They talked about their grandchildren one by one and then slept. Later, John woke with a bad cough. Jean rang the heart specialist and summoned an ambulance. But John died of heart failure.

The heavy blow of his death was intensified by its unexpectedness. The Indian ophthalmologist, Dr Venkataswamy, said that Wilson's sudden death was a great loss in his life. Dr Pararjasegaram, the WHO expert, said that those involved in the prevention of disability felt orphaned.

The funeral, for family and friends, took place at St Margaret's Church, Rottingdean on 1 December. On 23 March 2000, a memorial service was held at Southwark Cathedral which was packed with family, friends and former colleagues from many countries and several religions. It was a perfect English spring day. The sun shone. Daffodils were flowering and the trees were blossoming. Jane Martin, his younger daughter, read the words quoted towards the end of Chapter Seven, John Wilson's 1984 summary of his philosophy, which included the lines: 'To fear neither life nor death and, whilst seeking mitigation of suffering, to accept the inevitability of loss,' and 'To see the compassionate face and active force of God in every religion and, having chosen one way, to approach holy ground there – in the uncertain light of inadequate understanding – to see the majesty of God.'

A nephew, the Reverend David James, gave an address of thanksgiving for John Wilson's life. He quoted a message from the Philippines, one of the many received from abroad, describing him as 'the moving spirit who inspired everyone, the wind beneath our wings' and suggested that his legacy was to be found 'in his life's work, effective organizations and initiatives across the world which are dedicated to helping disabled people to find a fulfilling life in programmes which prevent blindness, restore hearing, increase mobility, reduce the rate of infant mortality, inoculate against deadly disease and empower many of the world's poorest people to contribute richly to life.'

Claire Hicks spoke on the theme 'A Legacy of Hope', quoting words her father had recently written: 'At the dawn of the new Millennium, prevention of needless disability is an option, a refreshing force for change, for hope, for potential action which could conserve the quality of human life now and for future generations.' A lesson was read by Lord (Alf) Morris of Manchester, a tireless campaigner on disability throughout a long parliamentary life, and a tribute was paid by Peter White, the BBC presenter often referred to in this book.

A memorial fund was established, the proceeds of which were to be used by Impact, Sight Savers (the Society's more familiar name since 1986) and other organizations to train people in medicine, education and management for the prevention of disability. Some £60,000 was eventually raised and projects were financed in Bangladesh, Pakistan, Nepal, Myanmar, Cambodia, Tanzania and Ghana. In America the trustees of Helen Keller Worldwide adopted a Resolution in John Wilson's honour, recalling that 'his luminous vision had served as an inspiration to his colleagues for more than

THE LEGACY

five decades,' and deciding to create a 'Sir John Wilson Fund for the
Future'.

An annual international memorial lecture series was instituted by
the World Eye Surgeons' Society, the first being delivered in 2000 by
the renowned Chinese ophthalmologist, Professor Yuan Jia-Qin, on
the elimination of cataract blindness in China.

Over the years, Wilson's achievements had been recognized by
a series of awards and honours. So numerous were these that I
mention only a selection. In Britain, he was made an OBE in 1955
and a CBE in 1965, and he was knighted in 1975. In 1991, the
Richard T. Hewitt Award of the Royal Society of Medicine and the
(American) Royal Society of Medicine Foundation was conferred
on him. Five years after that he and Jean jointly received the Hard-
ing Award, that was presented for outstanding work of immediate
and future benefit to disabled people, previous holders of which
included Lord Morris and Leonard Cheshire, the founder of the
Cheshire Homes.

But, given John Wilson's long love of Oxford and its importance
in his life, no British honour gave him greater pleasure than that
of Honorary Doctor of Civil Law of the University, conferred in
1995. The citation stated that the Royal Commonwealth Society for
the Blind 'had restored the power of sight to 1,000,000 people,
a benefaction on an almost unimaginable scale.' The University's
Chancellor said: 'I present the helper of the handicapped, the com-
forter of the sick, the unfailing support of the afflicted, Sir John
Wilson.'

As a global figure, his work was recognized by many inter-
national honours, including the Lions International Humanitarian
Award in 1978, the World Humanity Award in 1980, the Rotary
International Presidential Citation in 1984 and the Jose Rizal Gold
Medal of the Asia Pacific Academy of Ophthalmology in 1997, the
latter received jointly with Jean.

And then, of course, there was America. Wilson had always
been excited by the entrepreneurialism, inventiveness, power and
wealth of the United States. But, as he told an American audience in
1992, there was another quality to which he responded even more
readily: 'One of the things I find most exciting, most admirable, is
the optimism of your scientific community, the conviction that the
movement of history is still forward, that there need be no intellectual barrier which may not be crossed by the spirit of enquiry. More

than your power or your money, it is this optimism which most justifies your claim to leadership of the science of the modern world. Never has this optimism been more needed than in this querulous age, wielding Olympian powers in the hands of far from Olympian humans.'

The first American organization formally to mark Wilson's achievements nearly thirty years before his death, had been, fittingly, Helen Keller International. John Wilson did not claim to be an especially close acquaintance of Helen Keller, but they met fairly frequently and corresponded a good deal before her death in 1968 in her eighty-eighth year (sadly the archive containing the correspondence was lost as a result of the terrorist attack on the Twin Towers in New York in 2002). She, too, was an inveterate traveller, visiting thirty-five countries between 1946 and 1957 and embarking, at the age of seventy-five, on a five-month-long tour through Asia. She, too, had blazed a trail to help the disabled. She, like John Wilson, firmly believed that the emphasis must be placed on the *prevention* of disability.

Wilson once described her as follows: 'She has an extraordinary grasp of her impact on people. She knows just what will interest them. There is about her the essence of gaiety and vitality and, in a way, nobility and tranquillity, though it is difficult to avoid the sense that this is a carefully distilled essence, the result of a careful process of education. She leaves an impression on everyone she meets. Some are uncomfortable at the element of constant publicity. Others resent the lump which she raises in their throats. Yet others are uplifted and enriched by her presence.' He used to recall an early UNESCO meeting Helen Keller attended to present the new Braille code which the organization had formulated. She spoke not in English but in French, the first time, he says, that a deaf and blind person had learned a second language. 'The clapping was like the waves of the sea; even the interpreters joined in.'

These memories, and the strong sense of a joint cause, must have been present in Wilson's mind when in 1970 he was presented with the Helen Keller International Award. This had the distinction of not being presented annually or at a given interval of time, but only when an individual emerged whose contribution to the development of services for blind people and for the prevention of blindness, particularly at the international level, was so remarkable as to merit recognition. Only two people had received it before Wilson.

Nine years later, he was presented in New York with the Albert Lasker Special Public Service Award, a highly prestigious American decoration for medicine, conferred in this case 'for his dynamic leadership in organizing practical programs to alleviate, prevent and treat blinding eye disease'. The citation described him as a 'brilliant, dedicated and dynamic international health administrator'. In 1982, again in New York, he received the Pisart Vision Award. In 1987, the Dean's Medal of the Johns Hopkins School of Public Health and Hygiene was conferred on him. In 1989, he was made an honorary member of the International Council of Ophthalmology, the only non-ophthalmologist who had ever been given such membership.

In 1993 he visited Wilmington, North Carolina, to accept the Albert Schweitzer International Award for Medicine. This was presented every four years to those whose work was considered most to have reflected Schweitzer's spirit and ideals. A previous recipient had been Mother Teresa, whom Wilson had met several times in India and found 'amusing and charming'. In his acceptance speech, Wilson thanked the organizers for associating Jean with the award, describing her as his 'guide, philosopher, intellectual stimulus and essential partner'. He obviously found much to admire, and respond to, in Schweitzer's 'life-affirming philosophy', which he had studied for the occasion. He believed that Schweitzer's reverence for life would have led him to see the prevention of disability as part of the global imperative of conservation. As he speculated on the course of human evolution, he referred to 'that transcending mystery, "the white light at the back of the mind to guide us"' (a quote from the poet, Louis MacNeice, which he often used).

Referring to Schweitzer's work on the mysticism of St Paul and his analysis of the concept that the Kingdom of God is within us, Wilson asked: 'Might we go one step further and dare to think that the powers of the Kingdom could potentially be within mankind in a world where science was for healing and communication for understanding?' As so often, he ended his speech on a strong note of hope: 'As we approach the new Millennium, let us venture upon optimism. Maybe we are fallen angels, but still, thank God, with wings that can lift towards the sunrise.'

This array of awards, international and domestic, together with the praise and admiration of friends and colleagues that were displayed at the time of John Wilson's death, are a powerful testimony to his achievements. But beyond the heady oratory of citations and ceremonies lie harder facts. There are more rigorous tests we can apply in determining how significant his legacy is. One of his Indian colleagues said to me recently: 'It is not what John did. It is what he continues to do.' A few days later I was in Southern India, being conducted round the facility at Aravind where disability aids of one kind and another are manufactured for use in India and many other countries. As I looked at a partly assembled low-cost hearing aid, the words of my Indian informant came back to me. It was another Wilson project continuing after his death. This small example illustrates a test worth conducting on a larger scale: take the organizations Wilson founded, or was instrumental in founding, and examine what they are contributing today to the effort to cure and prevent disability.

One of his earlier schemes, it will be recalled, was to establish in each of the then British colonies an organization to work on problems of blindness. Initially branches of the Society, these organizations were to become autonomous and more often than not they were affiliated to the Society. Much has changed since those days. Most of the organizations have had their ups and downs. But a number are still in existence decades later and work actively to prevent and cure blindness. In Kenya, for example, the Society for the Blind hosts and runs the secretariat of the Kenya Ophthalmic Programme, provides a network of rehabilitation workers and promotes integrated education for blind children. Similar societies are active in Ghana and elsewhere in Africa and in a number of Asian countries such as Bangladesh, Malaysia and Singapore. In the Caribbean, the Council for the Blind is still a key organization and a number of national societies continue to work there as well.

A description and assessment of the activities of all these bodies alone would fill a book, but it is certainly the case that their work, over in many cases half a century, has helped to cure hundreds of thousands of cases of visual impairment, has prevented large numbers of people from going blind and has aided the education and rehabilitation of many irreversibly blind people. There is no precise way of apportioning part of that achievement to Wilson but without his efforts in the 1950s and 1960s many of the organizations would not have been established at that time and, in some cases, perhaps never.

One of the more remarkable examples is the Hong Kong Society for the Blind, whose offices I visited in 2004. I have described the dismay Wilson felt when in the 1950s he first saw the inadequate institutions for blind people in the British colony and the way in which he responded to Hong Kong's request for help by seconding a social worker who played a major role in establishing the Hong Kong Society for the Blind in 1957. It now occupies a large and elegant building in Kowloon from which it administers state of the art facilities for the visually impaired people of Hong Kong, runs mobile clinics in mainland China and also directs the work of the Asian Foundation for the Prevention of Blindness, which was itself a Wilson initiative and for which he helped to raise 10,000,000 Hong Kong dollars in one evening in 1981. It is of course hard to believe that Hong Kong, with its enterprise, efficiency and wealth, would not in due course have done much of this without Wilson's assistance. But that is idle speculation. The fact is that at a crucial stage of its existence, he helped a major charity which for nearly fifty years has produced highly beneficial results. Some of that achievement is John Wilson's.

Perhaps the principal part of the Wilson legacy lies in the continuing activity of the Royal Commonwealth Society for the Blind. In 1986 the Society was selected for a charity promotion by the BBC television programme for children, 'Blue Peter'. In the course of the programme-making the media experts complained that the Society's name was too much of a mouthful and did not convey sharply enough what its functions were. It was then that they proposed 'Sight Savers', this being a readily recognizable and easily memorable label. The name stuck. While formally and legally the organization is still the Royal Commonwealth Society for the Blind, it is now generally known as Sight Savers International.

Not everyone was happy with the change. Some felt that the historical title was so well established, so replete with memories, that it should not be modified in any way. Some argued that, in any case, 'Sight Savers' was an inaccurate description of the organization's role. The last point was, to an extent, correct. While the Society's main focus was certainly on preventing and curing blindness, the name did not encompass the work the organization did, and still does, for visually impaired people in terms of rehabilitation and education. But then the more formal title was not accurate either. The Society, from the beginning, had been more than an organization 'for the blind'. Its main objective quickly became one of preventing people going blind, or curing them if they were blind. The two titles, taken together, represent rather well what the modern Society does; but the term Sight Savers is now irreversibly fixed in the public mind – or that part of the public mind that thinks about these things – and I shall use it from now on.

An assessment of Sight Savers' work over the years is fundamental to an appreciation of the Wilson legacy. We have seen how he transformed a paper concept into the original working Society and then led it and built it up over thirty-four years. It is now, in 2006, fifty-six years old. What has it achieved?

At this point, statistics become unavoidable. Professor Alfred Sommer, Dean of Johns Hopkins Bloomberg School of Public Health, and a close colleague of Wilson, once heard him reciting some figures about the number of children in Bangladesh at imminent risk of blindness through vitamin A deficiency and asked him where the data had come from. Wilson told him not to quibble over data, just get on with the job. The broad figures Wilson often used in his speeches may sometimes have lacked a rigorous statistical basis. On the other hand, as seen earlier, it was he above all who pestered the WHO into beginning the task of providing reliable data on the global problems of visual impairment and he was always concerned, when addressing a practical task, to base it on the best data possible. Certainly, much effort at the Society's headquarters went into the collection and analysis of such figures. Nowadays, methods have been refined and great care is taken to produce reliable statistics.

Sight Savers calculates that, since the Society's foundation in 1950, its efforts have resulted in the treatment of over 65,000,000 people for potentially blinding conditions and the restoration of sight to well over 5,000,000 people. In the year 2004 alone, working through its partners, it helped 15,000,000, which included over 11,000,000 who were protected against river blindness and over 3,000,000 patients who were treated for various eye problems, over 200,000 of whom had eye operations. In addition, nearly 5,600 visually impaired people received training in mobility, orientation and life skills and some 7,600 blind and low-vision children were helped to receive mainstream education.

The need for trained staff in the developing world remains acute. In 2004 Sight Savers helped to train nearly 71,500 people in eye care and rehabilitation, ranging from community volunteers to specialist teachers and cataract surgeons.

Mounting statistics may dull the reader's mind as much as the writer's. However, it is worth reflecting on what just one new cataract surgeon can achieve in the rest of his or her career or on the transforming effect which other trained personnel can bring to the lives of those whom they will treat or teach in their professional lifetimes. The multiplier effect is good to contemplate. By the same token, the multiplier effect of Wilson's work throughout his life, and now beyond it, is impossible to calculate but it certainly changed for the better and often transformed the lives of tens of millions, and possibly several hundred millions. Such a statement could not, I suggest, be made with much confidence about many personalities of today or from the past. This achievement alone justifies the statement of one of his obituarists that he was one of the greatest humanitarians of the twentieth century.

Sight Savers is a much larger organization now than when John Wilson stood down as director in 1984. In 2004, its total income, excluding gifts in kind, was just over £23,000,000, still coming mostly from individual donors in the United Kingdom. It worked in thirty-two countries, nine in the Caribbean, four in South Asia and nineteen in Africa, its largest programmes being in India, Pakistan and Bangladesh and, in Africa, Kenya, Malawi, Ghana and Nigeria. It remained strongly orientated towards Commonwealth countries, but eight of the thirty (Togo, Guinea, Mali, Senegal, Guinea Bissau, Benin, Liberia and Haiti) were not members of the Commonwealth. Eye problems, like other things, do not stop at borders and, as John Wilson pointed out, it often makes sense to extend programmes into adjoining countries.

Unsurprisingly, policies and techniques have changed a good deal since Wilson's time with the Society. Today Sight Savers has about 175 staff working overseas, nearly all of them citizens of the countries where they work. At its Haywards Heath headquarters it has about 90 employees. The whole thrust of the organization's work now is to build up local capacity. Only when a developing country has acquired the facilities and trained staff it needs to provide the whole range of eye services can there be confidence that eye problems will be brought under control, and that people who are irreversibly blind will be properly assisted. Short-term projects run by white-gowned Western doctors may be photogenic and catch the headlines, but they are not a fundamental solution. So Sight

Savers, as a matter of policy, no longer conducts direct operations but instead provides finance, equipment, training and other forms of help to partner organizations in the country concerned so that they in turn can provide the necessary services. A partner will sometimes be one of those autonomous societies founded by Wilson half a century ago. However, it may be any one of a large range of candidates – a ministry of health, a church, a hospital, or a local non-governmental organization. In the smaller countries there may be just three or four partners. In India Sight Savers now works with more than 130.

Another key policy is the provision of comprehensive eye-care services. At earlier stages of its history, the organization tended to focus over a period on a major issue such as river blindness or the backlog of cataracts requiring treatment. The focus was never exclusive, other issues always receiving a certain amount of attention. But the present objective is, by working with and through local partners, and by encouraging governments, to arrive at a situation where in a given district the whole range of services – screening, treatment, surgery, education, training and rehabilitation – are available. It will be many years before the goal is reached everywhere, but today it is within reach in, for example, the Gambia and some states of India.

This policy does not mark a radical breach with Wilson's thinking but is rather a natural development from it. Before he left the Society in early 1984, its Planning Committee looked at the historical development of its policy. It noted a first phase where the concentration was on specific programmes such as river blindness and trachoma in Africa, and cataract and blinding malnutrition in India; then a second phase where mobile eye units addressed a number of ophthalmic problems rather than just one (and used paramedical personnel trained for the purpose); leading to the third phase, which the Society had then reached and which required small static facilities, preferably situated in general health-care units, an ophthalmic component in the training of all health-care personnel, and perhaps only the peripheral involvement of specific ophthalmic personnel. The committee's clear conclusion was that 'the primary challenge in the next five years and beyond it is to continue and to expand the process of providing Commonwealth countries with comprehensive eye-care services, particularly at the primary level, which are ultimately integrated with general health-care delivery systems, thus rendering unnecessary programmes dealing with single ophthalmic problems.'

Through these policies – of working with local partners to build up indigenous capacity and of developing comprehensive eye-care services – Sight Savers continues to address the range of problems to which Wilson devoted much of his life.

Cataract remains the world's leading cause of blindness. Support for local partners who are engaged in this field is a major priority, particularly given the huge backlog of cases across the world requiring treatment. India leads the world in cataract surgery, but Sight Savers continues its supportive work in that country, as in many others.

Despite the considerable progress made through international programmes, river blindness is still a major concern, principally in Africa where it remains endemic in nearly thirty countries and, to a lesser extent, in the Americas. Sight Savers is supporting treatment with the drug Ivermectin (trade name, Mectizan) in eleven African countries and plans to continue such work when the current international programmes described earlier come to an end.

Trachoma is responsible for one in six cases of blindness globally and is especially common in women and children because of cross-infection. Sight Savers works with its partners to implement the WHO's SAFE strategy, so called because of the initial letters of its four components – Surgery, an operation to turn the inward-turning eyelids outwards again; Antibiotics, used to treat the infection; Facial cleanliness, to reduce disease transmission; and Environmental hygiene, that is to say health education to promote improvements in water supply and sanitation.

A relatively new area of concentration is so-called Low Vision – a condition which results in a significant reduction in a person's vision that cannot be fully corrected through refractive services (spectacles, contact lenses) or through medical or surgical intervention. Well in excess of 100,000,000 people have low vision and this is likely to increase with the ageing of the population worldwide. The problem is tackled by assessment, counselling, the provision of low-vision devices and advice on non-optical devices such as lighting aids.

The organization now spends much less time on blinding malnutrition because this disease, on which the Wilsons worked so hard, has now largely disappeared as a public health problem. The education of blind children in mainstream schools continues to be promoted, though the proportion of such children reached by the international effort remains very small (a UN study in 1993 calculated that only 2% of people with disabilities in developing countries had access to rehabilitation and appropriate basic services). The techniques for rehabilitating blind people have developed since the Wilson days. In the 1980s Sight Savers, and other similar organizations, adopted a policy of community-based rehabilitation – training people, not in distant institutions of the kind which the Society organized in Africa in the early days, but within their own community and with the aim of giving them the appropriate skills to support themselves and their families, and involving both the disabled person and his or her community in the process of rehabilitation. As we saw previously, Wilson was moving towards this concept some decades earlier.

In 2004, I was taken to a village to the north of Dhaka, the capital of Bangladesh, to meet a blind middle-aged man who had been through this process. He told me that he had spent many years simply sitting in a room in his house, unable to do anything for his family, and without anything that could be called a life. Following his training, he now ran a village shop which gave him a worthwhile income (and of course greatly increased his confidence and self respect). Remarkably, when he needed to re-stock the shop, he walked several miles down a busy main road, bought what he needed and carried it back. Another life transformed.

In the early chapters of this book it was reasonable to focus on the work of the Society as an independent entity, since in many ways it was first in the field and blazing a trail for others to follow. But it is now more appropriate to see Sight Savers as part of an international collaborative effort. It works closely with a range of similar organizations around the globe on policy development, programming, advocacy and resource mobilization. Which is just what Wilson would have wanted. He once said: 'There is no competition. We are all in this together.' The instrument which he, more than anyone else, brought into being to enshrine that cooperation and direct it into effective activity was, as we have seen, the International Agency for the Prevention of Blindness: again a key part of Wilson's legacy. Now, firmly established as the overarching body and focal point for this work, it spans the globe through its regional structures in Africa, North America, South America, the Eastern

Mediterranean, Europe, South East Asia and the Western Pacific. Its board is stocked with international experts, many of great experience and repute. The twelve leading non-governmental organizations dealing with the prevention of blindness are all members. The IAPB held its seventh General Assembly in Dubai in September 2004.

I shall return to the IAPB in the final paragraphs of this book when I describe today's global plans for dealing with blindness in the future. Meanwhile, what of Impact, the organization Wilson created to pursue his campaign for the prevention of disability in general? The International Federation of Impact Associations now has member organisations in fifteen countries or regions: United Kingdom, United States, Denmark, Norway, the Eastern Mediterranean, Bangladesh, India, Pakistan, Nepal, Sri Lanka, Thailand, the Philippines, Hong Kong, Singapore and East Africa. It remains committed to promoting activities for the prevention of disablement and for the cure, mitigation and relief of disabling conditions. Its current priorities include: accessible surgery, the early identification and treatment of disabling conditions; the ending of hidden hunger caused by micronutrient malnutrition; measures to ensure safer motherhood and child survival; immunization against disabling diseases; and helping to break the link between disability and ageing.

In 2004, the Boat of Life in Bangladesh was used to examine and treat close to 30,000 people, to perform over 2,300 operations, and to offer training of various kinds. In India, the original Lifeline Express has to date provided over 370,000 people with treatment or surgery. As mentioned earlier, there are now three 'Lifeline Express' trains operating in China. Other Impact projects are currently being implemented in the United Kingdom, Bangladesh, India, Kenya, Tanzania, Zanzibar, Nepal, the Philippines, Sri Lanka, Thailand, Pakistan and the Eastern Mediterranean. The United Kingdom Impact Foundation is the powerhouse of the international programme. Jean Wilson is its president. Claire Hicks, its chief executive, worked closely with her father for years, first at the Society, then when she became director of Impact in 1986. 'The vision was John's,' she says. 'My role was to make things happen.' When her father died, she saw the continuation and development of Impact as her personal challenge.

Impact calculates that since its establishment, its various foundations, either directly or through partners, had by the end of 2003 carried out over 20,000,000 'interventions', a figure obtained by adding together the numbers of people who received treatment or surgery, or were immunized or trained, or helped in other ways. Some proportion of all that work must be regarded as part of John Wilson's legacy.

That said, Impact itself argues that disability remains a largely overlooked human tragedy. Depending on the definitions used there are now probably between 350,000,000 and 500,000,000 disabled people in the world, eighty per cent of them in developing countries, one-third of them children. Over the years, governments and agencies have gradually incorporated thinking about disability issues into development policies. In February 2000, for example, the British Department for International Development published a policy statement on disability, poverty and development. But blindness, and disability in general, still struggle to acquire the prominence in official thinking that Wilson advocated. In September 2000, 189 countries met at a Millennium Summit in New York and adopted a series of Millennium Development Goals. Three of the eight goals are health-related but none deals specifically with disability. Other health problems still take precedence in international thinking. This is not necessarily wrong. But if governments have higher priorities, then the main effort to deal with problems of disability will still have to come from non-governmental organizations.

The bare statistics of blindness and other disabilities prevented and cured, and persons rehabilitated, by the organizations Wilson bequeathed to the world are an unshakeable part of his legacy. But they are only a part. Two less tangible but still important elements in his continuing influence are the intellectual and the inspirational.

In an article in *New Beacon*, written shortly after Wilson's death, Kevin Carey, who worked for the Society for many years, argued that 'his legacy is greater than the sum of the individuals whose lives he has changed, for what he thought, reported, formulated and taught have become part of the humanitarian process.' Concepts and applications which are now part of conventional thinking are so largely because of his pioneering efforts. He was the first to grasp the scale of the problem of blindness in Africa. He saw more clearly than others the potential of eye camps in Asia. No one now argues that the *prevention* of disability should not have a very high priority, but it was Wilson who first saw the compelling need for, and power of, the concept and caused it to become part of the global health vocabulary, and then a common element in national health plans. If it is now generally accepted that well-trained paramedics should undertake ophthalmic surgery in places where qualified ophthalmic surgeons are not available, that is in large part because Wilson saw and advocated the possibility. Much of today's effort to tackle the problems of blindness and other disabilities uses the ideas and language he first formulated. In 2002, Professor Alfred Sommer delivered the fourth John Wilson Memorial Lecture in Sydney, Australia on the theme 'Visionary Leadership', in the course of which he described Wilson's life as 'a testimonial and roadmap for the future of global ophthalmology'. That is one important sense in which the legacy goes beyond the work of the organizations he created – his intellectual influence will affect eye-care theory and practice, and action on other disabilities, for generations to come.

A major theme of this book has been the influence Wilson exerted on the problems of visual and other kinds of impairment, not directly, but through his inspiration of individuals who then made key contributions through their own careers. In earlier chapters, I described Wilson's encouragement and assistance to Dr Venkataswamy who built up the very large eye-care complex in Tamil Nadu, India, to the point where it is now a world centre of excellence. I also recorded his influence on Sam Campbell who went on to run the Milton Margai School for the Blind in Sierra Leone and on Dr Pararjasegaram, long one of the main international players in the field and now a senior consultant with the WHO.

Many other such cases could be mentioned but I shall limit myself to two more, both from Africa and both particularly eloquent.

Moses Chirambo is from Malawi. In 1973, he was receiving training as an ophthalmologist in Israel when Wilson visited the country. The two met and Wilson talked to Chirambo about the eye problems of Central Africa. In 1974, the latter returned to Malawi where he became the only government ophthalmologist. At that time the Society provided a mobile unit to help with a small eye-care outreach programme. When Wilson visited Malawi in 1978, he was told by the Ministry of Health that eye problems were insignificant in that country. Wilson did not believe it. He asked to meet Moses again and questioned him for an hour. Moses was able to confirm from his own experience of the last few years that there were indeed significant problems of visual impairment. He had found in his own work that measles, vitamin A deficiency and traditional medicine were important causes of blindness.

They discussed what could be done to prevent visual impairment. At Wilson's suggestion, Moses established a National Committee for the Prevention of Blindness, which became affiliated to the IAPB. The Society undertook, from then on, to provide equipment for eye-care work and the funds to run a mobile unit. In 1983, it participated in a survey which confirmed that vitamin A deficiency was a major cause of blindness. Moses Chirambo meanwhile revived an earlier programme for the training of paramedics which, in the last twenty years, has produced over 700 such personnel for work on blindness in Southern Africa. Also in the 1980s, the Society gave Malawi five mobile units, which are now performing between 5,000 and 6,000 cataract operations a year. When Chirambo retired from Malawi government service in 1989, he was appointed by Sight Savers as its eye-care consultant for East, Central and Southern Africa, a post which he held until 2004.

He told me when I was writing this book that blindness from vitamin A deficiency and measles had largely been arrested in Malawi, though cataract remained a problem. I asked him how different his life would have been if he had not met Wilson. He was clear: 'I would have stayed in clinical ophthalmology and ended up in private practice.' John Wilson's emphasis on prevention and on a community approach to eye problems had changed his whole perspective. Had it not been for Wilson, it is plain, much of the effective work on blindness prevention which Malawi has now pursued for a quarter of a century or more would not have taken place. Tens, perhaps even hundreds, of thousands of people would have lived much worse lives.

My second case study comes from the other side of Africa. Hannah Fahl was born in 1945 in the Cross-River state of Nigeria. She passed through convent school and a boarding school for girls into the medical school of the University of Ibadan, largely by winning scholarships, because her parents could not have afforded to pay for such education. She started to train as an ophthalmologist in 1971, partly because this branch of medicine was open to women while others were not. She won a Commonwealth scholarship and continued her training in the United Kingdom.

At this point she was contemplating an academic career. She and her Gambian husband, an obstetrician, decided to move to his home country where they obtained government appointments as consultants. Hannah quickly faced a dilemma. She was confronted in Gambia with the reality of eye diseases and all the non-medical risk and contributory factors which result in those diseases. Her training hitherto had equipped her to deal with individual patients, but not for this experience. She felt inadequate. Her professional self-sufficiency was wounded.

She wanted to learn how to *prevent* blindness. A colleague who had links with the Society advised her to write to John Wilson. She hardly expected a reply. But she got one – and more. Wilson invited her to attend the 1982 General Assembly of the IAPB in Washington and undertook that all her costs would be met.

'The meeting had a major impact on my life,' says Hannah. 'Sir John was a most moving orator. For the first time I was exposed to what a blind person could do.' (She herself is fully sighted.) 'I learned about the enormity and tragedy of needless blindness. I heard what was being done in Kenya and Tanzania – poor African countries like mine. I met the leading figures in prevention of blindness. Sir John gave the vision and lit the passion.'

Hannah went back to the Gambia, wrote the first rudimentary eye-care plan for the country and advocated to all and sundry the cause of visually impaired people. With the Society's continued help, 'The vision of taking a population and reducing avoidable blindness through a plan of action was followed through in the Gambia and cascaded to West Africa and beyond.' In 1996-7, a survey and evaluation in the Gambia proved that that country had reversed the upward trend of blindness and reduced its incidence. It had demonstrated what Wilson had always insisted could be done.

In 1993, Hannah Fahl was appointed President-elect of the IAPB. 'I received the news with trepidation and considerable reluctance, feeling ill equipped for the stratosphere this global position represented.' When, in 1999, the time came for her to take over as President, she wrote to Wilson and asked if she could visit him to seek his advice. 'There was nothing I had read or heard about prevention of blindness that had not been expressed as a vision by Sir John.' She visited the Wilsons' home in Brighton. 'He encouraged me, gave me ideas, emboldened me and pointed out that it was my duty to knock on all doors, including that of Kofi Annan (the UN Secretary General).' She did not, in the event, feel quite bold enough to tackle Kofi Annan but she left the Wilsons 'encouraged and willing to give of my best to the presidency. If he could give all those years, travel as a blind person to all parts of the globe in very difficult circumstances and at his age retain the passion, the least I could do was my bit.' Hannah Fahl remained President of the IAPB until September 2004. For many years she has been, and still is, Sight Savers' eye-care consultant in West Africa. I have travelled with her across the Gambia and have seen the respect in which she is held at the highest reaches and in the simplest villages of that country, and the skill she brings to eye-care problems in the field. Her reputation in Africa at large and much more widely speaks volumes for her achievements.

The Wilson legacy is thus in part demonstrable, in terms of the activities of the organizations he bequeathed to the world, and in part intangible, in the enduring influence of his intellectual contribution and his inspirational effect on others. But one can almost hear him saying 'That is all very well. But what are you going to do now?' There is an answer.

In February 1999, the year of Wilson's death, a new international initiative, 'Vision 2020: The Right to Sight', was launched by Dr Brundtland, director-general of the World Health Organization. At the operational level, it is a collaborative effort between the IAPB and the WHO, particularly the latter's Prevention of Blindness Programme. But it aims to cement a larger global partnership of UN agencies, governments, eye-care organizations, health professionals, philanthropic institutions and individuals. The IAPB has set up a task force of some twelve non-governmental organizations, including Sight Savers International, to work with the WHO to plan and implement the Vision 2020 programme.

The goal is to eliminate all preventable and treatable blindness in the world by the year 2020. It is a bold target. When the campaign was launched there were calculated to be at least 45,000,000 blind people in the world, increasing in number by 1,000,000 to 2,000,000 a year. In addition some 135,000,000 people were thought to suffer from varieties of low vision, giving a global total of 180,000,000 with significantly poor vision. The strategy of those implementing the new initiative is to develop and coordinate global and regional work plans, to mobilize resources to fund the necessary activities and to monitor progress. The World Health Assembly in May 2003 called on all governments to support the initiative by setting up, not later than 2005, a national Vision 2020 plan, to start implementing it by 2007 at the latest, and to monitor and evaluate progress with the aim of showing a reduction in avoidable blindness by 2010.

During his lifetime, Wilson was associated with many international appeals for action and became used to inadequate responses. Will it be different this time? Possibly. Never before has there been such a strong international alliance pressing for action on visual impairment. Governments will be under greater pressure to respond. Stronger arguments for action are available. The right to sight is more deeply embedded in international thinking and more powerfully expressed. 2003 saw the publication of an authoritative study, 'The Magnitude and Cost of Global Blindness: An Increasing Problem That Can Be Alleviated' (*American Journal of Ophthalmology*, April 2003). Its authors, Kevin Frick and Allen Foster, calculated that if Vision 2020 achieved its aims, there would be 52,000,000 fewer blind people in 2020 and 429,000,000 blind person-years would be avoided. They estimated that the economic gain from this result would be $102 billion. If the governments of the world invested appropriately in this initiative, the economic returns alone would be highly significant.

Nor is it necessary to think that governments in general will resist. Things have moved on. While most administrations still face other health problems that they regard as more pressing than those of visual impairment, an increasing number are cooperating with the WHO and international agencies to develop and enhance prevention of blindness programmes. Some are delivering impressive results. The Gambia's success in reducing the incidence of blindness has already been described; Gambia is the smallest country in Africa and one cannot extrapolate too far from its success. But at the other end of the scale is India which, as Wilson always believed it would, is leading the world in action. The number of cataract operations in that country increased from 1,500,000 in 1993 to 3,800,000 in 2002. A national survey of blindness completed in 2002 recorded the first fall, albeit slight, in its prevalence in Indian history (and that despite substantial population growth over those years). India is thoroughly committed to Vision 2020 and has put in place nationwide structures and programmes to implement it. It has first-class institutions which have put their weight behind the initiative, not just Aravind which featured so strongly in Wilson's life but, among others, the renowned L.V. Prasad Institute which has played no part in this story only because it has developed since Wilson ceased to be directly involved in prevention of blindness activity (he nevertheless took a considerable interest in its progress). Pakistan has also made impressive progress in reducing problems of visual impairment.

But the most significant and encouraging development in recent years has been the publication of a new set of statistics by the WHO. Based on the world population in 2002, the organization now calculates that the number of blind people in the world has actually fallen to a total of 37,000,000, with a similar reduction in the numbers with low vision (124,000,000) and in the overall total of visually impaired people (161,000,000). These are still massive figures. Moreover, although progress can be recorded in dealing with the Four Giants, there are now formidable foes such as age-related macular degeneration, diabetes nellitus and glaucoma, which, with cataract, increasingly dominate the landscape. They are all conditions that primarily affect the elderly. As the longevity of populations continues to increase, these problems are likely to intensify. Visual impairment thus remains a major challenge for the world

But Wilson would have been delighted that, after a lifetime of watching the statistics rise inexorably, there is now good reason to believe that the corner may have been turned; that the global effort that he launched may have begun to reduce the problem. As the course of the Vision 2020 campaign is monitored in the years ahead, there will be many involved in it who will think of John Wilson. It is the most obvious current manifestation of his legacy. He could not have devised the technology that drives the campaign's work programme because much of it was not available in the 1980s. But the structure of the initiative is largely of his devising. Without him there would probably be no International Agency for the Prevention of Blindness, no WHO programme for blindness prevention, no collaboration between the IAPB and the WHO, no consortium of international non-governmental organizations working towards the same goal, no Sight Savers International.

Many who are devoting energy and thought to making this initiative succeed are stimulated and inspired by the Wilson legacy. Their aim – the aim of Vision 2020 – is a world free of avoidable blindness. For decades, that was John Wilson's vision.

Index